CH00922043

The Coming Economic Implosion of Saudi Arabia

David Cowan

The Coming Economic Implosion of Saudi Arabia

A Behavioral Perspective

David Cowan
Boston College
Boston, MA, USA

ISBN 978-3-319-74708-8   ISBN 978-3-319-74709-5   (eBook)
https://doi.org/10.1007/978-3-319-74709-5

Library of Congress Control Number: 2018934724

Cover illustration: Glyn Thomas / Alamy Stock Photo

Printed on acid-free paper

This Palgrave Macmillan imprint is published by the registered company Springer International Publishing AG part of Springer Nature
The registered company address is: Gewerbestrasse 11, 6330 Cham, Switzerland

To Hanny, David and Yasmin with love and thanks

Preface

In this book, I offer up the possibility of the implosion of Saudi Arabia, with the current economic situation it faces as the catalyst for this implosion. The Saudi monarchy and government are I believe aware of this possibility, though they may believe it to be more remote than I suggest by my title. Certainly the common Western perception is that such a failure is highly unlikely, but I suggest such a view in the academy is backward looking and complacent. Speaking to Saudis in different places, there is a concern that failure is a real possibility balanced by an optimism that God willing there will be success. The monarchy and government leadership are taking action, but I provide here an argument that posits more is needed. Analyzing the problems Saudi faces means understanding the economic, political and religious dimensions of the Kingdom. To do this requires an interdisciplinary approach of economic, political and religious disciplines, which I have humbly sought to provide. I say humbly, because no doubt, as with all interdisciplinary works, I may have missed some nuance and the various disciplinary experts will want to qualify some of my arguments. I ask their indulgence in order that all readers may see the bigger, albeit speculative, picture of what is a complex situation in a Kingdom beset with apparent contradictions. My conclusion may surprise some, in that I am suggesting in this era typified by secularism and Islamophobia that Saudi needs to be more Islamic rather than less so. As a Christian theologian by training, this may seem even more odd. However, I suggest that thinking more deeply about Islamic solutions to the problem the Kingdom faces will create a balance between the culture and the economic problems in the context of globalization. To this end, I offer a six-point agenda for discussion in the hope that this book will reach places where this dialogue is needed.

I have written, worked and thought about Islamic economics and societies for over two decades, my first writing appearing on the subject in the early 1990s. The last five years have been spent working in Saudi Arabia, training leaders and managers in one of the Kingdom's top corporations. Any errors in understanding are mine, but I have learned much from hundreds of discussions formal and informal with Saudi colleagues. There are many I could list, but I will single out two in particular to mention: first, my good friend Hisham in Riyadh and second I am indebted to conversations with Prince Turki bin Faisal Al Saud. I am also indebted to the Boisi Center for Religion and American Public Life at Boston College, which provided me with an intellectual home as a visiting scholar. Thanks go to Erik Owens, Associate Director, for his professional and personal friendship while at the Center, Alan Wolfe founder of the Center and administrator Susan Richard who was always on hand to help. Grateful thanks go also to my research assistant at Boisi, Alison Hiatt. The Boisi Center co-hosted with the Islamic Civilization and Societies Program and the Winston Center for Leadership and Ethics at Boston College my paper "Setting the Agenda for Global Dialogue: A Theoretical and Practical Approach to Business Ethics in Saudi Arabia," where I was able to outline some of the arguments and the six-point agenda pursued in this volume. My thanks go to the Islamic Civilization and Societies Program Associate Director Kathleen Bailey for her support. That lecture subsequently became a paper at the Gulf Research Meeting 2015 held at Cambridge University and subsequently published. I am indebted to Mohamed A. Ramady, Visiting Associate Professor, Finance and Economics, at King Fahd University of Petroleum and Minerals, Saudi Arabia, for his support and encouragement in thinking through the agenda I proposed there.

As ever there are the most personal debts, by which I refer to my family. My wife Hanny has given me her usual stellar support for my work, and without her I could not do what I do. My children David and Yasmin always have my deep love and support and I remain proud of everything they do.

Boston, MA, USA   David Cowan

Contents

1

Saudis Misbehaving?

Saudi Arabia represents global Islam by virtue of the Kingdom holding the custodianship of the two holy sites in Mecca and Medina, toward which the 1.6 billion Muslims[1] around the world are called to turn in prayer and submission to God's will. This presents a powerful image of a global faith, but also highlights that ownership of the two holy sites is a major global political and economic position to hold. If a new Caliphate or an Iranian-led destabilization of Saudi Arabia were ever to come about, and consensus says it won't, it would be because their forces will have driven out the house of Saud and taken custodianship of these sites. Current wisdom suggests this is a somewhat fanciful notion, though Saudis I have spoken to in recent years have certainly expressed the view they feel Iran is a real and credible threat. It is very much in the realms of possibility today we could see a destabilized Saudi Arabia. What heightens this threat is the emerging economic picture in Saudi, which is undergoing a paradigmatic change in its economy as it seeks to move from oil-dependency and the resource curse into a more diversified and sustainable economy. Whether, and how it might, fail or succeed is the question in this book. I posit the possibility that the Kingdom could very well implode within the timeframe the Saudis have set themselves of 2030 to reinvent their economy. Critics may argue implosion is unlikely, but

© The Author(s) 2018   1
D. Cowan, *The Coming Economic Implosion of Saudi Arabia*,
https://doi.org/10.1007/978-3-319-74709-5_1

economic implosion or failures are frequently seen in the light of that wonderful thing called hindsight, and consensus is a fickle thing. Many economists, as well as political scientists and others, did not foresee the implosion of the Soviet Union or the 2008 recession. There may be various reasons for this, but in part I suggest this is because they did not study the behaviors of the leaders and networks of people closely enough.

For many years the Saudi story has been a cyclical one of oil rises and falls since the 1970s oil boom. The Kingdom incurred deficits in each year in the period 1983–1999, peaking at a cumulative rate of 25% of GDP from 1981 to 1985.[2] The solution was always the same, the government threw money at solving the problem and relied on a strong relationship with America. The status of the House of Saud, with varying predictions of its demise,[3] has fluctuated as the Sauds consistently proved themselves adept at retaining a firm grip on power. Iran was annoying, but never perceived as a viable threat; a Shia minority after all could not overthrow the overwhelming Sunni majority. And so the story goes on. Until now. In this book, I will argue that this story is changing dramatically, and there is much in Saudi that could be up for grabs as the Kingdom shows itself more vulnerable to failure and implosion than at any point in its 80-odd-year history. This book is not a prediction, it is a speculation about how Saudi is vulnerable to implosion. The launch of the national economic strategy called *Vision 2030* was not just a statement of intent, it was a statement of leadership by the rulers themselves. A major test for the monarchy came in the midst of the economic downturn and the death of King Abdullah bin Abdulaziz on 23 January 2015. Aged about 90, he had been king since 2005, and a very popular one at that. According to the rituals of Wahhabism, King Abdullah was buried simply and in an unmarked grave. This was a far different style of marking the passing of regimes than we see in respect to leaders in many other parts of the world.

King Abdullah was succeeded by his half-brother Salman, aged 79. King Salman promised continuity, stating on national television "We will continue adhering to the correct policies which Saudi Arabia has followed since its establishment." There had been much speculation and commentary about the future succession plans in the latter years of the illness of King Abdullah, but this was eventually ended with the family succession and passing of power, in part due to Salman having undertaken many of the late king's duties and partly by the opaque way in which power is managed in this nation. After some power games from 2015 to 2017 the question was finally settled, though not to everyone's liking, on Prince Mohammad bin Salman, known by the moniker MbS.[4] The outcome is that this has settled the succession question for the foreseeable future. King Abdullah had been much loved and respected within the Kingdom, and he managed to initiate a number of reforms, albeit in many Western eyes at something of a snail's pace. While King Salman shows some of this continuity, he has acted with a certain degree of increased speed, and there is a more clearly detectable response to the economic challenges the Kingdom faces.

What immediately attracted the most attention to the new reign, however, were the human rights issues in the Kingdom. In the first year under the new king there was an increased number of beheadings and capital punishment in the Kingdom. In his first year, there were 150 executions, the highest for 20 years. The strongest reaction came, however, when King Salman started 2016 with the decree of death sentence for 47 people, including Sheikh Nimr al-Nimr, a Shia and outspoken critic of Saudi Arabia's ruling family. This set off some violent reactions in the Eastern Province, which is about a third Shia in population, and abroad. There was international outrage, but the lead attacks came from Iran, itself no stranger to such actions with a somewhat worse record than Saudi.[5] The Iran reaction coincided with a nuclear deal that rehabilitated Iran in the international political and diplomatic community enough to allow Iranian government and business officials to start a charm offensive and go on a global road-trip to do business with a world prepared to lift sanctions, and apparently to forgive and forget. Iran, used to attacking Saudi as American Islam, had done its own deal with the devil. The politics of the Saudi economic change revolves around three areas of influence: issues of human rights and gender, the relationships with United States and Iran and conflicts with Syria and Yemen. At the heart of these three areas is oil. The revolutionary changes taking place since King Salman became king has made the Kingdom fragile. The changes are coming about through the agency of his heir MbS, who is taking daring risks in a risk-averse culture. London School of Economics associate professor Steffen Hertog goes further, suggesting MbS has undertaken a task to "slaughter many holy cows of the Saudi distributive state."[6] These risks are a high stakes gamble that MbS believes will preserve the Kingdom, and maintain the tradition of the Saud's adroitness at keeping power.[7] On the other hand, and in the eyes of traditionalists, he is a young man in a hurry who is threatening the culture.

The title of this book posits an economic implosion and offers a behavioral perspective. Behavioral economics as an approach brings into play the psychological and behavioral impulses in the economy. Saudi Arabia makes for a very interesting case study for the behavioral economist, because it behaves differently from many economies and religious psychology is of great importance in interpreting economic activities. Saudi has what could be called a distinct ideological economy,[8] which is essentially an Islamic distributive welfare state. It is also one that is akin to the Soviet Union and China which emerged in the twentieth century as communist economies, suggesting there are other kinds of political economy than the capitalist economy. The Soviet Union failed as a communist state that was inept at employing economic tools of capitalism, while China thrives as a communist state by using the economic tools of capitalism effectively. These are critical reference points for Saudi Arabia, which has an ideology or faith, which is Islam, that fundamentally is at odds with capitalism[9] yet has been to date a profitable economy. The relationship between this ideology, faith or philosophy—however you wish to frame it—and the workings of the economy is what I find greatly interesting here. Saudi is in a period of change, which is not just an economic conundrum but involves social and behavioral change. Will it implode like the Soviet Union or reinvent itself like China? I will later argue that the aspiration of Saudi Arabia is to be like China, but the nature of the Saudi ideology may drag it down in ways akin to the Soviet Union, but I will conclude there is the option of pursuing an Islamic third way. We have a fascinating journey ahead of us in this book to explore the possibility of implosion, however remote economists may think it so. There are many aspects of economy, religion and politics to take into account. This book will doubtless irritate purists in each of the disciplines, but I ask them to indulge me in a speculative exploration of what might happen, which I realize goes against the grain of economists' distaste of hypotheticals. To which I can only say economists have been on the wrong side of history before, and perhaps this book will offer insights to help keep them on the right side of events on this occasion.

The speculation here is that Saudi Arabia could implode. Implosion means a sudden failure or collapse of an organization or system, such as a global financial implosion. While Saudi is facing the possibility of an economic implosion, it is not inescapable. The question to consider here is what the warning signs are of such an implosion, how might it be staved off and what social impact there will be in the Kingdom as it changes and if it were to implode. To its benefit, Saudi has a strong clan or family system and has a relatively high level of social cohesion, though this cohesion has been a process of diplomatic endeavor, intermarriage and threat, and as such could feasibly be unwound under conditions of conflict. In contrast, the Western economies have seen a breakdown in family systems, social cohesion and religion, yet their economies are among the elite capitalist economies. Saudi will want to maintain the best of both worlds and such cohesion could bode well for Saudi society, but it has been maintained by the coordination of the families during a sustained period of economic well-being. How will these families, and Saudis generally, respond to the real pressure of economic pain and crisis? What role will social networks and religious faith and law, the hallmarks of Saudi society, fare under such conditions? These are the questions I am approaching here. They are questions Saudi has faced before, but I will argue the situation has been quite different in the past to the current economic challenge.[10]

In this speculative approach, I have purposely used the dramatic and negative language of implosion, but my aim is firstly to take a constructive approach and secondly to avoid an academic tendency to look backward or get lost in the weeds of theoretical questions and thereby miss the trajectory of what might actually happen. This looking in the rearview mirror way of assessing a contemporary and uncertain situation is why academia and experts can often find themselves out of step with events. The title of this chapter takes a nod to Nobel economist Richard Thaler, because what I am interested in are the behavioral economic questions of how Saudis act and react. This means looking at Saudi behavior in the dimensions of religion, State bureaucracy, educational ethos, risk tolerance and heuristics. One of the issues that dogs economics is the "as if" statement, something which Thaler has examined in entertaining detail.[11] This book is both an "as if" and "what if" speculation. Economic models traditionally used in the West use an "as if" way of understanding behavior that I suggest is quite different from the way Saudis behave; thus it becomes difficult to posit "as if" in the Saudi context. The "what if" refers to what if Saudis behaved more Islamically. In this respect, Saudis do misbehave, as we will see later on. The objective here is to look at what behaviors Saudis exhibit and how that behavior helps or hinders the economic problems Saudi faces today, and whether the policy options combined with Saudi behaviors will lead to the current problems being exacerbated and ultimately to end in failure. If we take the issues down to the level of individual Saudis, there is an interesting set of questions surrounding their role as economic actors. To study the intrinsic and extrinsic motivations of Saudis, we need to take religious motives more seriously and deeply than Western economists and secular societies are used to doing in their work. I start with the assumption that Islam is normative and a serious faith. It is a faith that informs the daily behavior of Saudis and their activities in the economic sphere. We can see this quite visibly in the "disruption" of prayer times and the uniformity of dress, but also in the perspective taken such as the frequently voiced term "Inshallah." These are not incidentals, they are central ideas and actions.

If we move from the individual actor level to the state level of society, we need to look at the role of Islam in the exercise of power and social cohesion. The significant issue for Saudi and the world is not the often-speculated fall of the house of Saud through self-immolation, rather it is the potential for the fall of Mecca and Medina to a new global Islamic order. The way to effect this is to attack the house of Saud and encourage Saudis or others to lay siege to the two holy sites in the name of a new Islamic order, or even a more secular ideology. The current political and economic climate today provides for the first time since the founding of Saudi Arabia the realistic conditions for just such an attempt, and if any attack of this nature occurs the world will become a new Islamic battleground like never before. Many politicians and international organizations, with some degree of hypocrisy one might add, have been calling for change in Saudi, but they should be careful what they wish for, since the demands for change could result in a much greater danger. Underpinning this book is a realist appraisal of the Saudi problem that has emerged not from politics but from an economic source, and to find new ways to have political dialogue to address the problem, and one that foregrounds religion rather than seeks to tame it. Though its nemesis Iran would say it is already tamed.

The leader of the 1979 Iranian Revolution, and first head of the new Islamic state, Ayatollah Khomeini[12] in an attack on the behavior of Saudi Arabia called the Kingdom the "American Islam," stating:

> The ruling regime in Saudi Arabia wears Muslim clothing, but it actually represents a luxurious, frivolous, shameless way of life, robbing funds from the people and squandering them, and engaging in gambling, drinking parties, and orgies. Would it be surprising if people follow the path of revolution, resort to violence and continue their struggle to regain their rights and resources?[13]

This was a not too well disguised call to arms for Saudis to revolt, but to little avail. On a simplistic level, a Shia leader telling Sunni citizens to revolt is neither surprising nor realistic. That said, Iran's aim is a more realistic one about destabilizing effects than outright revolt. Hence, the same accusation has continued since then with regular attacks on Saudi as the "American Islam" and what the Iranians see as a corrupted form of the faith. Saudi is unfit they say to be custodian of the two holy sites of Islam. Khomeini had also branded Saudi as the Islam of aristocrats and Abu Sufyan, referring to the leader of the Quraysh tribe who had opposed Mohammed in Mecca.[14] Despite a handful of protests over the decades since, Saudi has not fallen yet to an Islamic revolution, but currently it is under threat from an economic one which could lead to a religious revolution after all. Iran is part of the Saudi problem and is a growing concern, along with the internal economic dynamics which could play into the threat posed by Iran.

While Iran calls for revolution in Saudi, there are many voices in the Western world calling for Islam to undergo a reformation.[15] It is important to assess this question of reform in the global debate surrounding Islam and see how it connects to Saudi Islam. This is also a behavioral perspective, suggesting that Saudis are misbehaving in their use of religion, and need to behave more like the rest of us, whatever that means, which they plainly do not wish to do. It is curious that so many have been calling for a "reformation" of Islam because of "fundamentalism." It is perhaps little wonder the West struggles with the Middle East and Islam, when all too often the terminology used does more to obfuscate than clarify the issues. The term "reformation" draws on references to the medieval Christian religion and the rejection of papal authority, which eased the path of the renaissance and started the decline of the church as a political power and then its acceptance as the primary moral authority. If we look at the impact of the reformation and secularization on Christianity, then we can understand the Saudis may be taking notes, even if there is not a direct parallel. The Saudis see Christianity as being destroyed in the West by secularization, and many would not like to see Islam going down that particular path. As we will see later, secularization and economy are closely linked, though not in all the ways covered by Weber's secularization thesis.[16] The loaded term "fundamentalism" is another Christian reference, which entailed another rejection, this time of modernity. Christian conservatives in the United States, inspired by a collection of largely scholarly essays called "The Fundamentals," were reacting to the teaching of evolution in schools. From this point on the term fundamentalist became an epithet, which is now applied to religious conservatives generally and Islamic conservatives specifically. However, the term does not cross smoothly, as conservatism in the two faiths mean very different things, and holding to the fundamentals could be viewed simply as holding to traditional doctrine and what believers understand to be the truth according to divine command. Islam is not monolithic, or even binary between Sunni and Shia; like Christianity it is one faith, but one that is dispersed and localized around the globe. Thus, the problem is one of defining doctrine and who can speak for Islam, because there are many Islams. To draw a parallel with Christianity in the American context, a conversation with the Vatican would not solve concerns that evangelicals in the Bible Belt "cling to their God and their guns."

Using a plethora of Christian terms to describe Saudi behaviors and tackle an Islamic set of challenges suggests the limitations of the Western approach to the rise of Islam globally. The point is that in Saudi Islamic religious behavior is normative, and so needs to be better understood if we are to find ways of understanding the future of the Kingdom. As I shall posit, Islam already had a reformation in Saudi Arabia and so a global debate about reform and fundamentalism is not going to fix anything in Saudi, and I doubt it will fix anything elsewhere either for that matter. The hope, or perhaps hubris, behind the use of these terms simply gives rise to seeing a mirage rather than the reality. It is also naïve in the extreme. The problem with foreign policy with respect to Islamic nations and movements is that it talks past its adherents. This has happened because of decades of political and social scientists believing religion was over and done with, and it was the Weberian secularization thesis which reigned supreme. Marx may have been wrong that religion is an opiate but it certainly performs a social function, and in Saudi the Islamic religion is integral to being Saudi and is also the basis of the strong social bond that binds the families and citizens together into a Kingdom. It is also a religiopolitical alliance, where religion is not a question of autonomy or individualism, it is social and reinforcing; though for how much longer this will be the case is one of the questions to consider. To start to answer this, I will offer a way of understanding Saudi behavior that may be more productive.

To understand Saudi Arabia, and the full import of a new emerging paradigm, I will utilize three dimensions of implosion to grasp the core strands that run throughout the Kingdom, its people and its organizations. These three dimensions are:

- Economic implosion (Chaps. 2, 3 and 4)
- Political implosion (Chaps. 5, 6 and 7)
- Religious implosion (Chaps. 8, 9 and 10)

I have put them in this order, prosaically in alphabetical order, because my starting point is the economy, but it is also unwise to prioritize one over the other, as they intertwine, with one aspect being more prominent than another in one context but then less so in another context. To explain the dynamics of coherence, we can say that the economic question centers on the economic spirit, the political question centers on diversity of people's wants and needs, and the religious question is one that centers on the tension between the economic and political. This role of religion, running throughout all these questions, is what I would call foregrounding rather than being a question of prioritizing religion.

In the midst of all the political problems, such as the war on Yemen and arms trade, that have become part of the diet of Western media coverage, there is a weakening economy for Saudi and a sense that the Kingdom needs to change. How the Kingdom navigates its way out of these economic troubles, in what is more accurately a religious, political and economic situation, makes it one of the most unpredictable states in the region, and by the same token one of the most fascinating. To discover the way forward for Saudi means being able to make sense of the religious, economic and political elements. There are those who may feel it makes good economic sense to work with Saudi, while others may feel it makes sense to tackle the political problems at the expense of Western economic interests. The economic problems currently facing the Kingdom and the faith of its people means we have to understand what is so different this time round in order to understand the future of the Kingdom and how this will impact the rest of us. Of course, there are those who say it makes moral sense to deny human rights abusers, but then all the major Western democracies would have to backtrack on Iran and Saudi specifically, and ask more about their own historical and contemporary role in creating and perpetuating the problem; but then again, in the world of political realism what has the morality got to do with it?

To help us we will look at Saudi identity, Islam and political thought as elements which predate the events of 1979 and 9/11, and tease out how that past relates to the present problems. Over 14 centuries, the political theory and practice of Islam has shared a diversity of normative ideas and contingent context, and today's conditions are another chapter in the Islamic story. I see the current economic challenge as a catalyst impacting the various stresses in the Kingdom's position today. At a time when the West is seeking to create a more social economy, Saudi has kept a social sense of economy as part of the Kingdom all along, which is implied in the first article of the Saudi Basic Law[17] because the constitutional sources stated therein have a theology that implies this. Islam is a social faith, meaning not just the community of faith and family but also the political society, and it is social in ways that differ from the approaches taken by the secular societies and also the other "people of the Book."[18] One may dismiss this as theocracy, but followers are addressed in faith and society more intimately, and we need to reach an understanding of what comprises a legitimate Islamic political range, before we can discover how individuals, groups and nations can be defined as within or beyond its reach. We also have to define the Islamic political and economic ideas that came to the forefront in the twentieth century generally and how this became part of the Saudi global outreach.

Saudi is politically monarchical and economically capitalist, albeit a rentier state, or as some might say a crony capitalist state. However, there is the emergence of a more free market capitalist strain of economic thinking being used to determine how Saudi needs to change. This raises the question of whether this is to the detriment of Islamic thinking and culture in Saudi, which may be a judgment depending on your views of, or allegiance to, Islam. Capitalism is viewed in many Christian quarters as having undermined Christianity and Christian values, though I would argue it is political thinking that has done the undermining not capitalist thinking, as there are ways to think economically in a Christian way without dismissing capitalism. Since the implosion of the Soviet Union there has been a greater engagement in Christian circles, but still somewhat woeful and begrudging in the dialogue, but this is for another discussion.[19] A similarly difficult dialogue will need to take place in Saudi as it opens its economy to market forces, which are already effecting more change in areas like gender than the perhaps overly prescriptive approaches taken by non-governmental organizations (NGOs) and others. Saudi Arabia is at the proverbial crossroads. The past policies cannot be reenacted, so the rulers of the house of Saud need to find a new way forward to avoid the economic, and subsequently political and religious, implosion of the Kingdom. The *Vision 2030* encapsulates the economic plan to make for a brighter future, but it may be inadequate to explore the road ahead for Saudi in any great detail. At the outset, I will look at the *Vision 2030* which is currently Saudi policy. In my conclusion, I will explore three trajectories by looking at the ideological approach taken by the former Soviet Union which led to implosion, the development of state capitalism using the Chinese model and an Islamic solution.

Saudi is untouched in certain respects by globalization, unlike the neighboring United Arab Emirates (UAE) which in contrast has long embraced globalization, with Dubai in particular becoming a major cosmopolitan center. The foreigner, in Dubai especially, is embraced so long as there is respect for the local culture. The sexuality omnipresent on the streets and beaches of the West is curtailed here, and instead what Islam defines as respectful dress is to be worn and public displays of affection not shown. Emirati women are dressed according to an Islamic style, but they are freer to act. Except for religious holidays alcohol is served in restaurants and hotels, and pork products are sold in stores, albeit behind closed doors somewhat akin to the way pornography was hidden away in days of old in the West. What is outlawed is homosexuality, and treatment of foreign workers is rightfully the subject of objections from human rights and labor groups. There are aspects of life shared by the two societies, but there are also distinct differences as well as nuance of difference. Culturally, in private conversations I have had with Saudis, they once looked down their noses at Dubai as being less than strict Islamically, but the new stark economic realities means they are increasingly talking about Dubai as a possible model to be adapted for the Kingdom's future. However, Hilal Khashan, professor of political science at the American University of Beirut, doubts the comparison:

> Energetic and avant-garde Dubai presents a particular challenge to Riyadh's Vision 2030. The two neighbors belong to two different worlds and temperaments when it comes to business. Unlike Saudi Arabia, where most of its merchant community hails from Yemen's Hadramaut region, Dubai has a strong and well-established entrepreneurial spirit. Its indigenous population follows the Maliki school of thought in Sunni Islam that is considerably more moderate than the austere Wahhabi doctrine of the Saudi ruling elite. Whereas in Wahhabism the ruler controls society and enforces piety, the Maliki ruler does not implement compliance with the faith, which rests solely with the individual believers. As a corollary to its control of society, the Saudi state drives economic development. In Dubai, the emirate facilitates and lauds the achievements of its vibrant private sector. For Riyadh, the innovative edge of Dubai's rip-roaring capitalism is too tall an order to emulate.[20]

Whatever the case, since 2014 Saudi Arabia's gradualist approach has been tested by an increasingly uncertain and challenging economy, suggesting the Kingdom is now facing a major disruption, economically driven rather than politically. The Kingdom is under stress from the declining revenues from oil,[21] which form 80% of its total revenues.[22] The collapse of oil prices in 2014 forced the Kingdom into double-digit fiscal deficits and a rapid drawdown of the overseas reserves held by its central bank the Saudi Arabian Monetary Authority (SAMA). The problem is compounded by internal pressures due to the cost of its Islamic welfare state arrangements,[23] a youth bulge and growing numbers of women entering the workforce.

That there is a problem is certainly recognized by the house of Saud. At least rhetorically the Saudi leadership is clearly stating that there needs to be a dramatic change, and recent decisions such as lifting the bans on women driving and cinemas suggest there is some substance to the rhetoric. MbS has been increasingly aggressive in making changes, both structural and symbolic or both, as in the case of the 2017 arrests of some of the Saudi elite.[24] By Saudi standards some dramatic policies have been introduced, including budget cuts, frozen contracts and temporary pay cuts for civil servants, and will continue to do so, such as the introduction of VAT in 2018, a possible income tax to be paid by foreign workers, and the sale of shares in Saudi Aramco.[25] This is clear evidence of some seriousness of purpose. However, the scale of the task is immense given the dynamics of change in the oil price and the dependency on natural resources rather than entrepreneurship. The changes and rhetoric suggest a high-level approach, but it is down in the details the problems will surface and this will be because of what I will discuss as the Saudi mind,[26] as we shall discover later. Suffice to say at this stage, the jury is out on whether the desired change will come about, in which case we need to explore what the trajectory is likely to be in order to respond to the current economic problems Saudi faces and what policies might work. The fear, and the author suspects it may well come to pass, is that the economy will implode in a way that parallels the latter option of the former Soviet Union, which would mean Saudi Islam will lose its position in global Islam and create great dysfunction for both the Islamic world and the global economy. However, it need not be the case.

The Challenge of Fideism in an Era of Diversity

These are all powerful dynamics to consider, but I can offer a connecting idea that ties the religious thinking to the political-economic dimensions of the problem in a more coherent way. In this book, I am looking at

Saudi Arabia as a nation with a culture, and with its own form of Islam interacting with various domestic, regional and global ideas and players. I seek to offer a narrative of the Saudi future which takes religion more seriously than I contend many policy approaches tend to take, and I will argue that Islam is not just part of the problem, it is also critically at the heart of the solution. So, allow me one more clarification before we proceed. I have already flagged that naming is at the heart of the media and the political problem with Islam. I will employ these various names without using "so-called," like "so-called Islamic State," because the damage has already been done. All these names point toward a useful single appellation that can help us pick our way through the threads of the issues, and it is one that best describes the core of Saudi Islam. This core, and the challenge at the heart of Islam and Islamic radicalism today, is ultimately a theological category, and to deal with it requires exploring a theological understanding. The appellation I propose which makes greater sense to explain Saudi religious thinking is the term "fideism." The philosopher of religion Alvin Plantinga defined "fideism" as "the exclusive or basic reliance upon faith alone, accompanied by a consequent disparagement of reason and utilized especially in the pursuit of philosophical or religious truth." The fideist therefore "urges reliance on faith rather than reason, in matters philosophical and religious," and therefore may go on to disparage the claims of reason, which does not mean to say it is irrational or ignores reason, but simply that it prioritizes faith. The fideist seeks truth, above all, and affirms that reason cannot achieve certain kinds of truth, and certainly not ultimate truths, which must instead be accepted only by faith.[27] Such fideism is a powerful motivator at all levels of society, from the head of a Kingdom to a disenfranchised Arab in the backstreets of Brussels. The theological problem is discerning how we are to understand a fideist interpretation of divine action in a world of diversity. The practical problem is that this fideism drives Saudi thought, and we cannot understand the economic and political problems without understanding the theological origin of the problems. To which one can add, economic problems are a theological category for Islam, with guidance in the Koran, Hadith and Sharia on how to live economically as a faithful Muslim.[28] One difficulty of addressing the place of Saudi Arabia in the world and international relations is that a great deal of Western criticism reacts to Islam as politically inflexible with global ambitions. In the case of Saudi, what it lacks in reality is religious flexibility while usually exhibiting political flexibility.

Saudi, as is often said and written, is a Kingdom of contradictions, and this will be a recurring note in this book. If we analyze Saudi through the Western lens it will always appear contradictory, and indeed often it does throw up contradictions, but if we understand the Saudi mindset there is considerably less inherent contradiction. It is also obviously a Kingdom, and one undergoing immense change that differs for a monarchy than it does for a democracy. One theme important for this analysis is authority, by which I mean the paternalist, authoritarian and male structure of power in Saudi. The relationship between economic and political relationships is a critical one. In the West, capitalism and democracy in relationship form democratic capitalism, and this is a major focus for understanding authority in Western societies. Saudi is a monarchy, and the Saudi economy is frequently cited as being a rentier economy which entails a different sense of authority based not just on principles of monarchy but its control of the dominant source of wealth. This authority is a political and religious authority which is essentially funded by the oil wealth. This authority is within the nation, supporting the house of Saud, and globally as the home of Islam, specifically the two holy sites. There are aspects of this in other religions, but the material and spiritual have a specific relationship in Islam, which is commonly termed, and criticized as, a theocracy. In Saudi Arabia this relationship needs to be understood if we are to get to the heart of the matter. The economy has created a political tremor, but it is religion that can either tear the Kingdom apart or provide a way to maintain stability. To grasp which of these approaches will triumph and how it can be championed is the goal of this book. My aim is to understand holistically how the Kingdom of Saudi Arabia is changing by looking through these three lenses and how the economic relates to the religious and political dimensions of the Kingdom in order to explain why the Kingdom is on the verge of a potential implosion that will not just impact Saudi, but will have a devastating impact on the region, the world and Islam.

Notes

1. http://www.npr.org/sections/thetwo-way/2015/04/02/397042004/ muslim-population-will-surpass-christians-this-century-pew-says, http://www.pewresearch.org/fact-tank/2013/06/07/worlds-muslim-population-more-widespread-than-you-might-think/
2. Saudi Arabia: IMF Country Report No. 15/286, October 2015 https:// www.imf.org/external/pubs/ft/scr/2015/cr15286.pdf
3. Including Aburish (2005). The possibility is also novelized in Richard A. Clarke The Scorpion's Gate (G.P. Putnam's Sons, New York 2005).
4. https://www.ft.com/content/f941e190-ee1e-11e4-987e-00144feab7de, https://www.nytimes.com/2017/07/18/world/middleeast/saudi-arabia-mohammed-bin-nayef-mohammed-bin-salman.html?_r=1 https:// www.washingtonpost.com/world/saudi-king-names-son-as-new-crown-prince-upending-the-kingdoms-succession-line/2017/06/21/ e66db88d-fecc-40fe-a902-7f9afa487de9_story.html?hpid=hp_hp-top-table-main_saudis230am%3Ahomepage%2Fstory&utm_ term=.53f84fa01bd3
5. http://www.economist.com/news/middle-east-and-africa/21695716-while-iran-reopens-west-repression-still-prevails-home-human-rights
6. http://www.lse.ac.uk/iga/events/2017/a-new-saudi-state
7. https://www.nytimes.com/2015/02/20/world/middleeast/saudi-king-unleashes-a-torrent-as-bonuses-flow-to-the-masses.html?_r=0. Throwing $32 billion at the issue didn't help King Salman, and reflects the old mindset. MbS appears determined to create a new mindset.
8. I accept capitalist and Western economies are ideological as well, but I am attempting to distinguish economies that have a different economic philosophy than the economic norms of the dominant market capitalism.
9. There are very fundamental problems with the Koranic injunctions on the charging of interest and futures trading, and the demand to give charity, and base the structure of contracts on principles of fairness. Interestingly at this level Islam has been subjugated to political and economic priorities with capitalist economic norms accepted in the economies of Islamic countries.
10. https://www.cnbc.com/2015/12/03/biggest-cash-issue-for-saudi-arabia-goes-beyond-oil.html
11. Thaler (2015).
12. https://www.theguardian.com/world/2016/jun/10/ayatollah-khomeini-jimmy-carter-administration-iran-revolution

13. http://nationalinterest.org/feature/irans-greatest-fear-american-islam-11951
14. Koya (2010).
15. Ayaan Hirsi Ali Why Islam Needs a Reformation Now (Alfred A. Knopf, Toronto 2015) is prominent among a number of books and articles calling for a reformation of Islam.
16. See Chap. 11 for discussion on Weber's thesis.
17. Article 1: The Kingdom of Saudi Arabia is a sovereign Arab Islamic state with Islam as its religion; God's Book and the Sunnah of His Prophet, God's prayers and peace be upon him, are its constitution, Arabic is its language and Riyadh is its capital. Basic Law of Governance (promulgated by the Royal Decree No. A/90 dated 27/08/1412H (March 1, 1992)) http://www.wipo.int/wipolex/en/text.jsp?file_id=200064#LinkTarget_158
18. Judaism and Christianity.
19. Some of my theological thinking on this topic is covered by David Cowan Economic Parables: The Monetary Teachings of Jesus Christ (IVP, Downers Grove, 2009, 2nd edn).
20. http://www.meforum.org/6397/saudi-arabia-flawed-vision-2030
21. https://www.brookings.edu/opinions/saudi-arabias-economic-time-bomb/ http://www.telegraph.co.uk/finance/economics/12071572/Saudi-Arabia-unveils-record-deficit-as-it-succumbs-to-oil-price-rout.html
22. http://www.telegraph.co.uk/finance/newsbysector/energy/oiland-gas/12012347/Saudi-Arabias-pockets-are-deep-enough-to-weather-oil-price-slump.html
23. WikiLeaks reports revealed the size of the welfare system beyond the formal economic arrangements; see https://www.huffingtonpost.com/2011/02/28/wikileaks-saudi-royal-wel_n_829097.html
24. https://www.reuters.com/article/us-saudi-arrests/future-saudi-king-tightens-grip-on-power-with-arrests-including-prince-alwaleed-idUSK-BN1D506P
25. http://www.nytimes.com/2016/10/16/world/rise-of-saudi-prince-shatters-decades-of-royal-tradition.html?_r=1
26. I do not intend to reference the so-called Arab mind, which was discussed in Patai (1973). This was rightly controversial, since it suggests a more monolithic Arab mindset than that exists in reality. However, I suggest the Saudi mind is more open to definition as it refers to a much narrower cultural identity analogous to Hofstadter's discussion of the "American mind."

27. Plantinga, Alvin (1983). "Reason and Belief in God" in Alvin Plantinga and Nicholas Wolterstorff (eds.), *Faith and Rationality: Reason and Belief in God*, page 87 (Notre Dame: University of Notre Dame Press).
28. More precisely so than in the other major religions, if one looks at the field of Islamic economics and finance.

Bibliography

Aburish, Said K. 2005. *The Rise, Corruption and Coming Fall of the House of Saud*. London: Bloomsbury.

Ali, Ayaan Hirsi. 2015. *Why Islam Needs a Reformation Now*. Toronto: Alfred A. Knopf.

Allawi, Ali A. 2009. *The Crisis of Islamic Civilization*. New Haven: Yale University Press.

Axworthy, Michael. 2008. *A History of Iran: Empire of the Mind*. New York: Perseus Books.

Barber, Benjamin R. 2001. *Jihad vs McWorld: Terrorism's Challenge to Democracy*. New York: Ballantine Books.

Black, Antony. 2001. *The History of Islamic Political Thought: From the Prophet to the Present*. Edinburgh: Edinburgh University Press.

Bremmer, Ian. 2010. *The End of the Free Market*. New York: Portfolio Penguin.

Bronson, Rachel. 2006. *Thicker Than Oil: America's Uneasy Relationship with Saudi Arabia*. New York: Oxford University Press.

Champion, Daryl. 2003. *The Paradoxical Kingdom: Saudi Arabia and the Momentum of Reform*. London: Hurst & Co.

Cowan, David. 2009. *Economic Parables: The Monetary Teachings of Jesus Christ*. 2nd ed. Downers Grove: IVP.

Craze, Jonathan, and Mark Huband. 2009. *The Kingdom: Saudi Arabia and the Challenge of the 21st Century*. London: Hurst & Co.

Fawcett, Louise. 2016. *International Relations of the Middle East*. 4th ed. Oxford: Oxford University Press.

Halliday, Fred. 2000. *Nation and Religion in the Middle East*. Boulder: Lynne Rienner Publishers.

Hamid, Shadi. 2016. *Islamic Exceptionalism: How the Struggle over Islam Is Reshaping the World*. New York: St. Martin's Press.

Hammond, Andrew. 2012. *The Islamic Utopia: The Illusion of Reform in Saudi Arabia*. London: Pluto Press.

Haykel, Bernard, Thomas Hegghammer, and Stéphane Lacroix. 2015. *Saudi Arabia in Transition: Insights on Social, Political, Economic and Religious Change.* Cambridge: Cambridge University Press.

Heggenhammer, Thomas. 2010. *Jihad in Saudi Arabia: Violence and Pan-Islamism Since 1979.* New York: Cambridge University Press.

Hertog, Steffen. 2010. *Princes, Brokers, and Bureaucrats Oil and the State in Saudi Arabia.* Ithaca: Cornell University Press.

House, Karen Elliott. 2012. *On Saudi Arabia: Its People, Past, Religion, Fault Lines – And Future.* New York: Vintage Books.

Kepel, Gilles. 2004. *The War for Muslim Minds: Islam and the West.* Trans. Pascal Ghazaleh. Cambridge, MA: Belknap Press.

Kerr, Malcolm. 1965. *The Arab Cold War, 1958–1964: A Study of Ideology in Politics.* Oxford: Oxford University Press.

Koya, Abdar Rahman, ed. 2010. *Imam Khomeini: Life, Thought and Legacy.* Kuala Lumpur: Islamic Book Trust.

Kropf, Annika, and Mohamed A. Ramady, eds. 2015. *Employment and Career Motivation in the Arab Gulf States: The Rentier Mentality Revisited.* Berlin: Gerlach Press.

Lacey, Robert. 2009. *Inside the Kingdom: Kings, Clerics, Terrorists, Modernists, and the Struggle for Saudi Arabia.* New York: Viking.

Lackner, Helen. 1978. *A House Built on Sand. A Political Economy of Saudi Arabia.* London: Ithaca Press.

Lewis, Bernard. 2002. *The Arabs in History.* New York: Oxford University Press.

Lippman, Thomas W. 2012. *Saudi Arabia on the Edge: The Uncertain Future of an American Ally.* Dulles: Potomac Books.

Nasr, Vali. 2009. *The Rise of Islamic Capitalism: Why the New Muslim Middle Class Is the Key to Defeating Extremism.* New York: Free Press.

Patai, Raphael. 1973. *The Arab Mind.* New York: Scribner.

Plantinga, Alvin, and Nicholas Wolterstorff, eds. 1983. *Faith and Rationality: Reason and Belief in God.* Notre Dame: University of Notre Dame Press.

Said, Edward W. 1979. *Orientalism.* Princeton: Princeton University Press.

Thaler, Richard H. 2015. *Misbehaving: The Making of Behavioral Economics.* New York: W.W. Norton.

Vitalis, Robert. 2009. *America's Kingdom: Mythmaking on the Saudi Oil Frontier.* London: Verso.

Yergin, Daniel. 1993. *The Prize: The Epic Quest for Oil, Money & Power.* New York: Touchstone.

Part I

Economic Implosion

2

Revolution or Obituary?

The economic problems facing Saudi Arabia, which started in 2014 with a drastic oil price drop of 44% in the latter half of the year,[1] led *The Economist* to suggest to the then Deputy Crown Prince Mohammad bin Salman in an interview[2] the need for a Thatcherite revolution in Saudi. The prince agreed, but such a revolution would be unprecedented for Saudi and would be socially disruptive not just economic, which is why I suggest that when the Crown Prince appeared to agree with the notion he did not fully grasp the resonance, as a British person might. MbS was talking to *The Economist* in his first on-the-record interview in January 2016, and the notion Saudi needed a "Thatcherite revolution" was perhaps a case of putting words into the interviewee's mouth. The question and answer recorded in the transcript between *The Economist* and MbS reads:

Q: *This is a Thatcher revolution for Saudi Arabia?*
A: Most certainly. We have many great, unutilised assets. And we have also special sectors that can grow very quickly. I'll give you one example. We are one of the poorest countries when it comes to water. There's one Saudi company that's an example among many companies, like Almarai dairy company, their share in the Omani market is 80%. Their share in the Kuwaiti market is more than 20%. Their share in the Emirati market than

© The Author(s) 2018
D. Cowan, *The Coming Economic Implosion of Saudi Arabia*,
https://doi.org/10.1007/978-3-319-74709-5_2

40%. In Egypt, where there is the Nile, their share is 10%. One Saudi company. We have other dairy, agricultural companies, and you can also do the same with the banking sector. The mining sector. The oil and petrochemical sector. There are many enormous opportunities to expand and develop.[3]

The economic questions are grounded in declining oil wealth inadequately balanced by other assets and services, and an economy dragged down by a large and increasingly onerous Islamic welfare system.[4] The Kingdom's vast oil wealth has been taken for granted, and certainly Saudi Arabia has never really gone to any great lengths to diversify its economy nor to account for a time when the oil wealth, if not running out completely, would be less valuable than in the past. Until now that is, with the launch of the Saudi *Vision 2030* which was approved by the Council of Ministers under the leadership of King Salman on 25 April 2016.[5] The *Vision 2030* was unveiled in 2016 as a blanket term for all the things that need to happen in economic terms for Saudi to diversify and reinvent its economy from being what is perceived as a rentier economy dependent on oil to becoming a more conventional free market economy or, more likely as we shall discover in this study, a state capitalist economy.[6]

The *Vision 2030* and the National Transformation Programme (NTP) 2020[7] were launched to create a roadmap for the economic future and build the institutional capacity and capabilities needed to achieve Saudi's ambitious goals. The NTP 2020 reaches across 24 government bodies operating in the economic and development sectors and sets strategic objectives linked to interim targets for the year 2020. These targets include a number of economic measures made necessary because of the Kingdom's decision in 2014 to abandon its policy of limiting production when needed to stabilize the oil price. On the economic question, it remains to be seen if Saudi will maintain market share as it moves toward 2030. The Kingdom gambled that huge foreign exchange reserves, along with debt issuance and fiscal austerity Saudi-style, will be enough to get the Kingdom's and the people through a major economic transformation. With each successive oil boom there has been a slowing of the pace of economic and social reform in Saudi, and the desire to be self-sufficient was not borne out by the previous attempt. The economic growth and high oil prices which ended in 2014 saw that in the previous ten years 2.7 million out of the 4.4 million jobs created went to foreign workers on temporary contracts, according to the management consulting firm McKinsey.[8] And of the 1.7 million jobs that went to Saudis, 1.1 million were in the public sector, where wages are 70% higher than those paid by private employers. Saudis were not getting the level of jobs aspired to, and those jobs created were public sector and not wealth creating. However, MbS is not just offering economic policies, he is looking at the structure of the Kingdom's economy and where behaviors need to change. One change was the acceptance, after many years of campaigning, for women to drive and thus improve their economic status. Another change that signaled his intent to reform came when he had senior princes and businessmen arrested and detained at the Ritz Carlton Hotel in Riyadh as part of a policy to tackle corruption.[9] However, as one Saudi business-man told the *Washington Post*, this is a risky approach because MbS is challenging both the princes and religious conservatives, and it appears "he's fighting too many wars at once."[10]

The Saudi economy can be discussed as a mix of capitalist, rentier and Islamic economics, and if we are to look into the broader economic problems of Saudi then we need to incorporate an understanding of the inter-relationship of religion, tribalism and power. Trade has always been a vibrant part of the Arab way of life, and Islam as the first Arab-produced religion embraced trade with the Koran offering a number of specific statements on trade and finance, which are at the core of an approach labeled Islamic economics with its own finance and banking operations. The Koran hadith and Sharia are not just beliefs and rules, they form the foundation of Saudi behavior, with religious norms defining how the citizen as believer should behave. What has sustained the house of Saud through economic change is the alignment of the monarch with promi-nent families, who also run family businesses in Saudi which account for some 90% of the private sector in the Kingdom.[11] Nimah Mazaheri[12] argues that the need to shore up the monarch means that power and deci-sion-making have operated in the Kingdom to protect the family elites, which in turn has depressed the emergence of the more highly function-ing middle class that is needed to propel the economy forward. The boom and bust cycles of oil have been managed differently in the past, but the very structure of the Kingdom is under stress now, because the economic uncertainty emerging from the oil price declines which started in 2014 is challenging this economy and cries out for new approaches other than calling on oil reserves and budget deficits. Not for the first time, Saudis have become worried, but it is different this time because of the nature of the uncertainty that is playing a new role. To tackle this problem MbS is pursuing a very different policy approach, and it remains to be seen if he will succeed or fail, and this book will attempt to answer this question.

It's the Oil Stupid

If there is one thing anyone can tell you about the Saudi economy, it is the oil. Saudi holds 22% of the world's proven oil reserves, produces some 226.46 billion barrels[13] and has led OPEC over decades of economic and political bargaining. In 2014, when the oil prices started to fall, Saudi Arabia's non-oil GDP stood at about 56% and the sale of hydrocarbons accounted for 85% of export revenues and 90% of government revenues.[14] Think Saudi, and people think oil. Think Saudi and America, and people think power. Some may go on to talk about "big oil" and America's relationship with a royal tyranny. This may in part true; but it was also nearly not the case at all. A recent retelling of events in the pre-oil strike days of Saudi Arabia is that the oil could have been British, not American. In 2014, it came to light the oil relationship with Saudi could easily have started with the British[15] in the late Spring of 1932, when King Abdulaziz sent his son, Faisal, on a European tour including London, arriving at Dover on Saturday 7 May and put up London's fashionable new Dorchester Hotel. Pilgrimage revenues from Mecca were sharply down, and though oil had been discovered in neighboring Persia and Mesopotamia (Iran and Iraq), geologists expressed doubt that Saudi Arabia held any reserves. The King's personal adviser, Fuad Bey Hamza, was asked to discuss the need for £500,000 in gold (several tens of millions of pounds in today's money) with a senior civil servant at the Foreign Office called Sir Lancelot Oliphant. When the question of a loan was raised, Sir Lancelot cited "difficulties in this time of most stringent economy." An American engineer had compiled a report on Arabia's mineral resources, but Hamza said King ʿAbd al-ʿAzīz "always preferred to deal with the British, and would welcome the assistance of British firms in exploiting the mineral resources of his country," but Sir Lancelot responded "British firms might hesitate to accept a report not drawn up by a British expert" and said British firms would be reluctant to invest in "a little-known country" at that time. Hamza said this was a matter of "great personal grief and disappointment," and he would look to other options, but Sir Lancelot dismissively said "it was a matter of great regret to His Majesty's Government also." Sir Lancelot was experienced in the diplomatic service and in foreign relations, specifically with Persia and Arabia. It was a matter of two weeks later that American prospectors struck oil in Bahrain, just off the Saudi coast. Within a year King Abdulaziz al Saud handed the concession to search for Saudi oil to an American consortium, and a few years later in 1938 they discovered the world's largest reserves of crude. The less prosaic version of events is that King ʿAbd al-ʿAzīz was not enamored of the British or colonial power, though financially desperate enough perhaps to talk to anyone. He had a British advisor St John Philby, father of the fabled British spy Kim Philby, who played go-between with the British and Americans. Either way, the Americans got the oil deal, and the rest—as the saying goes—is history.

I don't intend here to provide a detailed history of Saudi and oil, there are many volumes of varying quality that offer this to the interested reader.[16] What I want to highlight here is a trajectory of the economic life of Saudi, oil and capitalism, and how it fits with the contemporary problems being faced. Saudi has often run a budget deficit, and it has always been able to fund potential discontent through the soft power of financial measures. In the 1980s and 1990s, the Kingdom experienced 17 consecutive years of budget deficits. In the late 1980s, the average annual deficit was $13.3 billion, and in the early 1990s this rose to $16.1 billion. While the Gulf War had some impact on this level of deficit, it was by no means the cause of the problem. The treasury was able to draw down deposits in the central bank, which led to central bank assets falling from a 1982 peak of $145 billion to $69 billion by the end of 1987. In addition, the treasury borrowed $4.5 billion from a consortium of Western banks in 1991 and $1.8 billion from Britain the following year. State-owned firms like Saudi Aramco became borrowers as well, and there was "borrowing" through substantial delays in payments to foreign contractors by Saudi, including some $500 million in delayed payments to American consultancies according to a US Department of Commerce report in 1992.[17]

In the current climate, an assessment by the Brookings Institution[18] characterized the Saudi problem of the 2014–2015 collapse in oil prices as a time bomb which has cut deeply into Saudi's main source of revenue. *The Daily Telegraph*[19] reported a 77–88% reduction in total income. Saudi government economic data confirmed it indeed had incurred a huge budget deficit, which forced the government to draw on its foreign reserves and issue bonds for the first time since 2007. The year 2016 saw the deficit fall to 297 billion riyals ($79 billion), somewhat below the record 367 billion gap in 2015. It was also below the government's budget plan projection of a 326 billion riyals deficit.[20] Net foreign assets held by the Saudi central bank have fallen by an average $6.5 billion a month. The drop in January and February had been $11.8 billion and $9.8 billion, respectively, and by the end of the year showed a $10.8 billion fall between September and October to stand at $535.9 billion in October 2016, having peaked at $737 billion in August 2014 when oil prices were above $100 a barrel. The government had liquidated reserves to cover a large budget gap caused by the low oil prices. Reuters also reported "assets had tumbled by 16.3 percent from a year earlier to their lowest level since December 2011…The assets are believed to be held mainly in U.S. dollars, in the form of securities such as U.S. Treasury bonds and deposits with banks abroad."[21] The government started to implement a plan for a post-oil era to include subsidy cuts[22] and new taxes as well as a plan to expand its sovereign wealth fund into the world's largest.[23]

In the wake of these changes, the International Monetary Fund (IMF) reported that the Kingdom may run out of the financial assets needed to support expenditure within five years if the government maintained its current policies.[24] The fall in oil prices occurred in the midst of a perfect storm, with international and regional economic turmoil and a global economic slowdown in growth, combined with the emergence of alternatives becoming more mainstream. To add insult to injury, there was the return of Iranian oil production. To tackle the crisis, in 2015 and into the next year Saudi maintained over 1.5 to 2 million barrels per day of spare capacity on hand for market management.[25] The Kingdom has kept oil production at 10.3 million barrels per day, including 7.15 million for export and 3.15 million allocated for local demand. An added headache for the Kingdom was the increasing domestic consumption, according to Saudi Aramco estimates, and *The Wall Street Journal* reported that by 2030, local demand is likely to increase to around 8.2 million barrels per day.[26] Not that all this is entirely new. In 2011 a Chatham House report noted a number of economic studies had concluded that Saudi Arabia could be a net importer of oil before its centennial anniversary in 2032.[27] On the cost side of the balance sheet, the largest single allocation in the Saudi annual budget remains its inefficient military. The Strategic Defence Intelligence (SDI) estimates Saudi will become the world's fifth largest military spender by 2020, as it boosts its defense budget by 27% over the next five years.[28] The proverbial "guns over butter" trumps other expenditure as the leadership aims to maintain its grip on power in face of growing regional tensions, most notably the troubles in Syria, Iraq and the war in Yemen. In 2016, the budget was 213 billion riyals ($56.8 billion) for the military and security services, which was a considerable increase on the previous year, and according to the Saudi Arabia Monetary Authority (SAMA) makes up 30.5% of the budget.[29] The World Bank estimates specific military spending as a percentage of GDP to be 9.5%.[30] The cost rise was driven by additional salaries for civil and military employees, as well as increasing beneficiaries of social security and retirees.

The economic challenges present Saudi with three options, namely, cutting costs to reduce the deficits through austerity policies, raising revenues by introducing income tax and privatization or diversification with a combination of these policies. When the third option has been chosen in the past, Saudi never managed to escape the continued narrow policy of increasing dependency on oil, with large government subsidies given to industry and agriculture, which became the focus of public expenditure and attempts to diversify the economy. A report by the IMF in the 1990s[31] cast doubts on the effectiveness of such diversification plans, especially since subsidies and dependency were so deeply embedded in the Saudi economic system and the society psyche. These subsidies took various forms, direct and indirect, including direct cash to farmers and for utilities to cover operating losses. The subsidies for electricity, for instance, gave the Saudi people and businesses little incentive to econo-mize on utilities. State-owned refined oil products were also sold below the international price, including sales to consumers. To cut these subsi-dies, or introduce taxes, was seen to undermine the social contract in Saudi and the ethos of redistribution. Events since 2014 suggest more radical policies and diversification are required than these past attempts, and the oil-based economy needs to change.

The Saudi Choice of Policy Options

With the Vision 2030, what MbS and Saudi policymakers are banking on is the selling off of some state assets, primarily Saudi Aramco, and diversifying the economy into other sectors. The Thatcher reference is ironic in this sense, as her government sold off state assets in a process that one of her predecessors Harold Macmillan called "selling off the family silver." If *The Economist* interview is anything to judge by then there is great optimism this revolution can be undertaken, but as some of the interviewer's questions suggest there has to be doubts that this can be achieved smoothly, if at all. The reference to Thatcher probably did not fully resonate with the prince, as it would with the British readers of the magazine in various ways, but it does raise the question of how any revo-lution can take place given the Saudi approach and behavior. The con-cern has to be for Saudi that if such a revolution is to occur, then it has to foster different behaviors, which is as much a religious and cultural ques-tion as it is an economic question. If the Kingdom cannot change the behavior, then the success of any economic change will be limited. Economic failure will then become the catalyst that will bring about the fall of the house of Saud. We have to ask though how the behavior needs to change, and does this mean necessarily it has to be changed in a Western way? In other words, we can assess whether there is an Islamic economic behavior that can make the necessary change consistent with the Saudi Islamic worldview.

Previous speculations about the future of the house of Saud and Saudi Arabia have coincided with economic problems, but as noted the house of Saud has been able to throw money at the problems. Haykel et al.

argue[32] interestingly that these periods of discontent correlate to times of high oil prices, whereas intuition and evidence from other oil-producing nations would suggest such outburst should correlate to times of low oil prices, particularly if one wants to accept the rentier model as an explanation for Saudi. Yet on the past occasions when experts have speculated the house of Saud would fall, for this reason or that, each time crisis came and went. The Arab nationalism, led by Egypt's President Nasser, was expected to see the end of royalty. Then the Iranian revolution coupled with uprisings in Mecca and the Eastern Province were seen as signs of the end times for royalty. Again, the royal family survived. A decade later there was the emergence of Sahwa, an indigenous Islamist movement, which opposed royalty. Another decade on, and Al-Qaeda came on the scene, and again was seen as a challenge to the royal family and stability. Most recently, we saw the so-called "Arab Spring" come and pass Saudi by. In each instance, the royal family negotiated a way through the problems and kept a firm grip on power and the people. The point is that these were instances related to political movements. The current challenge is specifically economic, and this will not be quite so easy to navigate. It is not a case that the economic factors are the only factors, rather they are the factors I suggest that will ignite the various forces and interests of this contradictory and complex Kingdom. In these past instances the royal family used wealth to deal with the problems. In response to the Arab Spring uprisings, Saudi used its oil wealth to pump $130 billion into domestic subsidies covering salary increases, housing subsidies and other benefits, to calm unrest. However, this time it is wealth that is the problem, which is why this time economics will be the catalyst for any regime change that might come about within the next five to ten years or so. The economic minds in Saudi are set on the timeframe of 2030 to move to a new economic paradigm, and there are a number of policy areas where they are focused in their approach to effect the necessary changes.

Let us assess the key policies and reforms being undertaken. The first three are long-standing policies:

1. The Saudization Program
2. The Economic Cities

3. Joining the Global Club
4. Vision 2030
5. Women in the Economy

The remaining two are very much part of the change taking place under MbS, with the policy platform of Vision 2030, and opening up more opportunities for women, which has been an evolving process for some time now.

Policy 1: The Saudization Program

One morning, as usual, I was greeted by the sunshine of Riyadh and my usual Egyptian driver. He was a little guy who told me he had four wives to support, and obviously a lot more energy than I do. He had been part of the influx of Egyptians who arrived in Saudi following Anwar Sadat's *Infitah*, the Open Door policy of economic liberalization,[33] which led to the assassination of Sadat.[34] This morning though he was not expected because as he had told me that week he needed to use his friend, a Pakistani reserve driver, since he had other jobs that week. However, on the day in question the Saudi government had just implemented a crackdown on workers who did not have the correct papers, known as an *iqama*. Literally overnight many undocumented workers left the Kingdom, my reserve driver among them. Since then increasing numbers of skilled and semi-skilled expatriate workers have left the Kingdom. This is part of the policy of Saudization, an idea which in fact stretches back to the 1970s. It is also a significant policy in other Gulf economies as well, in UAE, Qatar and others with the names of emiratization, qatarization and so on.

Since the discovery of oil wealth, Saudi has had a high level of dependency on expatriate skills, knowledge and workers. There has long been a reliance on foreign labor to do jobs Saudis did not want to, or could not, do. On a simplistic level of calculation, if all the 9 million plus foreign workers were sent home today, the unemployment and poverty problem would be solved tomorrow. This is, however, too simplistic. For a start most of the unemployed Saudis do not have the necessary skills, and it is questionable whether they have the desire or energy to take over some of the work undertaken by foreigners. In the private sector, the problem has been that a mere 10% of jobs are held by Saudis, with foreign workers being preferred by firms. Because oil is such a major part of the economy and diversification has not been adequate, Saudi has maintained a very capital-intensive economy and thus not set down a lot of employment requirements. Added to which, Saudi is larger than its Gulf neighbors and is experiencing rapid demographic growth. A Euromonitor report entitled *Saudi Arabia in 2030: The Future Demographic* in 2017 stated, "In 2030, the population of Saudi Arabia will reach 39.1 million, an increase of 24.1% from 2015. Saudi Arabia's population growth is decelerating due to falling birth rates and fertility rates and increasing death rates, a trend that will continue up to 2030. Net migration will remain positive up to 2030, but will experience an overall decline. The population is ageing at a faster rate than the Middle East and Africa average and will be over nine years older by median age in 2030."[35] This is a set of demographic changes which is creating pressure to address youth and gender concerns. However, tackling this growth is undermined by a number of constraints, including family networks and a general lack of transparency.

Another area for concern is labor, with unemployment a big part of the Saudi problem. Again, the past does not offer a helpful guide in this respect which, like the subsidies just discussed, involved employment offered in the public sector even when the jobs did not exist. The problem now is that while official figures put unemployment at 11.7% for men and 32.8% for women, experts believe the figures are much higher. In an interview, a senior official at Saudi Aramco put the unemployment rate "closer to 27 to 29%, rising to 33% among youths between 20 and 24 years and 38% for 24 to 29-year-olds."[36] In 2016, unemployment in Saudi Arabia rose to 12.1% in the third quarter of the year, which was a four-year high. Although Saudis have been taking more jobs at a record level of 42%, the majority of jobs are still going to expatriates. Local investment bank Jadwa Investment in a report in the last quarter of 2016 painted the picture starkly, "during the first three quarters of 2016, total net employment in the Kingdom saw a significant rise of 892,000, compared with a 417,000 increase between 2014 and 2015. However, 95% of these positions went to non-Saudis."[37] This squeezes the Saudization objectives from two sides, the supply and demand side, because of the problem of the necessary expertise.

The Saudization program was created to increase the number of Saudis in employment, particularly in the private sector, and to decrease this dependency, but did not become a pressing matter until the 1990s, when unemployment started to rise significantly and the population grew, thus bringing young people into the job market in large numbers. To build its own skill base, many young people have been funded to go to foreign universities, principally in the United States, to gain the skills and knowledge necessary for a new generation of Saudi leaders and managers. The policy of Saudization aims to ensure all businesses in Saudi employ Saudis, based on a percentage formula according to size. As a target percent of total employment, Saudization was set such that by the end of 2009 Saudi nationals would comprise 51.5% in the eighth Development Plan (2005–2009). However, things did not work out that way, and even though in 2009 some 2.2 million new jobs had been created by the private sector during the five years of the eighth Development Plan, only about 8.9% of these jobs (195,755) were taken by Saudi nationals.[38] By 2011, the Ministry of Labour had admitted in its report that the program had stagnated. A move was made to breathe fresh life into the program, and in 2013 the decision was implemented that saw tens of thousands leaving voluntarily or being deported, encouraged with an amnesty offered to many workers; hence 5.2 million expats legalized their status during the amnesty period. Most of those who left or were deported were laborers, so the immediate effect was that many public works projects were halted temporarily because they didn't have the labor force to work on them and so again this was less than successful.[39]

Thus although the idea has been to create self-reliance, in reality there remains a great skills shortage and of course there are many jobs the Saudis don't wish to do. Saudis in the private sector amount to 1.26 million employees out of a total 8.7 million, that's one-eighth of the working population, and only a minority of this is women. The education minister Prince Faisal bin Abdullah has admitted that "Saudization and employment is not the solution…The solution lies in creating job opportunities. How can we do that? By developing the economy and expanding areas of work for Saudis to become productive."[40] Saudization, however, continues as a flagship policy and the Ministry of Labor and the Council of Saudi Chambers (CSC) have constituted a high-level joint panel aimed at boosting the Saudization drive and increasing the efficiency of the labor market.[41] The picture is complicated by the controversial fact that many private companies have been achieving their Saudization quotas through the so-called false employment of Saudis, involving tactics such as employing Saudis to stay at home just to make up the numbers.

These problems are recognized by the government and they have been attempting to stamp out the practice, because it is counterproductive to the Saudization aim and damaging to the local economy. In 2016, Saudi Arabia's minister of labor, Mufrej Al-Haqbani, announced the launch of a new phase in the Saudization program called "Guided Localization"[42] and urged leaders to get involved in supporting the program to overcome hurdles in achieving Saudization and to help in realizing total or partial Saudization in various sectors, especially the retail sector. Four stages were outlined. First, various sectors would be targeted for Saudization and training with the objective of a phased replacement of foreigners with Saudis in highly skilled and semi-skilled jobs in the private sector. The second stage involved regional intervention, with the provincial governors supported by the emirs calling upon support for the Saudization program so each province progresses according to the types of activities located in those regions. The third stage is total Saudization of specified trades in cooperation with other ministries, starting with Saudization of the sale and service sector of mobile phones. The fourth is linked to the "Balanced Nitaqat" program, which was to be launched by the ministry at a later date. Nitaqat, meaning "bands" or "zones," is designed to provide companies with more realistic targets. There are sanctions for companies in non-compliance, but also incentives are given to those in compliance with the advancement of the Saudization agenda. One problem is that the Nitaqat can put unnecessary burdens on the private sector because of the additional costs to companies.[43]

Policy 2: The Economic Cities

Another significant policy is the creation of economic cities, which if successful the Organisation for Economic Co-operation and Development (OECD)[44] has forecasted would generate $150 billion in new economic activity in 2020, a 50% increase in Saudi GDP. Again, there is a protracted history to consider. In 2006, King Abdullah inaugurated the economic city project and launched four mega economic cities in Rabigh, Hail, Madinah and Jazan to drive diversification and to attract domestic and foreign investment, which would then boost economic growth and create thousands of new jobs for its growing number of youth population. Each new city would be focused on specialized sectors using public-private partnership. The objectives of the six cities were stated as:

1. King Abdullah Economic City in Rabigh: Built off the Red Sea north of Jeddah and focused on port and logistics, light industry and services.
2. Prince Abdulaziz bin Mousaed Economic City in Hael: focused on logistics, agribusiness, minerals and construction material.
3. Knowledge Economic City in Madinah: near the Holy Mosque of the Prophet in Madinah, the city would attract Muslims from around the world and target knowledge-based industries with an Islamic focus and services.
4. Jazan Economic City: focused on heavy industry and agribusiness.
5. NEOM is a $500 billion "megacity" announced in 2017 and modeled on the "free zone" concept pioneered in Dubai, exempt from tariffs and having their own regulations and laws, hence operating separately from the rest of government.
6. Not so much a city as a region, the Red Sea coastline is to become a global tourism destination governed by laws "on par with international standards" and covering 50 islands and 34,000 square kilometers.

Though part of Vision 2030, these last two projects are essentially policy extensions of the four older cities.

The overarching objective is to grow the national economy and raise the standard of living for Saudis through enhancing the competitiveness of the Saudi economy and spurring foreign investment and thus tackle the Kingdom's reliance on oil. The Saudis recognized that regulatory reforms were needed to convince foreign firms that Saudi Arabia had more to offer than just cheap energy. They also recognized the need to create new jobs, which entailed improving Saudis' skill levels. Each city is to be developed around at least one globally competitive cluster or industry and adopt state-of-the-art means to create a growth engine for the city and attract other businesses. The idea is to move beyond simply an industrial free zone to create real investment.

The Saudi government portrayed these cities as "islands of change," explaining they are structured under relatively liberal terms, which means they can operate under new economic guidelines allowing foreign ownership of private companies, supported by a streamlined bureaucracy to reduce turnaround on fundamental needs such as visas and customs documents. They would also have more relaxed social rules to enhance women's roles and rights, and would thereby cultivate a better blend of Western and Saudi styles. The dream was to position Saudi Arabia among the world's ten most favored investment destinations within ten years, in other words by 2016. So much for the dream, reality took a different turn exacerbated by the oil downturn in 2014, a situation admitted by Deputy Crown Prince Mohammad bin Salman when he announced his Vision 2030 program in 2016, which also set out a plan to salvage the first four economic cities.[45] He subsequently announced the two new projects in 2017, recognizing the failures of the past in the hope they will not be repeated. In his vision statement, he stated "We are aware that the economic cities of the last decade did not realize their potential. Work has halted in several cities, and others face challenges that threaten their viability."[46] While some development has been taking place in King Abdullah Economic City in Rabigh, boosted by government support, the lack of funds and bureaucratic hurdles has stultified the other cities. In addition, the prince explained that the restructuring of the King Abdullah Financial District in Riyadh was to be another important goal, as work on the district had started in the last decade without considering its economic feasibility. He stated "We will seek to transform the district into a special zone that has competitive regulations and procedures, with visa exemptions, and directly connected to the King Khaled International Airport."[47]

Policy 3: Joining the Global Club

After the Second World War Saudi started to export oil and become part of global trade, long before the term "globalization" came into fashion. However, it was not until 11 December 2005 that Saudi acceded as the 149th Member to the World Trade Organization (WTO)[48] in order to enhance its competitive advantage in petrochemicals and strengthen its international market position. As main exporter, the Saudi petrochemical industry had much to gain. It took 12 years of negotiation and the introduction of 42 bylaws over four years. WTO membership provided Saudi with lower tariffs and subsidies on a wide range of goods and services, intellectual property rights protection and an international standard for trade grievances and disputes which gave foreign investors rather more comfort than domestic arrangements. It also reduced the cost of finance, insurance and transportation services. The then commerce and industry minister Hashim Yamani said:

> This is a high point in the programme of economic and structural reform that Saudi Arabia undertook. The accession will further integrate Saudi Arabia's economy into the world economy. It will also deepen the universality of the multilateral trading system…The accession will enhance the business environment in Saudi Arabia by adding more transparency and predictability. This we expect to lead to more investment and job creation.[49]

The significance of the WTO membership is that it symbolized international respect and acceptance for Saudi, which despite being the world's largest oil producer was to that point outside of the club, indeed the only GCC country not in the WTO. Saudi had not joined GATT, the WTO's predecessor global trade agreement either, because its sole export was oil, which was not part of GATT. When the Kingdom established its downstream oil and petrochemical capacity through the creation of SABIC, it became more critical for Saudi to join the WTO to protect its exports from higher tariffs imposed by high-cost producer countries. In short, WTO membership opens up the Saudi economy to greater transparency, gives protection of copyrights, places rule of law at the forefront of the economy and makes it more attractive to foreign investors. At the same time, it allows Saudi exporters equal and non-discriminatory access to other WTO countries.

Policy 4: Vision 2030

The newest policy option is the vision 2030 plan,[50] which incorporates in some form or other the first three policy options. The question is whether this is simply asserting a Western economic agenda from a cookie-cutter McKinsey study?[51] There are voices within Saudi who feel the Crown Prince is trying to push the pace too quickly.[52] The Vision 2030 plan for Saudi is aimed at economic diversification, though as we have seen it is by no means the first time Saudi has attempted to diversity its economy, and this Vision can be interpreted as a repackaging or recycling of old ideas, albeit using a single platform. There are some lofty aims set out by the Vision:

- Moving the economy from the current position as the 19th largest economy in the world into the top 15.
- Increasing the private sector's contribution from 40% to 65% of GDP.
- Raising the share of non-oil exports in non-oil GDP from 16% to 50%.
- Increasing non-oil government revenue from Saudi Arabian Riyal (SAR) 163 billion to SAR 1 trillion.
- Growing Public Investment Fund (PIF) assets, from SAR 600 billion to over SAR 7 trillion.
- Increasing foreign direct investment from 3.8% of GDP to 5.7%.

The Vision focuses on creating energy efficiency, fostering renewables, promoting foreign direct investment and developing the service sector.

- Building on the climate change agreement COP21 in Paris, the Kingdom aims to encourage research agencies to develop new technologies toward energy efficiency and to reduce the environmental impact of carbon.
- The Kingdom has set a target of introducing 9.5 gigawatts of power generation to the Kingdom's grid by 2030 through renewables, including wind and solar.
- American companies have been invited to increase their investments in the Kingdom.
- The service sector is seen a level above the traditional basic industries where Saudi can thrive, given its geographical location as a connecting land mass and its network of technologies, giving rise to a pivotal role in movement of materials and goods.

The main thrust of the Vision 2030 is the deputy Crown Prince himself, because he personifies the program and the idea of change, as Jane Kinninmont at Chatham House explains:

> …the main novelty lies in the fact that for the first time in Saudi Arabia they are being espoused by a leader who is both very senior in the royal family and very young, belonging to the generation that will face the post-

oil age in their own lifetimes. Previously such policies have usually been communicated by senior technocrats, such as the heads of SAGIA, the general investment authority, or ministers of finance or economy or industry. Ambitions to diversify the economy and develop the private sector have always been far in excess of implementation.[53]

Ambitious indeed, when the Vision 2030 was announced the International Monetary Fund (IMF) responded by stating that while the Saudi agenda was "ambitious" and "far-reaching," it would be difficult to implement the plan. There are some areas where the plan was decidedly silent, most notably no outline of steps to raise revenue from taxes and no proposed changes to the political structure of the absolute monarchy. Twitter was busy on the day, with a number of Saudis using social media, which is not heavily censored, to express their concerns on the need for political change, among other things, to make Saudi successful in the future.[54]

In Spring of 2017, a new set of programs were laid out by the Saudi Council of Economic Affairs and Development. They identified 11 programs specified as having strategic importance for the government to achieve Vision 2030.[55] The programs launched were defined as:

1. **Fiscal Balance Program 2020:** The program was launched to establish a balanced budget. Through the program, a number of procedures have been announced to benefit from the opportunities. It will also assign 200 billion SAR to support the private sector which will enhance a sustainable fiscal structure.

2. **Housing Program:** Providing a dignified life for Saudi families via enabling them to own houses that match their needs and financial capabilities which will be established through developing the sector with developed techniques. This will enhance its economic effect and thus create more job opportunities.

3. **Serving Pilgrims Program:** This program aims to provide an opportunity for the largest number of Muslims to perform pilgrimage and Umrah and visit the holy sites, which works on deepening and enriching the pilgrims' experience via preparing the Two Holy Mosques and achieving the global message of Islam. This program also ensures the effective role of private sector in enhancing the sector's economies.

4. **Improving Lifestyle Program:** Improving individuals' lifestyle by modernizing the means that enhance citizens' and residents' participation in activities related to culture, entertainment and sports among other events that generate job opportunities and promote the Kingdom's status among the best countries in the world. Cinemas have already been introduced under this policy.

5. **Strengthening National Identity Program:** The program is devoted to developing and strengthening individuals' national identity based on Islamic and national values. It also aims to strengthen personal characteristics that motivate people to succeed and be optimistic. In addition, this program will have an essential role in correcting the image of Saudi Arabia.

6. **Supporting National Leadership of Companies Program:** It aims to motivate more than 100 national companies that have promising chances in regional and international leadership and enhance their statuses in a way that positively reflects on the Kingdom's image and economy. This program aims to enhance the local level and enrich the economy by supporting small and medium enterprises and creating more job opportunities.

7. **Developing National Industry and Logistical Services Program:** This program was devised to develop national industry and local products, improving the infrastructure and developing the logistical services necessary for the Kingdom to be a distinguished industrial and logistical platform among the three continents. This program also aims to create promising job opportunities.

8. **Public Investment Fund:** A fund that aims at strengthening the role of the public investment fund as it is the efficient factor behind the diversity of economy in the Kingdom and developing specific strategic sectors via improving the influence of the fund's investments.

9. **Strategic Partnerships Program:** It will establish and deepen strategic economic partnership with strategic partnership countries which possess the basic components for contributing to accomplish Vision 2030. This is in addition to strategic relations with Gulf Cooperation Council countries and the region through facilitating the transfer of people, merchandize and capital smoothly in order to enhance and expand the different economic sectors.

10. **Developing the Financial Sector Programs:** This program works on developing the markets of Saudi capital and improving their status on the regional and global levels so that the Saudi market becomes the primary one in the Middle East and among top ten in the world.
11. **Privatization Program:** The program enhances the role of the private sector in providing services, improving their quality and lowering their cost generally. It also aims to reduce the cost and reestablish the government's organizational and legislative role. This program will also seek to attract more foreign investors.

Vision 2030 builds on changes in Saudization, the role of women and joining the WTO, and brings these themes and other economic ideas and plans under one flagship idea espoused by a senior national leader. Together these elements have the potential to bring Saudi toward its threefold ambition to be a vibrant society, a thriving economy and an ambitious nation, but it won't be easy and many cultural challenges lie ahead. There is a risk of doing too many things badly, rather than doing a few things well.

Policy 5: Women in the Economy

What will help Saudi change will be training and skills, but also Saudi women becoming more present in the workforce. By reason of cultural history, while the global proportion of women working has fallen the number of women employed in Saudi has increased, starting from a lower base, by 48% between 2010 and 2015. From 1991, the percentage grew from 14,228,000 (14%) of the working population to 20,059,000 (20%).[56] Compared to men, the last quarter of 2016 showed that 13,944,732 persons are employed in total, of which 11,935,646 are male (85.6%) and 2,009,086 are female (14.4%). Conversely, Saudi nationals who were looking for jobs reached 917,563 people, of which 177,573 are male (19.4%) and 739,990 are female (80.6%).[57] Particularly since early 2016, I have noticed in my personal visits more women in the workplace and greater interaction with men than was the case in the preceding years. In the stores saleswomen have come up and inquired if I needed any help, and on one occasion a young Saudi woman at the airport inquired if I was okay when a door shut on me. In teaching groups, I have found Saudi women to be very vocal participants and contribute a lot to sessions, and indeed often more forthcoming than their male counterparts. The growth of women-only offices, promotions and inclusion in mixed business meetings in major and lesser companies continues apace. These are commonplaces in life in most countries, but to Saudi they are new experiences that remain counterbalanced by conservative demands for the continued segregation of women. The changes that are occurring though show there is a class of young ambitious Saudi women who are prepared, if not demanding, to make a contribution to the economic future of Saudi Arabia. Saudi women are now permitted to work in hospitality and retail, and are finding jobs in the diplomatic services, military and media, while the first Saudi female lawyers were granted their practicing certificates in late 2013. The amended article 149 of the KSA Labour Code prohibits employment of women in what the Minister of Labour classifies hazardous and detrimental jobs, such as industrial production areas, construction and hazardous materials, though they can take administrative roles. The Human Resources Development Fund has a subsidy program for employers operating remote working for women, which includes funds for training and reimbursement of salary costs. Women are also working entrepreneurially at home. Women have a number of rights, including maternity benefits, and are entitled to the prescribed period of *Iddah*, which is four months and ten days from the husband's death date, in compliance with Sharia law. A 2013 report by Oxford Strategic Consulting, *Maximising the Employment of Saudi Females*, states there is:

> a significant economic, social and cultural opportunity. We calculate that raising female workforce participation in KSA to c40% (still lower than most G20 economies) could increase GDP by c$17 billion pa whilst it could add $58bn in revenues to Saudi companies as well as significant increases in productivity, engagement and innovation.[58]

The economic impact will be matched with broader social impacts, and part of how women's rights and roles change in Saudi will be affected by these economic advances, and this will be part of the answer of how Saudi achieves the Vision 2030 goals both in terms of the economic output and also mindset needed to move Saudi toward the goals. The success of women in the economy will be a decisive factor in its overall success.

A Policy to Foster an Islamic Economy?

Economics is essentially about scarcity and the competition, or cooperation, necessary to eke out a living based on what is available, what is not, and who needs or wants what. The Western free market system is the only real game in town today, after some decades where the alternative of communism suggested there could be an alternative economy based on a different understanding of economics. With the end of communism, free market capitalism has been the victor and few discuss an alternative economy today, only variants of capitalism, such as state capitalism. Many states in the Middle East have tended to "protect" themselves from capitalism and have state-controlled business, heavy taxation, a highly selective approach to business done with foreigners, all added to a good measure of xenophobia. Saudi belongs to a second group of Middle East states, those which have tried to be capitalist-like while treating the private sector as subjugated to government status. There has, however, long been an alternative economic view in Islam. The Islamic economic and financial system ideal is to allow a Muslim to be both pious and wealthy, while building a better society together. There have been radical approaches offered to promote an alternative Islamic economic system, but these often hooked their wagon to socialist economic thinking, discredited by today's trends and as a result they have not succeeded in taking much hold. If there were to be a "pure" Islamic economy, one can ponder how much such an Islamic financial and economic system may be a threat to the West, offering a new alternative to Western capitalism just as communism was in times past. In discussing secularism we have seen politically how for many followers the vacuum of secular ideas and consumerism can be filled with Islam, so the same could happen for the Islamic economic system. However, there may be more creative ways to work within the space of Islamic and conventional economic ideas. *Vision 2030* superficially appears to be an approach based on blending Islam with capitalism as practicably as possible, though it is more of a management consultancy solution than a cultural one. In this respect Saudi can learn much from the Dubai model, which has survived by running a parallel Islamic and capitalist economy blending the ways of the Islamic world with the secular or non-Islamic world by harnessing capitalism and pluralism.

However, perhaps Saudi is missing a trick here, in the sense they could develop a more ambitious and holistic Islamic program, a scenario I will return to in more detail later, but it is appropriate here to flag Islamic economics at this stage, because Saudi can certainly expand the Islamic part of its economic system. In its 2016 Country Report the IMF suggested there is great scope for Islamic financing as part of the Saudi solution:

Islamic finance in general, and Sukuk markets,[59] in particular has great potential in Saudi Arabia and an important role to play in financing the budget. Demand for Islamic financial instruments is growing very strongly, and this growth has the potential to support the implementation of fiscal and monetary policies and enhance financial sector development. The authorities have already expressed interest in tapping the abundant Islamic finance market liquidity by debuting sovereign Sukuk in 2016 with the intent to expand the investor base beyond what could be otherwise tapped through conventional finance.[60]

Saudi has 12 domestic commercial banks, four of which are Islamic banks (Al Rajhi, Alinma, AlBilad, Al Jazira), while a fifth is in transition to become Sharia-compliant. Together they account for around 25% of the domestic banking system assets, added to which there are the conventional banks who offer a mix of Islamic and conventional banking services. The IMF report that as of end-2015, the Islamic banking sector asset base in Saudi totaled some SAR 1151 billion, representing about 21.4% of global Islamic banking assets, representing a growth rate of 8% in 2014. This provides the investment funds to expand the offering of financial products, and perhaps innovate in some new directions. The Islamic side of the economy and Islamic economic ideas have the potential for greater dialogue between other economic systems and ideas to discover a path for Saudi that is a way forward through their current economic problems that can blend Islamic economics and capitalism. This could be a path to create an evolutionary path for Saudi Arabia, so that the values and outcomes of the Western consumer economy need not produce the same outcomes as Saudi. The Kingdom is accused of being conservative, but it is more accurate to say it is still in some ways a young society that is trying to come to terms with the globalized world in a way consistent with their Islamic faith and behavior, not just their economic experience.

Notes

1. https://www.eia.gov/todayinenergy/detail.php?id=19451   http://www.bbc.com/news/business-30223721. The average annual price fell from 99.29 in 2014 to 49.49 in 2015. https://www.statista.com/statistics/262858/change-in-opec-crude-oil-prices-since-1960/
2. http://www.economist.com/saudi_interview
3. Ibid.
4. http://foreignpolicy.com/2017/06/05/is-saudi-arabias-massive-economy-reform-coming-off-the-rails-mohammed-bin-salman/
5. https://www.oxfordenergy.org/wpcms/wp-content/uploads/2016/07/Saudi-Arabias-Vision-2030-Oil-Policy-and-the-Evolution-of-the-Energy-Sector.pdf
6. Bremmer (2010) defines "state capitalism as economies in which the state is the principal actor and judge, and uses the markets for political gains. China, Russia and Venezuela are among the examples." https://www.npr.org/templates/story/story.php?storyId=126835124. The emergence of a state capitalist economy is well captured in *The Rise of State Capitalism* http://www.economist.com/node/21543160 and *The Visible Hand*, a special report http://www.economist.com/node/21542931
7. http://vision2030.gov.sa/sites/default/files/NTP_En.pdf
8. http://www.mckinsey.com/global-themes/employment-and-growth/moving-saudi-arabias-economy-beyond-oil
9. https://www.nytimes.com/2017/11/04/world/middleeast/saudi-arabia-waleed-bin-talal.html?_r=0

10. https://www.washingtonpost.com/opinions/global-opinions/the-saudi-crown-princes-risky-power-play/2017/11/05/4b12fcf0-c272-11e7-afe9-4f60b5a6c4a0_story.html?utm_term=.8ea53780e068

11. https://mci.gov.sa/en/AboutKingdom/Pages/SaudiEconomy.aspx http://www.opec.org/opec_web/en/about_us/169.htm https://www.wsj.com/articles/saudi-arabia-faces-challenge-in-enlarging-private-sector-1465324961

12. See Mazaheri (2016). I reviewed the book in the *Times Literary Supplement* https://www.the-tls.co.uk/articles/private/economics-24/

13. http://www.opec.org/opec_web/en/data_graphs/330.htm

14. https://www.thenational.ae/business/saudi-arabia-has-diversified-but-economy-still-depends-on-oil-1.170006

15. The description of events here is based on a report from the BBC, which can be read in full at http://www.bbc.com/news/blogs-magazine-monitor-29954567

16. A selective list would include Lacey (2009), banned in Saudi; Bronson (2006), taking an historic sweep of the US/Saudi relationship; Vitalis (2009), a polemical history of oil development and Saudi Aramco; and Yergin (1993) offering a broad history of the oil history.

17. See *Petroleum Economist,* June 1994, pp. 86–87; *Middle East Economic Digest,* May 6, 1994, p. 4.

18. https://www.brookings.edu/opinions/saudi-arabias-economic-time-bomb/

19. http://www.telegraph.co.uk/finance/economics/12071572/Saudi-Arabia-unveils-record-deficit-as-it-succumbs-to-oil-price-rout.html

20. http://www.reuters.com/article/saudi-economy-budget-idUSD5N17S01X

21. http://www.reuters.com/article/saudi-cenbank-assets-idUSL8N1DT2YV

22. The IMF has estimated that energy subsidies cost Saudi Arabia $107 billion or 13.2% of gross domestic product in 2015. See https://www.ft.com/content/b9e1d072-893d-11e5-90de-f44762bf9896

23. Bloomberg – 06/04/2017 10:58 am.

24. http://www.bloomberg.com/news/articles/2015-10-21/saudis-risk-draining-financial-assets-in-five-years-imf-says

25. https://www.eia.gov/finance/markets/supply-opec.cfm

26. http://www.wsj.com/articles/as-saudis-keep-pumping-thirst-for-domestic-oil-swells-1435786552

27. https://www.chathamhouse.org/sites/files/chathamhouse/public/Research/Energy,%20Environment%20and%20Development/1211pr_lahn_stevens.pdf
28. http://www.defenseworld.net/news/13057/Saudi_Arabia_To_Rank_Fifth_In_Defense_Spending#.WQcNGol950s, http://government.defenceindex.org/downloads/docs/GI-MENA-Regional-Results-web.pdf
29. A discussion of the 2016 budget can be found at http://country.eiu.com/article.aspx?articleid=1373809921&Country=Saudi%20Arabia&topic=Economy
30. https://data.worldbank.org/indicator/MS.MIL.XPND.GD.ZS
31. Champion, Daryl *The Paradoxical Kingdom: Saudi Arabia and the Momentum of Reform* (London, C Hurst, 2003). Updated 2015 reports on diversification in oil economies and in Saudi can be found at https://www.imf.org/external/pubs/ft/scr/2015/cr15286.pdf https://www.imf.org/external/np/pp/eng/2016/042916.pdf
32. Haykel et al. (2015).
33. McLaughlin, Gerald T. *Infitah in Egypt: An Appraisal of Egypt's Open Door Policy for Foreign Investment* Fordham Law Review Volume 46, Issue 5 Article 1, 1978 http://ir.lawnet.fordham.edu/cgi/viewcontent.cgi?article=2311&context=flr
34. 6 October 1981.
35. http://www.euromonitor.com/saudi-arabia-in-2030-the-future-demographic/report
36. http://eaworldview.com/2016/03/saudi-arabia-feature-poverty-wealthy-land/
37. https://www.forbes.com/sites/dominicdudley/2016/12/08/saudi-unemployment/#23a0553b2022
38. http://www.wbiworldconpro.com/uploads/south-africa-conference-2016/management/1451461735.pdf
39. https://www.theguardian.com/world/2013/apr/02/saudi-arabia-expels-yemeni-workers, https://www.theguardian.com/world/2013/nov/29/saudi-arabia-foreign-labour-crackdown-migrants
40. http://www.albawaba.com/business/saudization-education-523901
41. http://www.saudigazette.com.sa/index.cfm?method=home.regcon&contentid=20140410201508
42. *Saudi Gazette*, Riyadh Tuesday, 8 March 2016.
43. Looney, R. *Saudization and sound economic reforms: Are the two compatible?* Strategic Insights vol. 3, no. 2, 2004, pp. 1–9. Ramady, M. *Gulf unemployment and government policies: prospects for the Saudi labour quota or Nitaqat*

system, International Journal Economics and Business Research, Inderscience Enterprise Ltd., vol. 5, no. 4, 2013, pp. 476–498.

44. http://www.oecd.org/mena/competitiveness/38906206.pdf
45. http://saudigazette.com.sa/saudi-arabia/saudi-vision-2030/will-strive-restructure-economic-cities/
46. Ibid.
47. Ibid.
48. https://www.wto.org/english/thewto_e/acc_e/a1_arabie_saoudite_e.htm. A 2006 paper: http://faculty.kfupm.edu.sa/FINEC/ramadyma/articles/ The%20impact%20of%20Saudi%20Arabia%E2%80%99s%20 WTO%20accession.on%20selected%20economic%20sectors%20 and%20domestic%20economies.pdf
49. http://news.bbc.co.uk/2/hi/business/4427880.stm
50. http://www.reuters.com/article/us-saudi-economy-idUSKCN0XM1CD
51. McKinsey was a major consultant on the creation of the *Vision 2030*. Brookings cite the report critically, stating "McKinsey's key report, full with glossy illustrations, contains consultant buzzwords ('transformation,' 'efficiency,' and 'synergies') that would make Marty Kaan in Showtime's *House of Lies* proud." https://www.brookings.edu/blog/ markaz/2016/05/11/saudi-arabias-mckinsey-reshuffle/ The *Financial Times* reported Saudi businessmen have sarcastically dubbed the Saudi Ministry of Planning as the "McKinsey Ministry." https://www.ft.com/ content/0f331bde-b784-11e5-b151-8e15c9a029fb#axzz44ji2fZYA McKinsey Global Institute report, *Saudi Arabia beyond oil: The investment and productivity transformation* https://www.mckinsey.com/ global-themes/employment-and-growth/moving-saudi-arabias-economy-beyond-oil
52. https://www.bloomberg.com/news/articles/2017-09-28/moving-fast-and-breaking-things-a-saudi-prince-tests-his-public, https://www. nytimes.com/2017/11/14/world/middleeast/saudi-arabia-mohammed-bin-salman.html, https://www.washingtonpost.com/world/middle_east/ an-ambitious-young-prince-wants-to-reimagine-saudi-arabia-and-make-it-fun/2017/05/18/41bf6640-3a5d-11e7-a058-ddbb23c75d82_story. html?utm_term=.5b692cc50804
53. https://www.chathamhouse.org/expert/comment/saudi-arabia-faces-its-future-vision-2030-reform-plan
54. http://www.bbc.com/news/world-middle-east-36134436

55. http://english.aawsat.com/theaawsat/news-middle-east/saudi-arabia/saudi-arabia-sets-10-programs-achieve-vision-2030
56. http://data.worldbank.org/indicator/SL.TLF.CACT.FE.ZS?end=2016&locations=SA&start=1990&view=chart
57. https://www.stats.gov.sa/sites/default/files/labor_market_fourth_quarter_2016_en.pdf, p. 16.
58. http://www.oxfordstrategicconsulting.com/wp-content/uploads/2015/05/Maximising-Saudi-Female-Employment-.pdf
59. Sukuk is the plural form of "Sakk" in Arabic, which translates as title deed, as it underscores ownership in the underlying asset.
60. https://www.imf.org/external/pubs/ft/scr/2016/cr16327.pdf, p. 21.

Bibliography

al-Rasheed, Madawi, ed. 2008. *Kingdom Without Borders: Saudi Arabia's Political, Religious and Media Frontiers.* London: Hurst.

Aburish, Said K. 2005. *The Rise, Corruption and Coming Fall of the House of Saud.* London: Bloomsbury.

Barber, Benjamin R. 2001. *Jihad vs McWorld: Terrorism's Challenge to Democracy.* New York: Ballantine Books.

Bremmer, Ian. 2010. *The End of the Free Market.* New York: Portfolio Penguin.

Bronson, Rachel. 2006. *Thicker Than Oil: America's Uneasy Relationship with Saudi Arabia.* New York: Oxford University Press.

Champion, Daryl. 2003. *The Paradoxical Kingdom: Saudi Arabia and the Momentum of Reform.* London: Hurst and Company.

Clarke, Richard A. 2005. *The Scorpion's Gate.* New York: Putnam.

Cook, M.A., ed. 1970. *Studies in the Economic History of the Middle East.* Oxford: Oxford University Press.

Craze, Jonathan, and Mark Huband. 2009. *The Kingdom: Saudi Arabia and the Challenge of the 21st Century.* London: Hurst & Co.

Cunningham, Robert B., and Yasin K. Sarayrah. 1993. *Wasta: The Hidden Force in Middle Eastern Society.* Westport: Praeger.

Gause, F. Gregory, III. 1994. *Oil Monarchies: Domestic and Security Challenges in the Arab Gulf States.* New York: Council on Foreign Relations.

Hammond, Andrew. 2012. *The Islamic Utopia: The illusion of Reform in Saudi Arabia.* London: Pluto Press.

Haykel, Bernard, Thomas Hegghammer, and Stéphane Lacroix. 2015. *Saudi Arabia in Transition: Insights on Social, Political, Economic and Religious Change*. Cambridge: Cambridge University Press.

Hegghammer, Thomas. 2015. *Saudi Arabia in Transition: Insights on Social, Political, Economic and Religious Change*. New York: Cambridge University Press.

Hertog, Steffen. 2010. *Princes, Brokers, and Bureaucrats Oil and the State in Saudi Arabia*. Ithaca: Cornell University Press.

House, Karen Elliott. 2012. *On Saudi Arabia: Its People, Past, Religion, Fault Lines – And Future*. New York: Vintage Books.

Kropf, Annika, and Mohamed A. Ramady, eds. 2015. *Employment and Career Motivation in the Arab Gulf States: The Rentier Mentality Revisited*. Berlin: Gerlach Press.

Lacey, Robert. 2009. *Inside the Kingdom: Kings, Clerics, Terrorists, Modernists, and the Struggle for Saudi Arabia*. New York: Viking.

Lackner, Helen. 1978. *A House Built on Sand. A Political Economy of Saudi Arabia*. London: Ithaca Press.

Lippman, Thomas W. 2012. *Saudi Arabia on the Edge: The Uncertain Future of an American Ally*. Dulles: Potomac Books.

Mazaheri, Nimah. 2016. *Oil Booms and Business Busts: Why Resource Wealth Hurts Entrepreneurs in the Developing World*. Oxford: Oxford University Press.

Nasr, Vali. 2009. *The Rise of Islamic Capitalism: Why the New Muslim Middle Class Is the Key to Defeating Extremism*. New York: Free Press.

Ramady, Mohamed A., ed. 2015. *The Political Economy of Wasta: Use and Abuse of Social Capital Networking*. Heidelberg: Springer.

Schwarz, Rolf. 2007. *Rule, Revenue, and Representation. Oil and State Formation in the Middle East and North Africa*. PhD thesis, Graduate Institute of International Studies, Geneva.

Vitalis, Robert. 2009. *America's Kingdom: Mythmaking on the Saudi Oil Frontier*. London: Verso.

Yahya, Sadowski. 1993. *Scuds or Butter? The Political Economy of Arms Control in the Middle East*. Washington, DC: Brookings Institution.

Yergin, Daniel. 1993. *The Prize: The Epic Quest for Oil, Money & Power*. New York: Touchstone.

3

Deconstructing the Saudi Economy

To understand the scale of the difficulties Saudi faces, there are six structural areas where policy and approaches need to change in order to solve the problems. As noted, the need to balance oil wealth and the need for diversification are not new ideas for Saudi Arabia, they have been policy issues for a long time and long understood as weaknesses in the Kingdom's socioeconomic model. However, the Saudi economic infrastructure has not made sufficient progress to date to counter the dominance of oil, the challenges of a unique business environment and a bulging welfare provision. Saudi faces internal and external threats, and there is little time or room for complacency this time round. Falling global demand and the rise of alternative energy, especially shale gas, are elements beyond Saudi control. The International Energy Agency released a report in November 2012 which predicted the United States would overtake Saudi and Russia as the largest oil producer by 2017, a prediction made more solid by a 4 July 2016 report that stated the United States now has the largest oil reserves. This puts a somewhat different complexion on the "America" and "big oil" argument as the basis for US-Saudi relations, as well as arguments about US oil independence. In conversations I have had with focus groups since 2014, I have witnessed complaisance turn to real concern over the economic changes occurring in Saudi.

© The Author(s) 2018   **53**
D. Cowan, *The Coming Economic Implosion of Saudi Arabia*,
https://doi.org/10.1007/978-3-319-74709-5_3

Problem 1: Diversification of the Economy and the Oil Dependency

When the oil prices started to fall sharply in the Spring of 2014 and it became clear by the end of the year the decline was deeper and longer lasting than expected, the question was whether Saudi Arabia and its OPEC partners would support the world oil price by cutting their own production. Saudi quickly gave the answer that they wanted the United States and others to cut production before cutting their own. This essentially signaled what some saw as the beginning of the end of the Organization of the Petroleum Exporting Countries (OPEC). Saudi remained determined to defend its market share against American shale, and thus abandoned its traditional position as a swing producer. The Saudi response was to try to stabilize prices by pumping more oil when prices went up and pumping less oil when the price went down, and continue to produce at normal output levels. The Saudis were quickly accused of having a political motive, using depressed oil prices to inflict more damage on their great rival Iran and on Russia than they did on Saudi itself. For its part, the United States was quite happy to go along with this Saudi strategy of brinkmanship. As noted, oil has long been the commodity that bound America and Saudi together in the region, and much has been written on "big bad oil," America and the Saudi elite, and much of it either exaggerated, unrealistic or idealistic. The narrative usually focuses on how Saudi is an important political partner in the region because it's the oil, stupid. Well, yes, it is the oil, and there is little need here to tread on such well-trodden ground, and for our purposes we can simply assume these two propositions as givens. The point is that Saudi cannot rely on "big oil," and instead needs to develop new areas of the economy and new diplomatic avenues in the political world.

A major policy option taken with partial success to date has been the diversification by moving downstream in petrochemical products and investing in other business areas, resulting in a small boom in plastics, packaging and technology markets, with some increased entrepreneurial activity in value-added goods and services. The policy dates back to 1999 when Saudi realized they were facing increased competition in the petrochemicals industry, higher production costs, shifting world trade patterns and a fall in petrochemical prices. The Saudis adopted a strategic plan to maintain and increase its competitiveness.[1] The plan included increasing production capacity, diversifying the product mix, more joint ventures, an emphasis on research and development (R&D), enlarging the role of the private sector and diversifying its petrochemical products further downstream. In 2006,[2] the Saudis announced they would enhance their position in the global market over the subsequent five years using five growth strategies, which was a tweak on the 1999 plans: diversifying the product portfolio, establishing more joint ventures with industry majors, placing greater emphasis on research and development, endorsing a larger role for private sector and diversifying into downstream. Hence, there is no shortage of policy options, but the boundaries must be shifted further in the direction of diversification if the Saudi economy is to become more robust. In seeking to push the boundaries, one cannot underestimate the potential gain from government ownership stake in the non-oil sector, with many large public enterprises and entities not listed on the stock market, including Saudi Airlines, the airports, Railroads Saudi, Gulf International Bank and SALIC (Saudi Agricultural and Livestock Investment Company).

Yet there remains the challenge of gas. Saudi suffers from a shortage of gas supplies which is creating difficulties for domestic growth, and $1 trillion in oil and gas investments have been deferred and canceled since the oil downturn began in 2014.[3] An Oxford Energy report argues:

> Saudi Arabia cannot afford to ignore this significant energy source given the size of its proven gas reserves estimated at 219 Tcf at end of 2001. Although small compared to the Russian 1,680 Tcf and the Iranian 812 Tcf the fact remains that Saudi Arabia's reserves rank fourth in size among gas countries (after Russia, Iran and Qatar).[4]

Sadad Al-Husseini, a former top executive at Aramco, explained "This means that resources in the Kingdom are not the problem, but rather how to discover, develop and produce such resources."[5]

There are other sectors which can help diversify the economy, especially agriculture, tourism and Islamic products. Tourist visas are planned for in 2018, though there is also growth in the domestic tourism sector to consider as well. A CNN Money report states Saudi "is aiming for 30 million visitors a year by 2030 (a sharp rise from 2016 figures of 18 million), while the country also intends to spend approximately £35bn on annual tourism by 2020."[6] The agribusiness sector is benefiting from a 2017 budget allocation of SAR78.1 billion ($20.82 billion) to the economic resources sector that include the Ministry of Agriculture and subsidiary industries. Agriculture contributes 5.2% to GDP, totaling SAR52 billion ($13.86 billion) and imports 80% of the Kingdom's food consumption.[7] Islamic finance can grow.[8] Fayaz Ahmad Lone and Salim Alshehri, at the College of Business Administration, Prince Sattam Bin Abdulaziz University in Saudi, argue there is a strong case for development of the Islamic economy:

> Islamic banking has huge potential for development of Islamic banking in Saudi Arabia. Although full-fledged Islamic banks have developed very recently in the world but its progress in Saudi Arabia is tremendous. It is because the market here is such where Islamic values are more important than anything else. But if we take profitability of Islamic banks in Saudi Arabia into consideration, it is also huge. It is expected that within few years every bank in Saudi Arabia might be fully Islamic and conventional banking will come to an end in Saudi Arabia. For this purpose Saudi economists are developing the economic models adopted by Malaysia and United Arab Emirates. As these two countries have become largest Islamic finance markets in the world. Although Saudi Arabia has competitive advantage to develop the Islamic financial system because of its Islamic laws and regulations as well as easy license for the establishment of Islamic banks.[9]

Whether this will spell the end for conventional banking is a moot point, but there is certainly scope for a larger Islamic finance sector in Saudi and for the Kingdom to become a larger player in the global Islamic market.

Problem 2: Corruption

On 4 November 2017, MbS ordered the arrest of prominent princes and business figures, ostensibly to cut out corruption, but many observers and critics have interpreted this act as a further power grab by an impatient prince.[10] King Salman stepped in, telling the Shura Council in Jeddah that corruption issues would be dealt with "in a fair and firm way so that our country enjoys the renaissance and development hoped for by every citizen."[11] An area of concern that is complex in Saudi is the range of activities that are categorized by international norms as forms of corruption. The use of payments in the form of "kickbacks" or "skimming" to do deals is legendary in Saudi and the region, and goes back a long way. It should be said this was in certain respects also entirely legal from the Saudi perspective. There are more complicated subsets to this issue, including familism, patronage and *wasta*,[12] a term that names something similar to what the English traditionally called "the old boys network," and which exists in many forms in all societies to a greater or lesser extent. In the Saudi case, *wasta* is said to result in people getting positions and preference based on family and tribal ties.

According to the GAN report, the picture of corruption can be captured thus:

Companies operating or planning to invest in Saudi Arabia face a high risk of corruption. Abuse of power, nepotism and the use of middlemen (*wasta*) to do business are particularly common. There is an overlap between business and politics, and the latter is generally based on patronage systems. The Combating Bribery Law and the Civil Service Law criminalize various forms of corruption, including active and passive bribery (*baksheesh*) and abuse of functions, but the government enforces these laws selectively. No law regulates conflicts of interest, and some officials engage in corruption with impunity. The royal family and social elite heavily influence the oil and petrochemicals sectors. Gifts are regulated under Saudi law, but facilitation payments are not addressed.[13]

In a report published by Reuters in London,[14] it was stated that some of the biggest handouts by King Abdullah over the past two decades have gone to his own extended family. The basis of the story was unpublished American diplomatic cables obtained by WikiLeaks, reviewed and checked by Reuters, dating back to 1996. The cables also highlight the true cost of the welfare program in the Kingdom both financially and socially. They also detail various money-making schemes some royals have used, including siphoning off money from "off-budget" programs controlled by senior princes, sponsoring expatriate workers who then pay a small monthly fee to their royal patron and simply borrowing from the banks without paying them back. The US embassy in Riyadh in a 1996 cable stated "of the priority issues the country faces, getting a grip on royal family excesses is at the top."[15] A prominent and wealthy Saudi businessman told the embassy that one reason rich Saudis keep so much money outside the country was to lessen the risk of 'royal expropriation.'"[16] A 2007 cable showed that King Abdullah started to make changes, since he did not wish to approach his judgment day with "the burden of corruption on my shoulder."[17] The confiscation of land extends to businesses as well, the cable notes.

To attract foreign investment requires abiding to higher standards of transparency, and stamping out corruption, seen by many international observers, including the World Bank and the IMF, as primary blockers to economic development. Usually this standard is discussed in relation to poorer countries, but it affects richer countries in need of diversification as well. Steps are being made by the Kingdom's top companies to strengthen compliance and regulation, and we can expect this activity to increase. However, the royal household is seen to be continuing playing by different rules, and the rate the Kingdom changes on this issue is very much tied to the rate practices are changed within the royal and family network. This is a complex dynamic, given the influence of royalty and family in the running of the social and economic fabric of the Kingdom. Of course, it goes without saying that corruption is un-Islamic and whatever policies put in place can be interpreted as a reinforcing of underlying Koranic principles concerning fair trading and behavior.

Problem 3: The Growth of the State

The problem is that the bureaucratization of government and extending the reach of the state into the lives of Saudis has been part of the way power has been accrued and maintained. Remarks about a "Thatcherite" revolution made by Crown Prince Mohammad bin Salman should signal a reversal of this problem and lead to more privatization and entrepreneurial activity, but whether the state sector will shrink is highly doubted if Saudi moves toward a state capitalist model. The Saudi state remained a minimal state rooted in basic and subsistence techniques in a village and tribal context until relatively late. As a state there was little in the way of resources to manage, and it was very much a ruling family rather than a state. Pastoral agriculture and trade were the main elements of the economy, with artisanal and commercial activities taking place in towns. There was a move toward institution building in the late 1940s and 1950s, starting in 1948 and aimed at overseeing the extraction of oil. The process became more deeply entrenched after the death of King Abdulaziz in 1953. Steffen Hertog nuances the rentier argument and states:

> The modern Saudi bureaucracy was created in the 1950s and early 1960s by an elite which was largely unconstrained by society or established bureaucratic structures… Saudi bureaucracy-building often seems to be a case not of "form follows function", but of "form follows family". Institutional reforms often were instruments in an intra-elite power game as much as attempts to modernize the state.[18]

Hertog makes the important observation that the "paradox of Saudi state development is that modern, differentiated bureaucracy and royal patrimonialism have grown concurrently."[19]

Saudi became a *rentier* economy as oil rents transformed both the economy and the nature of the relationship between the state and society. Regional development favored the central, eastern and Western provinces, with the south left somewhat behind. However, Steffen Hertog also nuances the rentier argument that the approach to rentier should refocus more on:

> contingency and agency, which are in turn crucial to understand the internal heterogeneity of the Saudi state: Oil income has in some cases allowed for the creation of very efficient bureaucratic islands – SAMA et al, where select commoners played crucial roles –, but in others has boosted neo-patrimonialism. As long as the system expanded, oil created great leeway to design institutions freely and in very different ways. Generalizations about the nature of the state are hence difficult.[20]

If Saudi is to restructure its economy the bureaucratization and growth of government needs to be checked, particularly in relation to the unproductive or entitlement jobs in the government sector, including nepotism or *wasta*. The Vision 2030 essentially demands the government redefine its roles and responsibilities, and ensure employees become more accountable to the people it serves. This also suggests a reorientation away from government being an outgrowth of the royal household toward being a servant of the people as a whole. This entails rethinking the power operations of the house of Saud, and the handing over of powers to public bodies, which in turn is a challenge to the royal and familial makeup of the Kingdom as it currently stands. The questions of form and elite power games posited by Hertog will be played out as the bureaucracy in Saudi evolves, but as the weekend changes and other change programs have evidenced this can be done quite quickly. Ironically the form as function, and more consensus among the elites that something needs to be done, is allowing the bureaucracy to be more flexible.

Problem 4: The Rentier State

As late as the 1940s the economy was still rooted in subsistence-based techniques, pastoral agriculture and trade, with production based on tribes and villages, entailing a minimal state. However, with the discovery of oil in 1938 came the oil rents, creating what critics commonly describe as a redistributive "rentier" state. By the end of that decade, Saudi had begun a process of institution building, though not with any overarching plan in place. The criticism of the impact on Saudi as a rentier economy since has been that the oil wealth has depoliticized its people, with government holding the wealth and being propped up by a seemingly endless supply of oil. As one Saudi Aramco executive put it to me as we walked around the company compound, everywhere we were walking we stepped on oil and we would be doing so for a very long time. Unlike tax-raising economies which derive funding from their populace to support state activities, which is what most economies do, Saudi and other oil states are rentier economies where the state is paid by an oil rent derived from its global customer base. This oil rent is then distributed and allocated to various parts of society, ranging from defense spending to social welfare solutions. This makes the state financially independent from the society, and does not trade tax and votes to survive or maintain power. Where the cry usually goes out, as Giacomo Luciani notes, "No taxation without representation" in Saudi it is reversed to "No representation without taxation."[21] Though most critics would agree the relationship is a little more complicated than this, the comment does capture the essential point they are making.

Let us deal first with the notion of the Saudi economy as a rentier economy. In classical economic theory, rent is defined in terms of the surplus remaining after all production costs are met, which is paid to the owner of the land, rewarding property ownership while giving the renter, entrepreneur or worker use of the resources they do not own, or what Alfred Marshall called "income derived from the gift of nature."[22] Adam Smith saw rent as a surplus arising due to some produce selling for a price in excess of the cost of production,[23] and Ricardo called rent "that portion of the produce of earth which is paid to the landlord for the use of the original and indestructible powers of the soil."[24] Such rental exists in varying ways in all economies, and it creates a degree of liquidity in the economy. However, in the concept of "rentier economy" rent is somewhat more fundamental, it is the percentage of rents in government revenues. The notion of a "rentier state" was first proposed by Hossein Mahdavy[25] in his study of pre-revolutionary Iran in the 1970s and is most widely used to describe the economies of the oil-rich Arab states, where rent is the dominant source of income and a minority group generates the source of rent and then distributes a portion of its income in some form to the majority. The sale of oil, and the attracting of foreign funds, has made rentier states sustainable up to now, but the dramatic disruption of the oil price and related economy has had deep effects on the rentier economies because of the dependency on the natural resources that produces the rent. The problem is that rentier states have also suffered historically from what is called the "resource curse,"[26] which refers to resource wealthy states which tend to experience less economic and political growth. Rolf Schwarz provides a useful picture of the problem Saudi faces because of such economic arrangements:

Seeing a simple dichotomy between grievances and greed, as evident in the recent literature on the 'resource curse', misses the point that lack of development, lack of economic growth, unequal wealth distribution and political inequalities are all secondary effects of rent-driven state-formation. They may create political grievances and these grievances may subsequently turn into violence or, as the cases treated in this article manifest, they may lead to stagnation, political incrustation, and lack of economic reform.[27]

As an aside, one aspect of this which is important to mention, but will not delay us further here, is the way in which a rentier economy is able to finance the military complex. We are familiar with President Eisenhower's notion of the military-industrial complex, but in the case of Saudi, we find the military-rentier complex, because the Kingdom can fund a level of defense and military based on oil revenues rather than from taxation and the populace as a whole.[28]

Problem 5: Restraint of the Middle Class

To take the point made by Schwarz further, the economic problems faced by Saudi are even more fundamental and problematic for economic reform as a rentier state, because a rentier economy creates a rentier mentality whereby individuals do not earn income because it is distributed to a large portion of them. It debilitates the middle class and is opposite to the entrepreneurial heart of capitalism. It also militates against the use of effort and reward as a way to propel the economy, and this in turn creates a level of expectation rather than achievement. In Saudi this in part takes the form of *wasta*. Such *wasta* does impact attitudes and expectations, but there is another dimension to add to the economic mentality. In rentier economies there are two kinds of workers, the indigenous population that receives the fruits of the rent without too much effort and the foreign or expatriate worker who works to get a share of the rent. All of this is fine, so long as the source of rents is plentiful, but it doesn't help when you are forced to diversify the economy, because the human capital available is suddenly found to be somewhat moribund and lacking in the required entrepreneurial nous.

The rentier problem took root in the period when Saudi's oil revenue increased some 25 times from 1970 to 1979. Over the decade, Crown Prince Fahd, regarded as something of a technocrat, oversaw the transformation of government from being small and poor to being large and extensive throughout the economy. This has created what has become a burdensome welfare state and a rentier economy that by the end of the 1970s saw the government-owned Saudi oil sector accounting for 65% of Saudi economic activity and 63% of total investment in physical assets, a level of state economy that could only be matched by the old communist and socialist economies. It was thus the beginning of the Kingdom as a state economy and the reduction of the merchant classes in Saudi to rent-seekers. The government heavily subsidized public utilities, state employment, a free education system and healthcare, which has tended to satisfy the Saudi middle class, until now that is. William Rugh has explained the mindset of Saudi's middle class:

> The Saudi New Middle Class member typically is ambitious to move up the economic ladder and improve his living standard. He is thus distinguished from the more fatalistic or passive Saudis in the lower classes. His stronger ambitions derive from a growing economy which increasingly rewards secular learning and the skills he has, and which opens up opportunities for him which did not exist before. But like other Saudis, he places higher value on the prestige or dignity of the job than on its monetary reward.[29]

As Hertog wrote "Patronage was not new to Saudi politics, but never before had it reached all strata of society. By 1979, the rentier social contract, in the making since the 1940s, had come to define national politics."[30] This state of affairs continued, indeed was extended, until 2014 and falling oil prices that went deeper and longer than ever expected started to force back the rentier control and has brought stricter market forces to operate, albeit gradually, in Saudi Arabia. Despite the emergence of a larger middle class, the average Saudi today is very much in the same position as they were back in 1979, and the Kingdom's political economy remains much today as it was in 1979, eerily echoing the election of Margaret Thatcher as prime minister in Britain that same year.

Gregory Gause III suggests Saudi is an exception to the rentier model, both in economic and political terms, explaining:

> Some of the earliest literature on the rentier state speculated that politics in such states would revolve around symbolic more than material issues, since the state's control over so much of the national wealth and its ability to spread that wealth to the citizenry would take economic issues off the agenda. We know that this extreme statement of the argument has not been borne out by the experience of oil states. Economic issues do arise, even in the richest rentier states. Saudi Arabia, unlike Kuwait and UAE, is not super-rich. In terms of per capita wealth, it is a middle-income country with some regional and class disparities of wealth.[31]

Hertog suggests that in discussing the rentier state there is greater contingency than the literature would have us believe. He distinguishes between what he calls the "meso-level" of politics and the micro-level of individual organization units and bureaucrats. Hertog explains bureaucrats "in large parts of the oversized state apparatus tend to be de facto distributive clients of the state, with job entitlements that sap individual motivation," and they tend to refer matters upward "while giving superiors little control over the day-to-day behavior of low-level administrators."[32] Thus, policies may be implemented but they are subverted at the lower levels. Hertog argues the heterogeneity of the Saudi state is exceptional, which has to do with how rents and royal power decisions are combined to shape the Saudi state.

A critical aspect to consider is that the rentier and middle-class question is essentially one of behavioral economics, and it has been a "tenacious" one. As Kropf and Ramady state "While it seems to be a mentality only, rentier mentality has also given rise to and nourished structures and mechanisms in businesses and administration that suited the mentality best."[33] As Hertog suggests "If anything constrained the shape the state took, it was pre-oil socioeconomic and political conditions, not the oil money with which the state was built." Thus, while diversifying the economy will lead to the end of the rentier aspects of the Saudi state and impact a range of relationships, especially that between the government and the people, we can assume some of these changes are leveraging off preexistent behaviors and mentality as well. It also means we can expect some evolution of these behaviors and mentality as the Saudis seek to engineer change. This means innovating the economy, which requires a creative and critical mentality. This effort is occurring against the backdrop of a higher cost of living and the rising specter of taxation in the Kingdom on the one hand and the weaning off the state and an end of dependency on the other. This could lead to social strife, and the difficulty of managing such a social transition cannot be underestimated. It is also Islamic to promote broad participation in social relations, and this the dominance of an elite to the detriment of the middle class appears to be contradictory to Islamic principles.

Problem 6: Poverty in Saudi Arabia

On 10 October 2011, two young Saudi bloggers Firas Buqna and Hussam Al-Darwish were jailed and served a 15-day sentence because they had uploaded a ten-minute YouTube documentary on poverty in Riyadh. It was the fifth episode of their Web TV show called "Mal'oub Alen" (translated as "we're being duped"), and it explored the living conditions of people in the poor neighborhood of Jaradiya, on the outskirts of Riyadh.[34] The video, which can no longer be viewed online, claimed that "over the past 27 years Saudi Arabia has donated 56 billion euros to developing countries, while 22% the country's own citizens were reportedly living in relative poverty in 2009 (local media put the number at 30% in 2008)."[35] The Saudi government does not reveal too much about the existence of the poor, but they do exist and you can see them sitting on the street corners of Riyadh and other urban centers or see the young boys begging at cars stopped at traffic lights. A press report in 2013 stated private estimates suggest that between 2 million and 4 million of the country's native Saudis live on less than about $530 a month, which is about $17 a day and considered the poverty line in the Kingdom. In the same year, the World Bank ranked Saudi Arabia as having the tenth lowest poverty rate worldwide, and gave it the highest ranking in the Arab region in terms of minimizing poverty,[36] though this is a contested point as the poverty rate continues to increase.[37] A more recent report in 2016 stated Saudi household income is around $3800 per month and the aver-age Saudi family comprises six members. According to the official statis-tics of the Ministry of Social Services, the poverty line stands at $480 a month. An economist at the King Fahd University of Petroleum and Minerals in Dhahran suggested otherwise, that "the government's figures are not really reliable. I reckon that 35 per cent of the population has to get by with much less than $533. They are poor."[38]

There are then challenges in the way poverty and extreme poverty are defined and measured in Saudi Arabia with little information to go on. However, the United Nations Development Program measures the state of things thus:

> The Kingdom's efforts to contain poverty have borne fruit. Data available under the National Social Development Strategy indicate that the propor-tion of Saudi households living under the extreme poverty line (food pov-erty) stood at 0.08% in 2004, but declined to some 0.06% in 2009, amounting to a drop of 25%. Thus, The Kingdom has achieved the 1 MDG goal of eradication of food poverty well ahead of the target year of 2015. Another positive aspect in this regard is that the Kingdom has set the extreme poverty level at near two US Dollars per person per day, which exceeds the MDG level of one US Dollar. In Saudi Arabia, the percentage of families living under extreme poverty was 1.63% in 2004 to 0.8 in 2008, Prevalence of underweight children under five 5 years of age decreased from *6.4% in 2006 to 5.3% in 2010.[39]

A more recent report by the United Nations Special Rapporteur on extreme poverty and human rights, Philip Alston, observed that most Saudis are convinced that their country is free of poverty, but the reality is that there are very poor areas in both the large cities and remote rural areas, and there is major neglect of the plight of many non-Saudi long-term residents. Only in 2002 was the existence of poverty in the Kingdom first acknowledged by the then Crown Prince Abdullah. While govern-ment programs have proliferated and charitable organizations working on poverty have flourished since then, Mr. Alston described the current social protection system for the poor as "a veritable hodgepodge of pro-grams which is inefficient, unsustainable, poorly coordinated and, above all, unsuccessful in providing comprehensive social protection to those most in need." He added, "In meetings with me the Government was severely self-critical of the shortcomings of its current social protection system and it appears to be making genuine attempts at reforming that system."[40] For its part, the Saudi Ministry of Economy and Planning, in what was labeled "a severe self-indictment," described the resulting challenges to the rapporteur in the following terms:

• Lack of a true understanding of the nature of poverty in the Kingdom;
• Weak targeting, overlaps and leakage in beneficiary coverage;
• Little account for geographic specificity and cultural variation;
• Social protection programs are not designed for graduation;
• Lack of a common vision across institutions;
• Weak coordination and fragmentation within and across delivery institutions;
• Institutional complexity and conflicting mandates;
• Little to no involvement from the private sector;
• Absence of arms-length monitoring and evaluation mechanisms across social protection programs;
• Absence of financial and social impact assessment of programs.[41]

This will be part of the Vision 2030 aim to fix the economy, but the UN Officer of the High Commissioner for Human Rights (OHCHR) believes some of the programs created could be troublesome for the poorer sectors of Saudi society, in the areas of subsidy reforms and the introduction of a cash transfer program, which OHCHR suggests affect the lives of those most vulnerable. The OHCHR in their report to the Saudi government highlighted actions in 2016 of making dramatic reductions of fuel, electricity and water subsidies and aims to cushion the negative impacts of those reforms by introducing a cash transfer program called the Household Allowance which is part of an overall Citizen Account system allowing for a greatly expanded data gathering capacity.

Concerns over poverty are not simply a matter of public policy, they are also a matter of faith. As Prince Sultan bin Salman, a son of King Salman, explained in an interview, "Living in Saudi Arabia is like living in a charitable foundation; it is part and parcel of the way we're made up."

Adding, "if you are not charitable, you are not a Muslim."[42] Charity forms one of the pillars of Islam, but Ismail Sirageldin extends this by outlining a useful axiomatic approach based on four basic tenants of the Islamic ethical system:

1. Unity (Tawhid): This axiom indicates the vertical dimension of the ethical system. It provides for freedom of action with the view that each individual is viewed as an integral part of the whole.
2. Equilibrium (Al'Adl wal Ihsan): The axiom provides for the horizontal dimension of equity leaving a lot of freedom for policy details, as, for example, striking an appropriate balance between the needs of present and future generations.
3. Free Will (Ikhtiyar): Although individual freedom is guided by broad guidelines, and individuals may travel their own paths, careful reflection is required "to interpret-reinterpret that freedom within specific societal contexts, and to suit the needs of changing times."[43]
4. Responsibility (Fard): The axiom states that although "Responsibility" is voluntary, individuals and society need to conserve for the public good, there is a social aspect of every asset owned or managed by private or public entities.

Sirageldin notes:

> These four axioms, taken together, lead to a universal ethical system that implies that policies should not lead to dependency, limit opportunities that develop capabilities to the few, or reduce individual responsibilities to take action. Policies should enhance motivation to seek knowledge, enhance productivity, and enhance transparency in government. They should also enhance intra- and intergeneration equity.[44]

The Islamic approach is deeply ingrained in the faith, perhaps somewhat more legally "required" than the notion of charity in the Christian faith, and not status-bound like the ostentatious giving and reward system of lotteries, celebrities and high society in the secular West. However, we should not idealize the Islamic approach, since like all religions what is preached is often at odds with what is practiced, and we cannot hold

Islam to a higher standard. This said, Islam has a theology of poverty which roots action in the notion of intent, and one should expect Islamic societies to place a high importance on looking after the people of the society.

Problem 7: Inshallah

It has long been commonplace to discuss the "American mind," and I suggest it is equally interesting to talk of the "Saudi mind." This is because the Islamic religion in Saudi is normative for behavior, just as Christianity was normative for America in times past and formed part of how America approached various economic and political challenges. In stark contrast to the rentier mentality, John Locke had stated man acquires property through the labor of his person, not through distribution or by rents:

> Though the earth, and all inferior creatures, be common to all men, yet every man has a property in his own person: this nobody has any right to but himself. The labour of his body, and the work of his hands, we may say, are properly his. Whatsoever then he removes out of the state that nature hath provided, and left it in, he hath mixed his labour with, and joined to it something that is his own, and thereby makes it his property.[45]

Thus to work was to be, and the spirit is joined between the physical and economic act. The twin set of Calvinist religion and enlightenment thought have popularly been called the "American mind," which gives the nation its self-understanding. For much of American history, the Bible and Calvinist religion were the dominant spirit of the mind, which went in tandem with the enlightenment thought of Locke, Rousseau and the European enlightenment.[46] The understanding of the American mind has come under strain in the last 40 years with challenges from the liberalization of culture and globalization, and American religious conservatives feel that the American mind is threatened by these cultural shifts and seek to defend what they see as a tradition dating back to the founding fathers of the nation. This evolution of thought spurred on the development of American democracy and the economy, with what has variously been called the Protestant work ethic and the American dream. More recently in 1987, the cultural critic Allan Bloom has noted this change in thinking as the close of the American mind, which was a critique of liberal education, which some students today might classify as elitist. The point is there was a way of thinking that seemed very American for a very long time, and it drove progress for better or worse. Such a mind, and the individualism it triumphs, is not the Saudi experience.

However, there are also deep cultural problems to assess as Khashan notes:

> Riyadh's cultural values do not support the objectives of Vision 2030. Saudi society is closed, status-oriented, and tribally structured. On the whole, Saudis are not law-abiding citizens, and they often violate it with impunity. They also tend to treat expatriates, especially laborers from poor countries, as nonentities unworthy of human dignity. Sordid abuse of hapless foreign workers is the norm rather than the exception.[47]

The current state of play in Saudi is one of a change in behaviors if the economy is to change, which means being self-reliant. Many foreign companies and individuals working in Saudi have a scathing view of the Saudi work ethic, which they see as a mixture of a rentier mentality and Inshallah. The rentier mentality resonates with this key attitude of Inshallah in Saudi. Like elsewhere in the Arab world, the word Inshallah is a constant in Saudi. It is a verbal key to understanding this intriguing and changing nation. It will punctuate conversations, and will frustrate foreign visitors trying to get something done. Its specific meaning is not always adequately grasped by foreigners: God has willed it, which means the one uttering the saying is recognizing that God wills it, not our individual will. It is part of the Islamic submission to God's way. The Koran reveals what God's way is, and hence the believer needs to obey what the Koran has revealed. Some Saudis will joke Inshallah means "if the boss wills it," and others use the word to indicate they will do nothing. In English usage the word most commonly means "hopefully," a kind of quasi-religious hope in God perhaps. In the business context the word reflects a sense of time that is quite different from the capitalist business culture of being very time sensitive, after all time is money as the saying goes. In Saudi time is more open, and it is God's time to dictate and not ours to second-guess. The prevalence of Inshallah indicates to me there is a level of efficiency in our Western business model that I don't believe is accepted and possibly not even desired in the Saudi business culture. Which brings us back to the role of religion, and the balance between economics and faith in Saudi and Islam.

From a capitalist perspective, the impact of Inshallah in economic terms is that it becomes somewhat fatalistic on the one hand, and militates against time as an efficient mode of economic conduct. However, while it can be dismissed as fatalistic or procrastination, to the Saudi its roots lie in a recognition of submission to God and the ownership of time by God. When we look at the consumerism and presentism of the Western world and globalization, Saudis suspect it is the capitalist economies which need a more enlightened sense of time. Either way, from the workings of the market economy, time is an important factor, and in a global economy, Inshallah is out of sync, whether in reality or as a perception, and so it presents Saudi with problems if it is to compete and be more efficient in the global economy. However, from the Islamic perspective it is not simply to be judged in terms of delayed time, it is God's time and is part of Islamic economic thinking and Sharia. Economically, it affects business planning, outlaws the futures markets, questions the paying of interest and underlines the need for a work/life balance. These are variables to consider if an Islamic economy is ever to be embraced.

New Opportunities?

Where the economic climate induced by the oil price drop is seen by some to be a problem, others see an opportunity. To take the example of the "youth bulge," many commentators see the boredom and lack of opportunity for young Saudis makes them prime candidates for radicalization or politicization. When I broached this topic with Prince Turki bin Faisal Al Saud,[48] former head of Saudi Intelligence and Ambassador to London and Washington DC, he responded to the contrary. Prince Turki sees the youth as potential candidates for the much-needed entrepreneurship, and the same holds for gender. I mentioned, at the time, women were

effectively banned from driving cars and limited socially, but Prince
Turki retorted that women were starting businesses from home. One
thing is certain with Saudi, the debate is polarized, and it is polarized
because the dialogue partners are usually talking past each other, and as
so often in human situations the truth lies somewhere between the two
positions.

It may well be assumed the economic challenge is whether Saudi can
reinvent itself in terms of westernized capitalist economics, but we also
need to look at whether it will result in state capitalism or if it is possible,
and desirable, for Saudi to become an Islamic economy. Reinvention
there must be, and the days of the rentier economy are all but over. If
Saudi is to survive the Kingdom must find a way forward that is appropriate, and for those outside of Saudi to interpret this means understanding what the spirit of Saudi is economically speaking. Weber argued,
usefully but not entirely accurately, that Protestantism was the spirit of
capitalism, and likewise we can study the role of Islam as the spirit at the
heart of Saudi economic change. We will discuss later in more detail how
Weber saw the Protestant work ethic and the spirit of capitalism as intimately related, but we can already pose the question: what of the Islamic
work ethic? In the Western tradition there is something religiously or
theologically inherently suspect about the economy and work, but it can
be contested that the Protestant work ethic is a question for Western
capitalism rather than economics generally. Economics is the part-science
of understanding the world of scarcity in relation to conflicting wants.
Theology looks at reconciliation, which is a reconciling of people firstly
to God and then to one another. While resources and money are often as
scarce as the milk of human kindness when we look at the tensions
between people generally, and in religious groups specifically, there is also
a world of abundance where the faithful believe God will provide us with
what we need in a world of scarcity, both economically and morally. We
just need to understand what constitutes abundance. In a Christian theological understanding of this tension between scarcity and God's abundance, there tends to be a separation of faith and economy in both liberal
and conservative circles, though for very different reasons. For this reason, books on economy do not tend to discuss theology and we don't
commonly talk about "Christian economics." Religious liberals tend to

see the economy and faith in oppositional terms and demand a protest against capitalism, while religious conservatives tend to see it in exclusive terms whereby the economy is not the place for redemption. However, some conservative groups believe in the so-called "prosperity gospel" whereby God helps those who help themselves to be successful. As we will see, the Islamic tradition sees the two as positively and inextricably tied together, rather than negative and in opposition, and of course there is something commonly called "Islamic economics" and "Islamic finance."

Notes

1. http://www.ogj.com/articles/print/volume-97/issue-33/uncategorized/saudi-arabias-petrochemical-industry-diversifies-to-face-challenges.html
2. http://www.ogj.com/articles/print/volume-104/issue-2/processing/saudi-petrochemicals-conclusion-five-strategies-drive-saudi-arabiars-quos-petchem-industry-growth.html
3. https://www.reuters.com/article/sabic-results-gas/saudis-sabic-says-natural-gas-shortage-limiting-domestic-growth-idUSL6N0NC04D20140420, https://www.ft.com/content/ed1e8102-212f-11e7-b7d3-163f5a7f229c
4. https://www.oxfordenergy.org/publications/saudi-arabias-natural-gas-a-glimpse-at-complex-issues/
5. http://www.arabnews.com/news/576361
6. http://money.cnn.com/2017/11/22/news/economy/saudi-arabia-tourist-visa/index.html?sr=fbCNN112217economy0438PMStory
7. http://saudi-agriculture.com/en-sa/about/about-saudi-arabia
8. http://jibfnet.com/journals/jibf/Vol_3_No_1_June_2015/4.pdf
9. Lone, Dr. Fayaz Ahmad and Alshehri, Salim *Growth and Potential of Islamic Banking in GCC: The Saudi Arabia Experience* Journal of Islamic Banking and Finance June 2015, Vol. 3, No. 1, pp. 35–43.
10. https://www.washingtonpost.com/world/saudi-arabia-detains-princes-ministers-and-billionaire-investor-in-extraordinary-purge/2017/11/05/ea0aa25c-c1fc-11e7-af84-d3e2ee4b2af1_story.html?tid=a_inl&utm_term=.ae6fee61687c, https://www.washingtonpost.com/opinions/global-opinions/the-saudi-crown-princes-risky-power-play/2017/11/05/4b12fcf0-c272-11e7-afe9-4f60b5a6c4a0_story.html?utm_term=.8ea53780e068

11. http://www.arabnews.com/node/1208436/saudi-arabia
12. Cunningham, Robert B. and Sarayrah, Yasin K. *Wasta: The Hidden Force in Middle Eastern Society* (Westport, Conn: Praeger, 1993). Ramady, Mohamed A. (ed) *The Political Economy of Wasta: Use and Abuse of Social Capital Networking* (Switzerland: Springer, 2016).
13. http://www.business-anti-corruption.com/country-profiles/saudi-arabia GAN Report?
14. http://www.reuters.com/article/us-wiki-saudi-money-id USTRE71R2SA20110228
15. https://wikileaks.org/plusd/cables/96RIYADH4784_a.html
16. Ibid.
17. https://wikileaks.org/plusd/cables/07RIYADH296_a.html
18. http://dro.dur.ac.uk/4561/1/4561.pdf
19. Ibid.
20. Ibid.
21. Luciani, Giacomo (ed) *The Arab State* (Berkeley: University of California Press, 1990), p. 75ff.
22. Marshall, Alfred *Principles of Economics* (London: Macmillan, 1920), p. 45.
23. Smith, Adam *An Inquiry into the Nature and Causes of the Wealth of Nations, Book I, Chapter XI "Of the Rent of Land"* (London: Methuen, 1904).
24. Ricardo, David *The Principles of Political Economy and Taxation* (New York: Dover Publications, 2004), p. 33.
25. Mahdavy, Hossein *The Patterns and Problems of Economic Development in Rentier States: The Case of Iran*, in Cook (1970). See also Beblawi, Hazem, The Rentier State in the Arab World *Arab Studies Quarterly* Vol. 9, No. 4 (Fall 1987), pp. 383–398. Luciani (1990). *The Oil Rent, the Fiscal Crisis of the State and Democratization* in Salame (1994) pp. 130–155. Matthew Gray, A *Theory of "Late Rentierism" in the Arab States of the Gulf.* Occasional Paper No. 7, Center for International and Regional Studies Georgetown University School of Foreign Service in Qatar, 2011.
26. Ibid, Mazaheri (2016); Steffen Hertog, Defying the Resource Curse: Explaining Successful State-Owned Enterprises in Rentier States, *World Politics* Vol. 62, No. 2 (April 2010), pp. 261–301.
27. Schwarz, Rolf *The Political Economy of State-Formation in the Arab Middle East: Rentier States, Economic Reform, and Democratization,* Review of International Political Economy, Vol. 15, No. 4 (Oct. 2008), pp. 599–621.

28. Further study of this point can be made by consulting Keith Krause, Insecurity and State Formation in the Global Military Order: The Middle Eastern Case, *European Journal of International Relations,* 1996, 3: 319–354. Sadowski (1993). Schwarz (2007). Rolf Schwarz, The Political Economy of State-Formation in the Arab Middle East: Rentier States, Economic Reform, and Democratization, *Review of International Political Economy,* Vol. 15, No. 4 (Oct., 2008), pp. 599–621.

29. William Rugh, Emergence of a New Middle Class in Saudi Arabia, *Middle East Journal,* Vol. 27, No. 1 (Winter, 1973), pp. 7–20.

30. http://www.mei.edu/content/rentier-social-contract-saudi-political-economy-1979

31. Haykel et al. (2015, p. 28).

32. Ibid, p. 11.

33. Kropf and Ramady (2015, p. 1).

34. http://observers.france24.com/en/20111107-there-are-no-poor-people-saudi-arabia-poverty-video-prison-bloggers-firas-buqna-Al-Jaradiya

35. http://www.albawaba.com/news/saudi-arabia-poverty-world-bank-531214. Other video reports can be viewed: https://www.youtube.com/watch?v=G7yuRNL37XU, https://www.youtube.com/watch?v=JmTiiC5s6qU, an ITV 2016 documentary https://www.youtube.com/watch?v=gLGrLiWFCg0

36. http://www.arabnews.com/news/472256

37. https://www.albawaba.com/news/saudi-arabia-poverty-world-bank-531214, http://www.adhrb.org/wp-content/uploads/2017/01/2017.1.06_SR-Poverty_Saudi-briefing_final-1.pdf

38. http://eaworldview.com/2016/03/saudi-arabia-feature-poverty-wealthy-land/

39. http://www.sa.undp.org/content/saudi_arabia/en/home/mdgoverview/overview/mdg1/

40. http://www.ohchr.org/en/NewsEvents/Pages/DisplayNews.aspx?NewsID=21099&LangID=E. UN Officer of the High Commissioner for Human Rights (OHCHR).

41. Ibid.

42. https://www.theguardian.com/world/2013/jan/01/saudi-arabia-riyadh-poverty-inequality; http://borgenproject.org/poverty-riyadh-saudi-arabia; http://www.albawaba.com/news/saudi-arabia-poverty-world-bank-531214

43. Naqvi (1994, p. 31).

44. http://www.irti.org/English/Research/Documents/IES/115.pdf
45. Locke (1764, p. 209).
46. https://www.theatlantic.com/international/archive/2017/10/muslim-reformation/544343/
47. http://www.meforum.org/6397/saudi-arabia-flawed-vision-2030
48. Interview 10 July 2016.

Bibliography

Aburish, Said K. 2005. *The Rise, Corruption and Coming Fall of the House of Saud*. London: Bloomsbury.

Barber, Benjamin R. 2001. *Jihad vs McWorld: Terrorism's Challenge to Democracy*. New York: Ballantine Books.

Bremmer, Ian. 2010. *The End of the Free Market*. New York: Portfolio Penguin.

Bronson, Rachel. 2006. *Thicker Than Oil: America's Uneasy Relationship with Saudi Arabia*. New York: Oxford University Press.

Champion, Daryl. 2003. *The Paradoxical Kingdom: Saudi Arabia and the Momentum of Reform*. London: Hurst and Company.

Chapra, Mohammed Umer. 1985. *Towards a Just Monetary System*. Leicester: Islamic Foundation.

———. 1992. *Islam and the Economic Challenge*. Leicester: International Institute of Islamic Thought.

Cook, M.A., ed. 1970. *Studies in the Economic History of the Middle East*. Oxford: Oxford University Press.

Craze, Jonathan, and Mark Huband. 2009. *The Kingdom: Saudi Arabia and the Challenge of the 21st Century*. London: Hurst & Co.

Cunningham, Robert B., and Yasin K. Sarayrah. 1993. *Wasta: The Hidden Force in Middle Eastern Society*. Westport: Praeger.

Darlow, Michael, and Barbara Ibn Saud Bray. 2012. *The Desert Warrior Who Created the Kingdom of Saudi Arabia*. New York: Skyhorse Publishing.

Gause, F. Gregory, III. 1994. *Oil Monarchies: Domestic and Security Challenges in the Arab Gulf States*. New York: Council on Foreign Relations.

Hammond, Andrew. 2012. *The Islamic Utopia: The Illusion of Reform in Saudi Arabia*. London: Pluto Press.

Haykel, Bernard, Thomas Hegghammer, and Stéphane Lacroix. 2015. *Saudi Arabia in Transition: Insights on Social, Political, Economic and Religious Change*. Cambridge: Cambridge University Press.

Heggenhammer, Thomas. 2015. *Saudi Arabia in Transition: Insights on Social, Political, Economic and Religious Change*. New York: Cambridge University Press.

Hertog, Steffen. 2010. *Princes, Brokers, and Bureaucrats Oil and the State in Saudi Arabia*. Ithaca: Cornell University Press.

House, Karen Elliott. 2012. *On Saudi Arabia: Its People, Past, Religion, Fault Lines – And Future*. New York: Vintage Books.

Kropf, Annika, and Mohamed A. Ramady, eds. 2015. *Employment and Career Motivation in the Arab Gulf States: The Rentier Mentality Revisited*. Berlin: Gerlach Press.

Lacey, Robert. 2009. *Inside the Kingdom: Kings, Clerics, Terrorists, Modernists, and the Struggle for Saudi Arabia*. New York: Viking.

Lackner, Helen. 1978. *A House Built on Sand. A Political Economy of Saudi Arabia*. London: Ithaca Press.

Lippman, Thomas W. 2012. *Saudi Arabia on the Edge: The Uncertain Future of an American Ally*. Dulles: Potomac Books.

Locke, John. 1764. In *Two Treatises of Government*, ed. Thomas Hollis. London: A. Millar et al.

Mabon, Simon. 2016. *Saudi Arabia and Iran: Power and Rivalry in the Middle East*. New York: I.B. Tauris.

Marshall, Alfred. 1920. *Principles of Economics*. London: Macmillan.

Mazaheri, Nimah. 2016. *Oil Booms and Business Busts: Why Resource Wealth Hurts Entrepreneurs in the Developing World*. Oxford: Oxford University Press.

Mitchell, Timothy. 2013. *Carbon Democracy: Political Power in the Age of Oil*. London: Verso.

Naqvi, S.N.H. 1994. *Ethics and Economics: An Islamic Synthesis*. Leicester: The Islamic Foundation.

Nasr, Vali. 2009. *The Rise of Islamic Capitalism: Why the New Muslim Middle Class Is the Key to Defeating Extremism*. New York: Free Press.

Ramady, Mohamed A., ed. 2015. *The Political Economy of Wasta: Use and Abuse of Social Capital Networking*. Heidelberg: Springer.

Ramazani, R.K., ed. 1990. *Iran's Revolution: The Search for Consensus*. Bloomington: Indiana University Press.

Ricardo, David. 2004. *The Principles of Political Economy and Taxation*. New York: Dover Publications.

Sadowski, Yahya. 1993. *Scuds or Butter? The Political Economy of Arms Control in the Middle East*. Washington, DC: Brookings Institution.

Salame, Ghassan, ed. 1994. *Democracy Without Democrats? The Renewal of Politics in the Muslim World*. London: I.B. Tauris.

Schumpeter, Joseph A. 1954. *History of Economic Analysis*. New York: Oxford University Press.

Schwarz, Rolf. 2007. *Rule, Revenue, and Representation. Oil and State Formation in the Middle East and North Africa*. PhD thesis, Graduate Institute of International Studies, Geneva.

Smith, Adam. 1904. *An Inquiry into the Nature and Causes of the Wealth of Nations*. London: Methuen.

Thaler, Richard H. 2015. *Misbehaving: The Making of Behavioral Economics*. New York: W.W. Norton.

Vitalis, Robert. 2009. *America's Kingdom: Mythmaking on the Saudi Oil Frontier*. London: Verso.

Yahya, Sadowski. 1993. *Scuds or Butter? The Political Economy of Arms Control in the Middle East*. Washington, DC: Brookings Institution.

Yergin, Daniel. 1993. *The Prize: The Epic Quest for Oil, Money & Power*. New York: Touchstone.

4

The Islamic Welfare State

Saudi Arabia has an Islamic welfare state, this needs to be stated simply and in some respects it works in ways similar to other welfare systems. Like people in other economies, Saudis are increasingly worried about job security and the cost of living. In the past, the labor market and welfare state largely insulated them from any long-term economic impacts, as the state threw money at the people and allowed extended families to afford to support their relatives comfortably without jobs. In December 2015, there was a rude awakening for the citizens of Saudi when the government announced a tight budget, raised electricity rates for the largest consumers and ordered higher fuel, gas and water prices for everyone.[1] The following year, in September, austerity went deeper when the government cut public sector pay.[2] However, in a popular move in April 2017, King Salman rescinded the public sector pay cuts by royal decree and backdated pay to October 2016, thus restoring the cuts made in the first place. This was the first reversal in two years of such austerity measures. To date it appears austerity measures have been accepted, especially with the added sweetener of reversals, but Saudis I have spoken to about the changes remain deeply worried about the future impact of these recent policies and what changes may lie ahead. As one Saudi executive told me it is more than just the money it is also the social fabric, which he explained

© The Author(s) 2018
D. Cowan, *The Coming Economic Implosion of Saudi Arabia*,
https://doi.org/10.1007/978-3-319-74709-5_4

in terms of family relationships. When inviting extended family to visit, it is customary to lay on quite a spread, including sacrificing a goat for all the family to share. This can be expensive but is now becoming more demanding on the household budget with less family gatherings likely to become the norm; to which he added, if it gets even worse, they might be lucky to buy a KFC chicken family bucket to share! He may have put it amusingly, but there is obvious concern about these types of budget changes, though one should put this into the context that such worries are commonplace in most economies, so it is perhaps more of a case that Saudis simply need to learn to deal with the plethora of bills and charges that people are used to in other economies. The concern is not, however, just the increased cost but the changes in welfare provision and the sense of security the welfare system allowed which is now undermined. We can expect to see growing resistance to these changes and policies.

One should not confuse Islamic notions of welfare with Socialism, which most Islamic commentators reject on the grounds of its humanism, though attempts have been made to marry the two.[3] Capitalism is theoretically rejected because of the role of interest or usury, called *riba* in Islam, but of course all Islamic countries have practically accepted capitalism; though Saudi, Malaysia and others effectively have a partially dual system and many other Islamic countries have Islamic financing arrangements. Intrinsic to Islamic welfare is the requirement of believers to pay *zakat*, the obligatory charitable tax defined as one of the five Pillars of Islam. The *zakat* is levied on property (food grains, fruit, camels, cattle, sheep, goats, gold and silver) and movable goods. It provides for the poor and needy, those who collect the *zakat* and "those whose hearts it is necessary to conciliate," such as discordant tribesmen, debtors, volunteers in *jihad* and pilgrims. *Zakat* is a microeconomic and individual tool, but the intention behind it looms large in Saudi as a component of the macroeconomic and political function within the Kingdom. The welfare state and health system in the Kingdom is in trouble.[4] Writing in the FT on the contradiction of austerity Saudi-style, *Financial Times* deputy editor Roula Khalaf provides a rather succinct picture of the problem, "Saudi rulers – and to some extent the people too – have long recognised that oil cannot guarantee the Kingdom's prosperity forever. A lavish welfare state that breeds indolence and apathy must one day come to an end."[5] There have been a number of significant changes taking place in welfare provision in the past decade.[6] In 2011, the "Hafiz" program, which pays unemployed Saudis 2000 riyals ($533) a month for up to one year, was introduced, and 1 million Saudis are now receiving unemployment benefit.[7] Further attempts to shore up the system were made in 2014.[8]

Healthcare budgets have increased dramatically, jumping from $8 billion in 2008 to $27 billion in 2016 and forecasts that the final figure for 2017 would top $46 billion.[9] In January 2014, the Saudi government announced a series of welfare programs,[10] which included an unemployment insurance scheme and a housing loan support program. The introduction of unemployment insurance was aimed at providing job security to some 1.5 million Saudis working in the private sector and to make it more attractive for young Saudis to seek jobs in private companies, where the starting salary and other benefits are less generous than in government departments. While the official unemployment rate is less than 12%, economists say only 30–40% of working age adults participate in the labor force. Under the new scheme, all Saudi workers are charged 1% of their monthly salary as a subscription. Their employer pays the same amount into the scheme. Those who lose their jobs are entitled to up to 12 months of compensation, set at 60% of the average salary they earned in the previous two years for the first three months and then 50% for the following nine months. Benefits are capped at SAR9000 for the first three months and SAR7500 for the rest of the year. There is a minimum payment of SAR2000. There is also housing help, with a new housing scheme aimed at ensuring transparent distribution of loans among deserving citizens such as widows and divorced. It also aims to encourage more investment in the housing sector and reduce rents. Applicants should be married and aged not less than 25 and should not have previously benefited from a government or private housing scheme. Women can also apply if they are responsible for their families.

Welfare in Saudi has been a major cost center for the domestic budget, but there may be other ways to fund the burden. This can be tied to how one assesses welfare needs and impacts, with one area identified for welfare development being the environment. The Vision 2030 has, as one would expect perhaps, prioritized environmental opportunities for economic development. The King Abdullah Petroleum Studies and Research

Center (KAPSARC) report "Gasoline Demand, Pricing Policy and Social Welfare in Saudi Arabia" has argued the importance of environmental improvement as a measure of welfare. The report explains that when gas prices rose from nominal prices for the 91 and 95 octane grades from Saudi Riyal (SAR) 0.45 and SAR0.60 per liter to SAR0.75 and SAR0.90, respectively:

> The gasoline price increase could potentially result in a net gain in social welfare of as much as SAR 2 billion annually at 2010 prices, which is equivalent to 0.1 percent of the Kingdom's gross domestic product (GDP) in 2015… Furthermore, the estimated welfare gain does not take into account the external costs of gasoline demand and driving. Therefore, the gasoline price increase, which would lead to a reduction in both gasoline demand and distances traveled, also offers additional welfare benefits in the form of reductions in greenhouse gas emissions, air pollution, congestion and accidents. In summary, the welfare estimates suggest that the recent gasoline price increase would yield an overall increase in social welfare, although consumers do incur some loss. Given that producers (mainly Saudi Aramco) gain surplus and that spending on gasoline imports falls, the net positive impact on the government budget and the structure of the Saudi labor market together suggest that the gains would probably be distributed back to Saudi citizens.[11]

A last point to make is one made in the 2017 Chatham House report *Vision 2030 and Saudi Arabia's Social Contract Austerity and Transformation.* A welfare approach requires social agreement about where people come into and fall out of the system. The report argued:

> The risks of growing inequality and social exclusion are significant, and pose a number of political risks in a system where the rulers have traditionally been seen by their supporters as the providers of economic largesse. More effective social safety nets thus need to be established.[12]

Whatever one says about the structure and economic future of the Saudi welfare state, there are three areas of welfare and social thinking normally thought of as central in welfare thinking which requires more in-depth attention. The modern notion of welfare involves more than distribution issues, there are also areas of social engineering. In the Saudi context these are destabilizing areas to consider as the Kingdom moves toward 2030. The three key items of the agenda we can look at are:

1. Human Rights
2. The gender Revolution
3. The youth Bulge

The first two areas are particularly controversial for Western critics, and I will address each in turn.

Human Rights

Implicit in a welfare approach to the wealth of a nation is an assumption there is a premium on the rights of people to benefit from welfare in different ways according to need. One can debate levels of welfare funding and rights, but while the Kingdom has historically had generous welfare provision for Saudis this has not been extended to non-Saudis. Worse still, Saudi is recognized as one of the most high-profile nations targeted for human rights abuses by observers. According to Human Rights Watch, campaigns to free a Saudi blogger shows how "Saudi Arabia repeatedly demonstrates its complete intolerance toward citizens who speak out for human rights and reform,"[13] while a case of a transgendered Pakistani demonstrates "Saudi Arabia's aggressive policing of the private consensual activities of Saudis and foreigners diverts resources from actual problems such as preventing and solving crimes."[14] The Human Rights Watch report, 2012, stated:

> Saudi Arabia in 2012 stepped up arrests and trials of peaceful dissidents, and responded with force to demonstrations by citizens. Authorities continue to suppress or fail to protect the rights of 9 million Saudi women and girls and 9 million foreign workers. As in past years, thousands of people have received unfair trials or been subject to arbitrary detention. The year has seen trials against half-a-dozen human rights defenders and several others for their peaceful expression or assembly demanding political and human rights reforms.[15]

In a similar vein, the 2013 Amnesty International Report on Saudi Arabia stated:

> The authorities severely restricted freedoms of expression, association and assembly and clamped down on dissent. Government critics and political activists were detained without trial or sentenced after grossly unfair trials. Women were discriminated against in law and practice and inadequately protected against domestic and other violence. Migrant workers were exploited and abused. Sentences of flogging were imposed and carried out. Hundreds of people were on death row at the end of the year; at least 79 people were executed.[16]

Then the 2015 Freedom House Report, which classifies Saudi among the worst of the worse, states:

> Saudi Arabia tightened restrictions on dissent and freedom of speech in 2014, and intensified criminal penalties for religious beliefs that veer too far from official state orthodoxy. A sweeping 2013 "antiterrorism" law took effect in February, enabling authorities to press terrorism charges against anyone who demands reform, exposes corruption, or otherwise engages in dissent. A royal decree in April penalized atheism with up to 20 years' imprisonment. Making use of these and other laws, authorities continued to crack down on dissidents, human rights defenders, artists, and journalists.[17]

Year on year, reports on human rights in Saudi attract major criticism, and leads to calls for boycotts and other sanctions to be taken. However, the dominant political policy of allies remains one focused on having influence on these issues by doing business with Saudi, and human rights abuses have had little impact on US foreign policy or economic relations.[18] President Obama was one who did say more than the norm about Saudi abuses, which his hosts dismissed as preaching at them. Increasingly the international standard today for businesses is to draft them in to tackle such abuses in partnership with government. In human rights, businesses and others operating in the Kingdom are not invited to solve these problems directly, and such partnerships would be especially problematic in an economy like Saudi because the major businesses are either part government-owned or have close ties to government and the royal family. This leaves lobbying and economic pressure at the political level as the main option, but as a 2014 visit to Saudi Arabia by President Obama[19] demonstrates, there is often little appetite for human rights diplomacy. While the president ended his 2014 trip to Saudi with a brief symbolic private ceremony in which he presented an International Women of Courage award to a Saudi woman who works to prevent domestic violence in the Kingdom, it was merely low hanging fruit. This ceremonial display had come a day after the president chose not to raise the issue of human rights during a two-hour discussion with King Abdullah.[20] If that is the best the "leader of the free world" can do, then what hope has a business or the people subject to such a regime? We are left with either continuing advancing largely ineffectual external political pressures or the government itself deciding to address human rights in a new way. The former is less than influential and the latter preferable option is highly unlikely for the foreseeable future.

The Gender Revolution

Traveling down Airport Road in Riyadh, you pass for some distance the expansive and architecturally stunning Princess Nourah Bint Abdulrahman University. This is a university for women only and was inaugurated in 2008 by merging a number of colleges and universities for women into one impressive campus, which was formally opened in 2011. At the ceremony, King Abdullah stated:

> Women carry a responsibility that is more than a duty, to maintain the stability of society and contribute to building the economy of the nation, and to represent the community and the nation to the highest standards, outside and inside the country. To be the caring mother, exemplary citizen and productive employee. Outside the nation, to be the ambassador of her country and community, and to represent well her religion, faith and our values.

The vision of the university is "to become a beacon of knowledge and ethical practices for women" and its mission is "to become a comprehensive university for women, distinguished with its academic leadership and scientific research that contributes to building a knowledge economy with societal and international partnerships." Despite such lofty ambitions, the contradictions of Saudi are clearly illustrated by an incident where the death of a student was reported in 2014. A young female Saudi student, 24-year-old Amena Bawazir, died of a heart attack after waiting for nearly two hours because male medical staff were not allowed to attend her.[21] This was because when an ambulance was summoned to help the crew turned out to be male and thus unable to enter the campus, and so a female crew had to be summoned, which took too long. In the intervening time the young woman died.

On the gender front, in 2016 Saudi Arabia was ranked 141 out of 144 on the Global Gender Gap Index,[22] and critics scoffed at the Kingdom being elected by the United Nation's Economic and Social Council (ECOSOC) to a four-year term on the Commission on the Status of Women.[23] The committee is "exclusively dedicated to the promotion of gender equality and the empowerment of women."[24] If you ask many young Saudi women about her top priorities, they are increasingly likely to talk about expanded job opportunities, increasing training for women, reforms in the practice of family law and protection from domestic violence and child abuse. Saudi women are less likely to argue about dress and driving cars, seemingly the defining issues for foreign critics, and many opposed lifting the driving ban or wanted limits attached.[25] A Gallup poll revealed 66% of Saudi women wanted to lift the ban, while equal rights attracted 79% and right to work outside the home 82%. The poll also revealed 89% of women want to keep their earnings while their husbands maintain them and also believe husbands should support their children 100% in cases of divorce. On the points of earnings and child support Saudi men also agree, while there is more of a gender gap on the other issues. Interestingly, the poll also reveals the gender gap in attitudes is narrower in Saudi than Iran and Egypt, where according to survey results the men in those two countries express opinions more opposed to equality for women.[26] Evidence suggests women do want to see a change in some cultural and societal attitudes, and to see the stigmas attached to public discussion of social realities removed. A 2015 survey in Riyadh also suggested that for women driving was not as important as education and participation in community development projects, and offered a picture of optimism about the progress of gender equality in the Kingdom.[27] Some views from Saudi women stated in the report reveal the difficulties they face:

> Saudi society is increasingly in support of women entering to the labor market; it is an economic need for most new couples; it is also related to the increasing education of women who are demanding to have jobs. (Female, 30)

> While women are now entering the work force, they are facing many obstacles as they are demanded [by men] to do all the house work and child care and at the same time suffer from discrimination in the workplace. (Female, 48)

> If a woman wants to participate, she must pay a heavy price and must jump through many hoops including the resistance of her family, the employers, the politicians and the religious leaders. (Female, 38)

> Women are now making progress in all fields; they are competing with men over levels of education, working in most fields, becoming active in creating their own businesses and leading NGOs. (Female, 51)[28]

In other words, they are seeking deep and long-lasting changes.[29] There are workplace changes in Saudi on a continuous basis, albeit gradual rather than dramatic. An industrial city for women has been established outside of Jeddah to encourage women to invest and work in manufacturing, which is also seen as helping to diversify the Saudi economy. "Saudization" of certain jobs for women have been legislated and attempted with mixed success, as in the case of requiring female salespersons for lingerie and training Saudi women as housemaids. In these cases, the jobs already exist. The challenge lies in finding Saudi women who are highly educated and trained and willing to do them, as well as in creating a social and cultural environment where men accept women working in these jobs. Given the presence of more than 1.5 million foreign female domestic servants in Saudi Arabia, some believe that Saudization of the domestic servant industry is critical to reducing foreign remittances, dependence on foreign labor and resolving the high rates of unemployment among Saudi women.

The education and changes in policy are certainly steps in the right direction, but they are not radical enough to go deep in to the culture. As Madawi Al-Rasheed states "hardly any aspect of the female body, behavior, or life is left unregulated by a fatwa."[30] She cites Anwar Abdulla's book which records that the Saudi *ulama* has produced more than 30,000 fatwas on women in the second half of the twentieth century. Al-Rasheed puts this in the context of the state's battle to maintain an Islamic identity, arguing that women are a symbol, "the visible signs of adherence to Islam need to be promoted and privileged to inscribe in the imagination the centrality of the pious state. This is dependent today on the visible signs of piety, and women in particular are doomed to be such signs. Their invisibility in the public sphere is, ironically, a visible token of state piety and commitment to Islam."[31] When I ask Saudi males about why women have to wear the hijab they explain it is part of their identity as Muslim women, which, with a somewhat different resonance, is the point Al-Rasheed is making. The Koran in Sura 24:31 states:

And say to the believing women that they should lower their gaze and guard their modesty; that they should not display their beauty and ornaments except what (must ordinarily) appear thereof; that they should draw their veils over their bosoms and not display their beauty except to their husbands, their fathers, their husband's fathers, their sons, their husbands' sons, their brothers or their brothers' sons, or their sisters' sons, or their women, or the slaves whom their right hands possess, or male servants free of physical needs, or small children who have no sense of the shame of sex; and that they should not strike their feet in order to draw attention to their hidden ornaments. And O ye Believers! turn ye all together towards Allah, that ye may attain Bliss.

In terms of international norms, this sura makes women appear submissive and as second-class citizens. However, just as Mary as a woman is made a counterpoint in some Christian theologies, the example of the Prophet Muhammad's first wife Khadija is offered as a counterpoint and role model for women. Mary, incidentally, is also seen as a role model in

Islamic theology, and often more highly thought of than even the most committed levels of Mariology.

Economic change is the main motivator for changes in the attitudes toward women, not any ideological victory or theological change of heart. Prince Salman in *The Economist* interview, explained his view of women in economic terms, and they are commonplace among Saudi men:

So why is Saudi Arabia's rate of women in the workforce, 18%, one of the lowest in the world?
Culture of women in Saudi Arabia; the woman herself. She's not used to working. She needs more time to accustom herself to the idea of work. A large percentage of Saudi women are used to the fact of staying at home. They're not used to being working women. It just takes time.

Do you think having a greater proportion of women in the workforce would be good for Saudi Arabia?
No doubt. A large portion of my productive factors are unutilised. And I have population growth reaching very scary figures. Women's work will help in both of these issues.

If women are critical to the success of Saudi's *Vision 2030* then, from a global stance, the marginalization of women in society means women will have to break free to avoid having a severely limited role in business. It is only in 2017 that women can now drive to university or work. This came after years of sustained protest, including a major incident on 26 October 2013 when more than 60 Saudi women's activists got behind the wheel of their cars to protest against a ban on women driving.[32] When I discussed the protest with one of the women[33] who were arrested she was adamant the driving ban was not trivial, it signified the plight of women in modern Saudi Arabia, and if such a policy changed then there would be hope for further changes. The change to driving ban was made,[34] but many obstacles remain. Women generally cannot work alongside male colleagues, instead they have a partitioned section for their offices. Often basics are not well provided for, such as restrooms which may be some distance away from an office or meeting room. Women are required to wear the *abaya* and *hijab* to work, which not only separates them from men but also makes it impossible to undertake some roles. Foreign women are excused some of this rule, and other Gulf countries have the *abaya*, so what seems to distinguish Saudi is that it imposes this restriction on non-Muslim women as well. Foreign women may have more rights, but even then they are severely limited compared to the freedoms they are used to at home or in most other countries, and need to be chaperoned by male colleagues. There are deep concerns that women must obtain permission from male guardians to work, travel, study, seek medical treatment or marry, and that the Saudi labor code, which came into force in 2006, incorporates an earlier stipulation decreeing that in line with article 4 of the code, which requires adherence to Sharia, "women shall work in all fields suitable to their nature" (article 149). The Committee on the Elimination of Discrimination against Women (CEDAW) in their 2008 shadow report argued that this principle of "imposing the guardianship of a male over the woman all her life in Saudi Arabia is linked to the inferior look to women and her traditional role in society and family."[35]

Gender issues in Saudi presents a problem for foreign companies operating locally, both in the locality and at home. To illustrate this difficulty, we can look at a story involving the Swedish furniture multinational IKEA,[36] which ran into trouble in the Kingdom when they released a local version of their catalogue which photoshopped women out of the global catalog. This became known in Sweden and the news went viral, causing the company to apologize and explain that excluding women from the Saudi Arabian version of the catalog was in conflict with the IKEA Group values.[37] What was right in Saudi was condemned by public opinion in their home nation and abroad. Saudi Arabia's Princess Ameerah al-Taweel said in 2013 on a panel discussion at the World Economic Forum (WEF) in Jordan that many conservative men in Saudi say "we don't want women to work, we want her to maintain her dignity... I think the main reason is fear from women and not for women, because they are afraid of women. We know that women are stronger than men in our society because they're a minority and the minority usually wants to prove itself."[38] However, the WEF's annual Gender Gap Index for 2014 now ranks Saudi Arabia ninth among Arab countries in terms of gender equality, stating that Saudi Arabia has improved the income of Saudi women compared to their male counterparts, with higher levels of political and economic participation, and improvement in education, health and living standards.[39]

While gender politics are changing somewhat, it is slow and what you won't get in Saudi is a sudden turnaround. However, pressure does seem to have some effect, and international observers may conclude it seems largely a matter of time, but in the meantime the position of women remains difficult in the home. This is especially so in the area of domestic violence. There is increased willingness to engage meaningfully in the issue, which surfaced with the 2004 case of a television personality Rania al-Baz who was disfigured by a severe beating inflicted by her husband. A national debate ensued when television images of al-Baz's brutalized face shocked people into facing the realities of spouse abuse. However, the religious and cultural questions remain, and women's Islamic identity is a central reflection, because they may want to keep their faith while challenging the cultural and social apprehension of that faith in Saudi and elsewhere. Al-Rasheed offers an intriguing conclusion when she states:

> Whether women choose conformity or silent rebellion, they live their modernity in a country that has not yet resolved big questions about its identity. Despite the slogans of Arab and Islamic heritage, Saudi Arabia lacks a local nationalism that unites fragments. Calling upon regional (Arab) and global (Islamic) heritage is not sufficient to make Saudis what they are. Women are what make Saudis unique and different from the other Arab countries or the numerous Islamic countries worldwide. Those women who assert their piety and defend their own exclusion are making a plea about what it means to be women in an Islamic state, thus confirming the state's legitimacy narrative about its piety.[40]

The role of women will not only drive the economy, it will drive the religious narrative as well, and the likelihood is that both these dynamics can only be positives for Saudi and Islam. As Amina Wadud-Muhsin, a specialist in gender and Islamic interpretation, explains the Koranic evidence advances a view that stresses the significance of each to the other, stating:

> With regard to social justice, it becomes necessary to challenge patriarchy – not for matriarchy, but for an efficient co-operative and egalitarian system

which allows and encourages the maximum participation of each member of society. This system would truly respect each gender in its contributions, and all tasks that are contributed. This would allow for the growth and expansion of the individual and consequently for society at large. As such, women would have full access to economic, intellectual, and political participation, and men would value and therefore participate more fully in home and child care for a more balanced and fair society.[41]

The lifting of the drive ban and going to football matches are incremental steps on the path, and as Manal Al-Sharif, an activist imprisoned in 2011 for defying the ban, stated in her memoir *Daring to Drive*,[42] "There can be no modern Saudi Kingdom as long as women are still ruled by men. It may take a long time, but I do believe that Kingdom will come…." Referring to lifting the driving ban, she concludes "The rain begins with a single drop." I have certainly noticed over the past year or two the steady fall of rain in the Kingdom.

The Youth Bulge

The current economic problem Saudi faces means that the pressure on youth will only increase, and this raises the issue of whether Saudi youth, well-educated but often bored, will protest for their own economic advancement or for radical religious objectives. This has long been a fear that marginalized youth will become disaffected and lose economic hope leaving them to resort to radical religious and political action. This is recognized, which is why in recent years there has been investment in deradicalization programs, focused on teaching moderate Islam and helping young people to get jobs. However, the coming economic storm will render them ineffective if there is no economic hope to displace radical ideologies. More so than in many other Arab countries, young Saudis are youth raised in a conservative religious culture that prioritizes Islam and the obligation to help Muslims in countries where Islam is not so privileged. This sets the scene for a possible uprising of radical and well-educated youth, more inspired by religious ideas than wishful thinking and empty promises of economic well-being. The youth question is common in other Muslim countries, which according to a 2011 Pew Research Center study have populations under age 30 that typically comprise 60% of the population.[43] In Saudi the statistic is higher, with two-thirds of the Kingdom's 29 million population are under age 30 and 37% of all Saudis 14 years old or younger. This means there is something of a youth "time bomb" to contribute to the economic problems Saudi faces.[44] It means that Saudi Arabia will have 1.9 million Saudis entering the workforce over the next decade, and already the unemployment rate for Saudis between ages 16 and 29 is 29%.[45] The CIA's *World Factbook* highlights the resulting problem that Saudi Arabia's youth population "generally lacks the education and technical skills the private sector needs." With less money to throw at the problem, it is conceivable that Saudi youth could be at the heart of its first economically driven uprising.

Saudi is aware of the skills problem and has invested over recent years in education and the training of its young people, allocating nearly a quarter of its budget to the problem, some SAR191.6 billion ($51 billion). Foreign exchange programs have been in place for some years now and are seen as a way to keep youth inspired and loyal. One of King Abdullah's projects was the modernization of the education system. In 2007, he launched the King Abdullah Project for the Development of Public Education, run through a company called Tatweer. The company spent about $3 billion to improve the quality of educational provision. Funds were used to beef up extracurricular activities, train teachers and develop curriculum. Interestingly, the Tatweer reform program was also designed to change the way students learn. Instead of just memorizing facts, students were encouraged to problem-solve. Two years later, the late King founded the King Abdullah University for Science and Technology with a $10 billion endowment and increased the 2015 Saudi national budget to allow increased spending on education by 3%. Of the roughly $58 billion the country allocated toward education, about $108 million was allocated toward general school rehabilitation projects, and $3 billion toward higher education, according to the US-Saudi Arabian Business Council.[46] There is a recognition that youth unemployment is a critical socioeconomic problem that not only risks undermining society but undermining the government's hold on power and the very future of the house of Saud. Part of the solution is that Saudi Arabia needs to create at least 3 million new jobs by 2020.[47] However, this is looked at as an opportunity in some quarters. In a conversation I had with Prince Turki bin Faisal Al Saud,[48] Prince Turki portrayed the Saudi youth as an exciting prospect rather than a challenge, as it is usually portrayed in Western literature. He argues that Saudi youth represent energy and new technology, tying into the Vision 2030 emphasis. Whereas Western youth are often assumed to be progressive or rebellious, in Saudi the youth are rather more conservative, which makes the positive view offered by Prince Turki all the more intriguing.

Research by Saudi Arabia's Depth Consulting, a new private research company in Riyadh, offered three core findings:

1. Saudi youth are surprisingly disinterested in foreign affairs relative to domestic matters. Their main worries are the proxy conflicts of Iraq, Syria and Yemen, Saudi's relationship with America and Britain.
2. In respect to Vision 2030, Saudi youth seem to vacillate between confidence in its ultimate success and anxiety about its immediate impact. Most share a reflexive desire to continue enjoying the benefits of the welfare state. Meanwhile, though a package of new socioeconomic projects has been launched for the purpose of benefiting Saudi youth, few are aware of it.
3. As the survey was before the change of succession, the research found most young people preferred that Deputy Crown Prince Mohammad bin Salman succeed, as opposed to the then Crown Prince, 57-year-old Mohammed bin Nayef. Mohammad bin Salman's popularity was reflected on Twitter.[49] His popularity remains high among the youth since his succession.

This raises the question whether young Saudis are prime targets for radicalization or not, assuming the economic collision course Saudi is on the question remains how young Saudis will respond. Prince Turki and others are hopeful that the Saudi youth will take up the entrepreneurial challenge and advance capitalism, consumerism and opportunity. The Vision 2030 is trying to capture this new mood and create excitement and an objective for their young. However, Saudi youth have been the target for radicalization in the past and have been recruited as part of mobilization against the house of Saud. This was especially so in the Islamist reform movement that emerged after the first Iraq War, when large numbers of Saudi youth became part of oppositional activities due to the royal family's support for foreign troops to handle the situation. Will MbS turn the youth this time toward the Sauds? One young Saudi man, speaking on the condition of anonymity, told the *Financial Times*:

> It seemed to me that whomever worked on it [the national transformation plan] cared more about how it will look when announced than for whether this vision can actually prosper… I now think that the announcement for the vision was actually just a political campaign in disguise. It was a huge PR stunt.[50]

Conversations I have had with young Saudis are a little more nuanced than this view but not much different, where I hear the combined messages of hope and skepticism. The hope is that a young leader can drive the change the young believe is necessary, while the skepticism is that conservative forces will hold him back and the lack of skills and opportunities will dampen prospects. The *In Depth* survey and another survey conducted by the King Salman Youth Center,[51] chaired by MbS, confirmed my conversations. The Youth Center report revealed that young Saudis are optimistic about their future but skeptical about job opportunities.

A Saudi Welfare Ethic

The social picture presented here of rights, gender and youth offers a mixture of optimism and pessimism for the Kingdom. External pressure on human rights and internal pressure from women and youth are key dynamics of the Saudi welfare state. In some respects, there are high levels of welfare from an Islamic point of view. The use of zakat, charities taking food left over from households out to the poor and the presence of faith in the workplace are all seen as points of proof for Islamic welfare. Such Islamic welfare is visible not just in social community activities by employees and corporate charitable sponsorship, but also the presence of places of prayer in the workplace. In major companies very large mosques, often much larger than many of the neighborhood mosques their employees normally attend, tend to be at the heart of the building complex and are well-used. American companies, like Exxon or Coca-Cola, do not provide such Christian church facilities and adhere strictly to a separation between such public spaces and religion. The working day is not stopped in its tracks to allow the workforce to attend to their prayers, nor are meetings interrupted or scheduled to allow a manager to go down the corridor and set down a prayer mat to pray. It is not completely regimented, meetings do go on at prayer times and a manager will make up prayer time at another time. Religion is a welfare ethic that is present everywhere in Saudi society, but again this is not to say that religion is all-pervasive, but to point to its continual presence in the economic space. In the business context it is influential but it does not rule the roost, though its position may evolve as economic pressures mount and an international code of business ethics take deeper hold. This raises the question of whether it is economic issues that will ultimately challenge the Saudi welfare state, and with it the dominance of Islam itself in the Kingdom.

Kayed and Hassan have undertaken a detailed study which argues that Saudi Arabia in business terms is driven by Western economic dynamics, principally profit maximization, rather than Islamic prescriptions.[52] This requires some clarification, because the Islamic and cultural influences make Saudi companies appear still quite different from their Western counterparts. Superficially, seeing employees at prayer in a corridor or the centrality of the mosque may give a misleading impression of religion in the workplace. To understand the real economic challenges, I would argue that the religious aspects of Saudi are an important aspect of resolving the problem in way that may harmonize economy and religion rather than create a separation. The objection made by critics of Saudi companies is that, because of issues such as gender, the attitude of *Inshallah* and Saudization, Saudi businesses in a purely economic consideration of their challenges are being run at a sub-optimal performance level. As stated at the outset, there is a lot for Saudi to worry about economically, yet the Basic Law demands economic challenges to be handled "according to a fair, wise plan." Vision 2030 seeks to grapple with some fundamental problems, such as a growing younger population that is less skilled and weaned on a welfare principle that cannot possibly support them much longer. Human rights, gender and youth are policy areas which need to change, and there are Islamic ways of doing so, and ways will need to be found if the Kingdom is to avoid an economic implosion.

Notes

1. https://www.kapsarc.org/wp-content/uploads/2017/08/KS-2017-DP018-Reforming-Industrial-Fuel-and-Residential-Electricity-Prices-in-Saudi-Arabia.pdf. The objective is to move closer toward parity with international standards; see https://www.bloomberg.com/news/articles/2017-09-18/saudis-said-to-weigh-raising-gasoline-prices-by-end-of-november
2. https://www.reuters.com/article/us-saudi-economy/saudi-arabia-slashes-ministers-pay-cuts-public-sector-bonuses-idUSKCN11W1VS
3. See Chapra (1992).
4. http://apps.who.int/iris/bitstream/10665/119213/1/emhj_2002_8_4_5_645_653.pdf
5. https://www.ft.com/content/077e83a8-b070-11e5-b955-1a1d298b6250
6. Also undermined by inequality https://www.huffingtonpost.com/2011/02/28/wikileaks-saudi-royal-wel_n_829097.html
7. https://www.reuters.com/article/us-saudi-unemployment-subsidy/more-than-1-million-saudis-on-unemployment-benefit-idUS-BRE82R0L320120328
8. https://www.albawaba.com/business/saudi-arabia-unemployment--545543
9. According to estimates from the Saudi asset management firm NCB Capital https://www.reuters.com/article/saudi-healthcare/saudi-healthcare-booms-as-state-scrambles-to-close-welfare-gap-idUSL5N0KQ0F220140119
10. http://www.arabnews.com/news/505026
11. https://www.kapsarc.org/wp-content/uploads/2017/03/KS-2017-DP04-Gasoline-Demand-Price-Policy-and-Social-Welfare-in-Saudi-Arabia.pdf

12. Authored by Jane Kinninmont https://www.chathamhouse.org/sites/files/chathamhouse/publications/research/2017-07-20-vision-2030-saudi-kinninmont.pdf
13. https://www.hrw.org/news/2017/02/20/saudi-arabia-imprisoned-activist-earns-human-rights-award See also the report *Shrouded in Secrecy: the human rights situation in Saudi Arabia following arrests in September 2017*, http://tgchambers.com/wp-content/uploads/2018/02/KSALegalOpinion31.1.18-Full-Report.pdf
14. https://www.hrw.org/news/2017/04/13/saudi-arabia-investigate-transgender-womans-death
15. http://www.hrw.org/world-report/2013/country-chapters/112341
16. http://www.amnesty.org/en/region/saudi-arabia/report-2013
17. https://freedomhouse.org/report/freedom-world/2015/saudi-arabia
18. FRUS 1951 Vol. V pp. 1027ff set US policy in this respect and has been operative to the present day.
19. http://www.nytimes.com/2014/03/30/world/middleeast/obama-saudi-arabia.html?_r=0
20. March 29, 2014.
21. http://rt.com/news/saudi-arabia-segregation-women-110/
22. http://reports.weforum.org/global-gender-gap-report-2016/rankings/
23. https://www.unwatch.org/no-joke-u-n-elects-saudi-arabia-womens-rights-commission/, http://fortune.com/2017/04/25/un-womens-rights-saudi-arabia/
24. http://www.unwomen.org/en/csw
25. https://www.theguardian.com/commentisfree/2013/nov/02/saudi-protest-driving-ban-not-popular
26. http://news.gallup.com/poll/103441/saudi-arabia-majorities-support-womens-rights.aspx
27. http://www.iri.org/sites/default/files/wysiwyg/2015-08-26_public_opinion_poll_of_womens_role_in_public_life_in_saudi_arabia_may_10-31_2015.pdf
28. Ibid.
29. http://www.mei.edu/content/freedoms-saudi-women-really-want
30. Al-Rasheed (2008, p. 295).
31. Al-Rasheed (2008, p. 296).
32. https://www.theguardian.com/world/2013/oct/26/saudi-arabia-woman-driving-car-ban
33. 6 November 2014.

34. https://www.nytimes.com/2017/09/26/world/middleeast/saudi-arabia-women-drive.html?_r=0
35. http://tbinternet.ohchr.org/Treaties/CEDAW/Shared%20Documents/SAU/INT_CEDAW_NGO_SAU_40_10011_E.pdf, p. 1.
36. http://www.theguardian.com/world/2012/oct/02/ikea-apologises-removing-women-saudi-arabia-catalogue
37. http://global.wharton.upenn.edu/post/ikeas-women-free-catalogue-in-saudi-arabia-misses-the-picture/
38. http://www.arabianbusiness.com/saudi-princess-says-men-are-too-afraid-allow-women-s-rights-503045.html#.VFJeMfnF-uk
39. http://www.arabnews.com/featured/news/652321
40. Al-Rasheed (2008, p. 301).
41. Wadud-Muhsin (1992, p. 103).
42. Al-Sharif (2017, p. 283). Reference taken from an advanced proof copy provided to me by the publisher.
43. http://www.pewforum.org/2011/01/27/future-of-the-global-muslim-population-main-factors/
44. Woodrow Wilson International Center for Scholars in Washington, DC. https://www.wilsoncenter.org/sites/default/files/Saudi%20Arabia%E2%80%99s%20Youth%20and%20the%20Kingdom%E2%80%99s%20Future%20FINAL.pdf
45. http://www.ibtimes.com/saudi-arabias-youth-unemployment-problem-among-king-salmans-many-new-challenges-after-1793346. The Saudis launched a committee to assess unemployment and develop policy http://english.alarabiya.net/en/business/economy/2015/10/15/Saudi-Arabia-launches-committee-to-tackle-unemployment.html
46. http://www.us-sabc.org/custom/news/details.cfm?id=1645#.VMKID0fF9HU
47. https://www.brookings.edu/opinions/saudi-arabias-economic-time-bomb/
48. Interview in London, July 10, 2016.
49. https://www.fpri.org/article/2016/10/surveying-saudi-arabias-youthful-majority/
50. https://www.ft.com/content/50503280-618f-11e7-8814-0ac7eb84e5f1
51. http://www.ksyc.org.sa/?lang=en
52. Rasem Kayed & Kabir Hassan, Islamic entrepreneurship: A Case Study of Saudi Arabia. *Journal of Developmental Entrepreneurship* Dec 2010, Vol. 15 Issue 4, pp. 379–413.

Bibliography

Aburish, Said K. 2005. *The Rise, Corruption and Coming Fall of the House of Saud*. London: Bloomsbury.

Al-Rasheed, Madawi, ed. 2008. *Kingdom Without Borders: Saudi Arabia's Political, Religious and Media Frontiers*. London: Hurst.

Al-Sharif, Manal. 2017. *Daring to Drive: A Saudi Woman's Wakening*. New York: Simon & Schuster.

Allawai, Ali A. 2009. *The Crisis of Islamic Civilization*. New Haven: Yale University Press.

Black, Antony. 2001. *The History of Islamic Political Thought: From the Prophet to the Present*. Edinburgh: Edinburgh University Press.

Bowering, Gerhard, ed. 2015. *Islamic Political Thought: An Introduction*. Princeton: Princeton University Press.

Champion, Daryl. 2003. *The Paradoxical Kingdom: Saudi Arabia and the Momentum of Reform*. London: Hurst and Company.

Chapra, Mohammed Umer. 1985. *Towards a Just Monetary System*. Leicester: Islamic Foundation.

———. 1992. *Islam and the Economic Challenge*. Leicester: International Institute of Islamic Thought.

Cook, M.A., ed. 1970. *Studies in the Economic History of the Middle East*. Oxford: Oxford University Press.

Cowan, David. 2009. *Economic Parables: The Monetary Teachings of Jesus Christ*. 2nd ed. Downers Grove: IVP.

Craze, Jonathan, and Mark Huband. 2009. *The Kingdom: Saudi Arabia and the Challenge of the 21st Century*. London: Hurst & Co.

Cunningham, Robert B., and Yasin K. Sarayrah. 1993. *Wasta: The Hidden Force in Middle Eastern Society*. Westport: Praeger.

Gause, F., III. 1994. *Gregory Oil Monarchies: Domestic and Security Challenges in the Arab Gulf States*. New York: Council on Foreign Relations.

Hamid, Shadi. 2016. *Islamic Exceptionalism: How the Struggle Over Islam Is Reshaping the World*. New York: St. Martin's Press.

Hammond, Andrew. 2012. *The Islamic Utopia: The Illusion of Reform in Saudi Arabia*. London: Pluto Press.

Haykel, Bernard, Thomas Hegghammer, and Stéphane Lacroix. 2015. *Saudi Arabia in Transition: Insights on Social, Political, Economic and Religious Change*. Cambridge: Cambridge University Press.

Hertog, Steffen. 2010. *Princes, Brokers, and Bureaucrats Oil and the State in Saudi Arabia*. Ithaca: Cornell University Press.

House, Karen Elliott. 2012. *On Saudi Arabia: Its People, Past, Religion, Fault Lines – And Future*. New York: Vintage Books.

Kropf, Annika, and Mohamed A. Ramady, eds. 2015. *Employment and Career Motivation in the Arab Gulf States: The Rentier Mentality Revisited*. Berlin: Gerlach Press.

Lacey, Robert. 2009. *Inside the Kingdom: Kings, Clerics, Terrorists, Modernists, and the Struggle for Saudi Arabia*. New York: Viking.

Lackner, Helen. 1978. *A House Built on Sand. A Political Economy of Saudi Arabia*. London: Ithaca Press.

Lippman, Thomas W. 2012. *Saudi Arabia on the Edge: The Uncertain Future of an American Ally*. Dulles: Potomac Books.

Marshall, Alfred. 1920. *Principles of Economics*. London: Macmillan.

Mazaheri, Nimah. 2016. *Oil Booms and Business Busts: Why Resource Wealth Hurts Entrepreneurs in the Developing World*. Oxford: Oxford University Press.

Mernissi, Fatima. 1987. *Beyond the Veil: Male-Female Dynamics in Modern Muslim Society*. Bloomington: Indiana University Press.

Mitchell, Timothy. 2013. *Carbon Democracy: Political Power in the Age of Oil*. London: Verso.

Naqvi, S.N.H. 1994. *Ethics and Economics: An Islamic Synthesis*. Leicester: The Islamic Foundation.

Nasr, Vali. 2009. *The Rise of Islamic Capitalism: Why the New Muslim Middle Class is the Key to Defeating Extremism*. New York: Free Press.

Ramady, Mohamed A., ed. 2015. *The Political Economy of Wasta: Use and Abuse of Social Capital Networking*. Heidelberg: Springer.

Ricardo, David. 2004. *The Principles of Political Economy and Taxation*. New York: Dover Publications.

Salame, Ghassan, ed. 1994. *Democracy Without Democrats? The Renewal of Politics in the Muslim World*. London: I.B. Tauris.

Schumpeter, Joseph A. 1954. *History of Economic Analysis*. New York: Oxford University Press.

Smith, Adam. 1904. *An Inquiry into the Nature and Causes of the Wealth of Nations*. London: Methuen.

Vitalis, Robert. 2009. *America's Kingdom: Mythmaking on the Saudi Oil Frontier*. London: Verso.

Wadud-Muhsin, Amina. 1992. *Qur'an and Woman*. Kuala Lumpur: Penerbit Fajar Bakti Sdn.

Yahya, Sadowski. 1993. *Scuds or Butter? The Political Economy of Arms Control in the Middle East*. Washington, DC: Brookings Institution.

Part II

Political Implosion

5

Oil Dependency and Cold War Politics

Ahmed Zaki Yamani, the one-time oil minister, famously quipped that the Stone Age didn't end because of a shortage of stone, meaning that the oil age, and certainly Saudi's privileged position because of oil, will not end because of a shortage of oil but because of other factors.[1] Concerns about 2030, and if not the end of the oil age at least a more competitive economic environment, are creating a dynamic of economic tension that will increasingly pervade government and society. To change requires a more international outlook, but does it mean Saudi needs to become more Western? Less Islamic? Saudi Arabia is attempting to establish a modern business culture while grappling with globalization's challenges to Islamic teaching and social welfare values. Saudi political and business leaders are acutely aware that the Saudi economy needs, on the one hand, to diversify, while on the other needs to become more self-reliant, in terms of skills and resources. As a wealth creation resource, oil was found and extracted by foreigners. My reason for emphasizing this is that the Saudis basically had oil-based wealth handed to them on a platter. Compared to America, the nation that collaborated with the Kingdom to create this oil-based economy, Saudis never developed a sense of pioneering for wealth or belief in the manifest destiny of national growth, and there was no Protestant work ethic. They have long relied on expat

© The Author(s) 2018
D. Cowan, *The Coming Economic Implosion of Saudi Arabia*,
https://doi.org/10.1007/978-3-319-74709-5_5

expertise and management, and it is only comparatively recently they have sought increased self-reliance. It is this conundrum of oil and the wealth curse, with the manner of welfare provision in Saudi, that goes to the heart of the needed change, and is responsible for the economic behaviors which go back to the first days of oil. The history of oil is inextricably bound with a political history of Saudi dominated by the relationship between America and Saudi to create the kind of economy Saudi has grown up with and still exists today.

The relationship between oil and democracy has been much studied, and America and Britain in particular have been complicit in maintaining the Saudi status quo according to critics.[2] In the Saudi context, oil rents have held democracy at bay since government is able to repress dissent, fund political support to assuage different constituencies, maintain the house of Saud and the family elite power structure of society and release funds when needed to stifle resentment. It can be difficult to decipher whether Saudi economic behaviors are rooted in religious fatalism or political docility. However one argues the origins, the changing politics of oil today means the structures and behaviors will need to change or adapt, and the economic demands require there be a more active political agency and a vibrant middle class. To look forward we need first to look back. There are three eras into which we can break down the history of oil and the Saudi/American relationship, which in turn can be framed within the context of the Cold War. The first is the nascent period of Franklin D. Roosevelt through to the end of the Cold War. A second phase came with the post-Cold War through to the administration of George W. Bush. We are now in a third phase starting with Barack Obama and continuing into the Trump presidency. The first era created the oil-dependent economy in the context of the bipolar world of the United States and the Soviet Union, and secondly complicated by the question of Israel which is an issue that has continued as a strand through to the current phase of relationship. High pressure points were the Arab-Israeli wars. The second era centers on the Iranian revolution and takes us to 9/11 and the ensuing "War on Terror." The third and current era is the legacy of the Cold War; what some have defined as a new Arab Cold War. The oil has been the basis of domestic and international politics, able to fund whatever policies the Saudis wanted to pursue, and inflected the attitude and policies of America toward the region. Throughout these three eras, it is worth bearing in mind that Saudi has been the longest and most consistent regional ally of America. The aim here is not to offer a detailed history of this relationship, but to pick out some useful elements we can use in looking at this history of oil dependency which can help us understand contemporary behaviors.

First Era: Oiling the Cold War Partnership

Whatever the exact dynamics of foreign involvement in Saudi oil, the national oil company named Saudi Aramco is parsed as American, not British. Power was also parsed, as Saudi Arabia became an oil giant partnering with America, and the United States started to supplant British power in the Gulf.[3] Recent events can be interpreted in the context of the US and Saudi relationship in the Cold War years and the end of Cold War. In this context, we have to consider a tension between the Saudi/US common distaste for communism and a difference of attitudes between Saudi and the United States toward the Jews and Israel, which has always been a sensitive point of policy for the Saudis. Roosevelt had established a relationship with a king who resented the British and their rule of other regional Gulf states. Until 1947, the Gulf Arab states of Kuwait, Bahrain, Qatar, Abu Dhabi, Dubai, Sharjah, Ajman, Umm al-Quwain, Ras al-Khaimah, Fujairah and Muscat/Oman all formed part of Britain's Indian Empire, controlled from British India. Crucially, this was before America emerged as a superpower and Saudi already had shown the potential of oil reserves, which would later turn out to be the world's largest. On 14 February 1945, two months before his death, US President Franklin D. Roosevelt met with King ʿAbd al-ʿAzīz at which, followed up in writing in April, Roosevelt gave the king his twofold undertaking that the United States would consult with Arabs and Jews on the Palestine question before taking any decision and the United States would not act against the interest of the Arabs. It was the start of a "beautiful relationship," but one that is now suffering as the Saudi economy changes and its geopolitical position evolves.

Roosevelt's successor Harry S. Truman was to be less committed to these positions,[4] snapping at American diplomats based in the Middle East "I'm sorry Gentlemen, but I have to answer to hundreds of thousands who are anxious for the success of Zionism; I do not have hundreds of thousands of Arabs among my constituents."[5] However, what Roosevelt had done was not undone by Truman or the eventual recognition of Israel by America, though it did cause problems. John B. Judis offers the case in his book[6] that flaws in American policy dating back to the Truman era (1945–1949) set the course for the Middle East up to the present day, quoting Truman saying in 1948 he was "the best friend the Jews had in America."[7] Though regarded by some critics as a Christian Zionist, Truman was responding to accusations he was not helping Jews and was essentially changing his position, from recognizing a Jewish state of Israel to a federated Palestine administered by Jews and Arabs. America had taken an isolationist stance after the First World War, but the Second World War led to the establishment of strategic air bases in the region, with specifically a major base at Dhahran, the very area where oil would be discovered. America had negotiated the oil and strategic locations, and the existential threat of communism gave the Christian US and the Islamic Saudi Arabia a shared enemy and global concern. After the Second World War, America became expansionist and more dominant in the region. America as a nation fighting godless communism thus found a natural partner in Saudi, a religious state that also vehemently opposed the godless communism of the Soviet Union, as King ʿAbd al-ʿAzīz once told a US general if he "could find a Communist in Saudi Arabia, I will hand you his head."[8]

During the 1950s, Truman's successor President Dwight D. Eisenhower and the Dulles brothers—CIA Director Allen Dulles and Secretary of State John Foster Dulles—rebuffed Soviet treaty proposals to leave the Middle East a neutral zone in the Cold War and let Arabs rule Arabia. Instead, they mounted a clandestine war against Arab nationalism— which Allen Dulles equated with communism—particularly when Arab self-rule threatened oil concessions. They pumped secret American military aid to regimes in Saudi Arabia, Jordan, Iraq and Lebanon favoring puppets with conservative Jihadist ideologies that they regarded as a reliable antidote to Soviet Marxism. At a White House meeting between the

CIA's director of plans, Frank Wisner, and John Foster Dulles, in September 1957, Eisenhower advised the agency, "We should do everything possible to stress the 'holy war' aspect," according to a memo recorded by his staff secretary, Gen. Andrew J. Goodpaster.[9] The Eisenhower doctrine was articulated and agreed to by the Saudi king in 1957. This was a doctrine which stated America would support any Middle East nation targeted by "overt armed aggression from any nation controlled by International Communism."

In that same year, a secret committee was charged with investigating the CIA activities in the Middle East, and the Bruce-Lovett Report[10] produced. The report described CIA coup plots in Jordan, Syria, Iran, Iraq and Egypt, all of which were common knowledge in the Arab world but largely unknown to the American people, especially as they had been denied by the US government. The report blamed the CIA for the rampant anti-Americanism that was taking hold "in the many countries in the world today."[11] While the alliance was still going strong between the US and Saudi Arabia, it was also set at odds with Egypt and other nations in what Malcolm Kerr, the prominent Lebanese-American professor killed by gunmen in 1984, called the "Arab Cold War."[12] Egypt under Gamal Abdel Nasser came to be allied with the Soviet Union, and Arab nationalism and anti-colonialism was sweeping the region. In July, again in the same year, following a failed coup in Syria by the CIA, Senator John F. Kennedy upset the Eisenhower White House, the US political establishment and America's European allies when he gave a speech endorsing the right of self-governance in the Arab world and an end to America's interference in Arab countries.

Kennedy was pro-Israel and believed they had a right to land, and as president he took this stance in the hope of achieving an even-handed solution to the Palestine problem, while his State Department was more pro-Arab. In a 1960 speech, in which Kennedy stated "The Middle East needs water, not war; tractors, not tanks; bread, not bombs," the then senator explained he stood within the Democratic Party tradition on Israel:

It was President Woodrow Wilson who forecast with prophetic wisdom the creation of a Jewish homeland. It was President Franklin Roosevelt who kept alive the hopes of Jewish redemption during the Nazi terror. It was President Harry Truman who first recognized the new State of Israel and gave it status in world affairs. And may I add that it would be my hope and my pledge to continue this Democratic tradition – and to be worthy of it.[13]

However, Kennedy also maintained support for Saudi, and visited King ʿAbd al-ʿAzīz on 27 January 1962, at the residence of Jean Flagler Gonzalez in Palm Beach, Florida, where King Saud stayed following an eye surgery in Boston. The following month, the king visited Kennedy at the White House on 13 February 1962. Further trouble brewed when Nasser sent United Arab Republic (UAR) forces to support a palace coup in 1962 in the Yemen, which distracted Saudi and Jordan from developments in Palestine. Nasser's UAR was thus pitted against Saudi and Jordan in proxy war[14] and to raise the threat further he had done arms deals with the Soviet Union. This put Saudi as an Islamic state unencumbered by colonial memories in a unique position as partner for America in its push against communism. As Rashid Khalidi explains:

The radical wave in the Middle East seemed to place the United States and its allies in a highly unfavorable position. To this apparently unbalanced situation, Saudi Arabia brought the powerful ideological weapon of Islam. This was something the Saudis were uniquely positioned to do, given the centuries-old alliance between the royal family and the rigidly orthodox Wahhabi religious establishment, and given the kingdom's special place as the location of two of the most holy places in Islam, Mecca and Medina. Particularly after the much more competent and more pious and ascetic King Faisal took over from his profligate older brother Saʾud in 1962, Saudi Arabia focused much more intensively, and more plausibly, on Islam as the backbone of its resistance to the self-proclaimed "progressive" Arab regimes.[15]

The presence of UAR forces and interference in Yemen remained a problem Saudi and America needed to face together. Responding to the situation in a letter to King Faisal on 24 April 1965, Lyndon B. Johnson reassured the Saudis:

This is a concern we share. As you are aware, our goal continues to be to bring about a withdrawal of these troops and a cessation of foreign interference in Yemeni affairs. In pursuing this goal, the security of Saudi Arabia has been uppermost in our mind. We have at no time espoused a policy toward the United Arab Republic which we believed was in any way injurious to the interests of your country. On the contrary, our actions throughout the Near East have continued to be aimed only at promoting harmonious dealings and the reduction of frictions among the countries there.[16]

The notion of harmony in the region was about to get a whole lot worse. The Nixon doctrine, which emerged out of the costly and unpopular Vietnam War that Kennedy and Johnson had started, pushed for America to develop regional allies to act as proxies in the ongoing Cold War standoff with the Soviets, a standoff that almost led to a nuclear catastrophe. The proxies were Iran, Israel and Saudi Arabia. The high point was the 1973 Arab/Israeli War, variously known as the Yom Kippur, Ramadan and October War. In the period 1969 to 1970, the Soviet Union ramped up its support for Egypt after the war, and when Anwar Sadat started to distance himself from the Soviets, they threatened direct intervention in the 1973–1974 conflict. The response from Nixon was to set America on a DEFCON 3 footing,[17] causing the Soviets to stand down and the Arabs to lose another conflict. On another front, Nixon supported the Shah of Iran, whose position in Iran was becoming increasingly fragile.

Gerald Ford continued the Nixon doctrine, and maintained good relations with the Saudis. Writing to King Faisal on 29 August 1974, Ford explained:

I agree with you that what has been achieved thus far has checked the efforts that the Soviet Union has expended during the past twenty years. We will continue to make a major effort to move the negotiations forward as rapidly as the complexities of the situation allow. Meanwhile, we are urging all concerned to maintain the atmosphere of calm in the area which is so important to the success of efforts to achieve peace.

Henry Kissinger had advised in a memo to Ford that the president should be pushing for Saudi to use its influence on the Palestine question:

> Although Saudi Arabia is not one of the immediate parties to the dispute, it has been in a position to exert increasing influence on the Arab states which need to negotiate with Israel. It is therefore important that we do what we can to keep King Faisal on our side so that he will counsel restraint at critical points.[18]

Of course, the two issues were related, which had been made clear in the previous year when King Faisal had warned that if US policy toward Israel didn't change, then there would be a reduction in oil supplies. Ford urged the king to stop damaging the Western economy:

> It is my hope that, with Your Majesty's leadership as an example, the principal oil-producing countries will adopt a statesmanlike posture that will lead to a pricing structure more in accord with the capabilities of the world economy.[19]

Thirty years of close alignment with the Saudis had survived a number of crises with the principal tension being over Israel, but a new challenge was about to best the relationship, and this was more of an existential threat for the Saudis. Kissinger wrote what was a fair summary of the Saudis in these 30 years, stating Saudi had:

> ...navigated between the pressures of Arab radicalism, Palestinian irredentism, its own fear of covetous neighbors, and Communist designs. Its leaders knew that, in the end, Saudi security – indeed, Saudi survival – depended on American support, but they had less confidence in our judgment and were concerned lest our impetuosity upset the subtle calculations by which they survived. Saudi Arabia was too experienced to feel secure in isolation and too weak to become a principal player in Middle East diplomacy.

He also noted that the Saudis may have publicly said harsh things, but in the back channels they were helpful to American diplomacy. The forces experienced in the contemporary world were being unleashed, and it started with the Carter administration.

Carter[20] was to find himself on the political front line of the pivot between the outcomes of the Cold War and the emergence of Islamic radicalism as religious leaders took control of Iran. When the Soviets entered Afghanistan in 1979 it was an attempt to protect their own Muslim population against such Islamic radicalism. The emergence of Islamic radicalism was not something well understood at the time by the Carter administration, and Carter still saw things through the prism of the Cold War. Carter "suspected communists might take over the country – this still being the Cold War, albeit in a state of détente – but never mullahs and Islamic fanatics."[21] Instead, he warned of the way Afghanistan were putting the Soviets a step further toward Turkey and articulated the Carter doctrine that the United States was committed to deploy military force to counter Soviet intervention in the Persian/Arab Gulf. The success of the rebels in driving the Soviets out of Afghanistan was seen as a victory for America, but it was a victory that came back to haunt them and the world. The main priority for Carter in the region had been the Egypt/Israel peace treaty, but Saudi supported other countries in opposition to the accord.[22]

The perceived ongoing threat of the Soviets was also at the center of President Ronald Reagan's foreign policy, with a belief in the domino effect of nations falling into communism, meaning the United States had to resist nations supported by the Soviets. The Reagan administration got involved in Lebanon, supporting the Israeli plan to invade the country in June 1982 and drive the Palestinian Liberation Organization (PLO) out. This was attractive to the Americans, and supporting Israel while defeating the PLO and Syria at the same time seemed a good outcome. Reagan had sent Marines to Lebanon on a peacekeeping mission. However, in 1983 a truck bomb killed 241 American marines, along with a second attack on multinational forces, in Beirut. The Americans withdrew a few months later in February. The attack was traced back to Hezbollah at the direction of the Iranians.

In the midst of this the American and Saudi relationship remained solid. Reagan met King Fahd on 11 February 1985, the first time a Saudi monarch had been entertained since Nixon met with King Faisal in 1971. Reagan exulted the usual relationship, saying in his address:

> King Fahd and the Saudi Royal Family, reflecting the values at the heart of their society, have been sharing and generous leaders. In addition to their humanitarian aid throughout the world, they contribute to such cultural and educational institutions as the American University in Beirut, for example.[23]

President Reagan said the time had come to "turn the page to a new and happier chapter" in the region and asked Fahd to use Saudi Arabia's influence and moral encouragement to bring forth direct negotiations between Israel and its Arab neighbors. In return, Fahd said it was also a matter of the Americans needing to support the Palestinians. Fahd explained the Palestinian problem differently to the Western analysis, stating that the majority of Arabs had gained their freedom since the Second World War but not the Palestinians, who had "committed no wrong that can justify what has befallen them."[24] He gave no assurance to Reagan that Saudi Arabia would respond to Reagan's call for talks with Israel. Fahd concluded that "the Palestinians, who were never aggressors or invaders, found themselves through no fault of their own, the victims of unjust aggression. The Palestinian question is the single problem that is of paramount concern to the whole Arab nation and affects the relations of its people and countries with the outside world."[25] With the cohesive force of anti-communism giving way, the only common goal for Saudi and America now was oil stability and a complex relationship on the Palestinian question.

Second Era: Post-Cold War

The Cold War ended in 1989, the year George H. W. Bush took office. One year later Iraq invaded Kuwait, only to lose it rapidly to the alliance and strategy of Bush, a former director of the CIA. The success of Desert Storm provided an opportunity for another attempt to bring the Israelis and Arabs together, again with the help of the Saudis. Bush I visited Saudi twice while in office visiting Jeddah and Dharan on 21–22 November 1990. He first visited with King Fahd and the Amir of Kuwait and to address US and British military personnel in eastern Saudi Arabia. By this time, there were 230,000 US troops inside the Kingdom, but King Fahd and Bush I agreed in their meeting that the American forces would leave immediately once the invasion crisis was resolved or at the request of the Saudi government. His second visit was to Riyadh to meet with King Fahd on 31 December 1992. Both Bush I and Bush II were criticized for their relationship with the Saudis and saw big oil at the core of the narrative. Author and journalist Craig Unger in a highly controversial book *House of Bush, House of Saud* documents $1.4 billion that has "made its way" from the Saudi royal family to "entities tied" to the Bush family. Much of his book was seen by critics as being strong on supposition and isolated facts, but inconclusive in establishing a causal connection. However, it was a smear that stained the perception of both the Bush presidents and played into the "big oil" narrative. One critic, Jonathan D. Tepperman, senior editor at the policy journal *Foreign Affairs*, who had published a critical review of Unger's book in *The New York Times Book Review*, explained in an interview with CBS that "these connections" (such as President Bush hosting Bandar at his Crawford ranch, an honor usually reserved for heads of state) do "look bad," but he explained:

> what I don't see is any evidence that the Bush family ever let their personal financial concerns dictate U.S. policy… The fact of the matter is that the Saudi royals are deeply unpleasant people and frankly they are not great allies for Washington to have. The problem is they are less bad than all the other alternatives.[26]

The world changed little after the first Iraq war, as the Iraq president Saddam Hussein resumed abuse of his people and Kuwait remained a wealthy monarchical state. There was no regime change, just the old wild west motif of the stranger who comes into town and chases the bad guys out of town to fight another day, which of course was to happen some decades later when Bush II entered the White House.

In 1993, Samuel P. Huntingdon, who had served under Johnson and Carter, published his *Clash of Civilization* thesis. The same year America had witnessed the first World Trade Center bombing on 26 February. The Clinton administration chose to treat this act of terrorism as a crime rather than a security or military issue. The same approach was taken when in October later the same year 18 American servicemen were killed by terrorists. Thus was born the Clinton doctrine, announced by Martin Indyk on the National Security Council on 19 May 1983, committing the United States to "dual containment" by placing sanctions on both Iran and Iraq. The Saudis saw Clinton as someone in pursuit of their money but not giving anything much in return. He successfully lobbied Saudi to spend $6 billion[27] to replace its fleet of commercial jets with American planes. He later asked the Saudi king to award a lucrative contract to AT&T to modernize the Kingdom's aging telecommunications system. AT&T was soon awarded the $4 billion contract.[28] The Saudis delayed the deal until Washington worked out an agreement to reschedule $9.2 billion in payments due for Saudi arms purchases from five US companies. Falling oil prices had forced Saudi to cut annual spending by 20% and required a prolonged payment plan. Clinton traveled to Riyadh to meet with King Fahd, and in a letter to the King, Clinton wrote "I hope AT&T, which has long been a market leader, will receive every opportunity to establish itself as Saudi Arabia's preferred partner, both for quality and cost, in this project."[29] Clinton also managed to secure substantial funds for his Foundation and Library, something which every president has managed to secure since the Nixon library received funds. He was not in favor of using power, though he launched two attacks in Syria, but certainly was not inclined to get overly involved or put boots on the ground. With the Cold War over and national fervor kept in check, he didn't seem to see the need to act. A Brookings Institute commentary saw the Clinton approach as a change from the previous presidents going back to 1943:

> It began to go sour in 2000 when President Bill Clinton failed to get both a Syrian-Israeli peace at the Shepherdstown peace conference and a Palestinian-Israel peace at Camp David. Then Crown Prince Abdullah felt Clinton failed to push Israel hard enough to make territorial concessions. The Saudis believed a Syrian deal was especially ripe in 2000 and would have weaned Damascus away from Iran, isolated Hezbollah, and paved the way for a Palestinian deal.[30]

Though a grand White House lawn photo opportunity, his involvement in the Oslo peace agreement was limited, having joined the party after negotiations had long started. Clinton played the part of peacemaker, and seemed to have achieved a solution to solving the intractable problem of Israel and Palestine faced by his predecessors. Although he phrased the point differently after his first meeting with Benjamin Netanyahu in 1996, when he talked about his role in a private conversation he asked "Who the fuck does he think he is? Who's the fucking superpower here?"[31] At the tail end of the Clinton administration, a hole was blown into the Oslo agreement.

Warning bells about Islamic terrorism as a global threat to American interests did not seem to ring when the US destroyer *Cole* was attacked with the loss of 17 sailors and 34 wounded. Little was done to respond to the attack, nor was much done about Islamic terrorism, either by the Clinton administration or in the first months of the Bush II administration. Despite these warning signs, the sole superpower came under attack on 9/11 in an act of terrorism mostly carried out by Saudi nationals funded from organizations in Saudi and under the leadership of Saudi Osama bin Laden. While Bush I had successfully dealt with Iraq, his son George W. Bush took a more troubled path that would see him ally himself to a neoconservative agenda. This resulted in outcomes that has had ongoing reverberations in the world, and has resulted in a more complex political dynamic in the region. Bush II articulated his doctrine in State of the Union address in January 2002 and in a booklet published in September of that year, *The National Security Strategy of the United States*. Bush II promised to fight terrorism, deal with countries developing weapons of mass destruction and advance the neoconservative agenda of inspiring democratization in the Middle East. In all this time Bush never escaped the heavy criticism of his links with the Saudis and big oil, similarly with his Vice-President Dick Cheney.

There are any number of books and commentaries about the world in the wake of 9/11 generally, which question the role of Saudi Arabia in the atrocity directly and argue it continues as a state sponsor of terrorism,[32] though Hegghammer explains Al-Qaeda actions in 2003 did not gain public acceptance in the Kingdom.[33] Edward Clifford in the *Brown*

Political Review offers a succinct summary of the claims against the Kingdom:

The exact impact of Saudi support for terrorist groups remains unclear, as understanding of terror networks is, at best, nebulous. Operating in the shadows, Islamist terrorist organizations, aware that financial flows have the potential to be the weakest links in the armor that secrecy provides, closely guard their benefactors' identities and the channels through which they are funneled cash. What is known, however, is that many terrorist organizations are capable of running on relatively meager budgets that can be easily supported by only a few wealthy patrons, such as members of Saudi's elite... The immense wealth of Saudi Arabia has been leveraged globally to fund all manner of Sunni extremism, most disconcerting of which includes links to 9/11 and the growing threat posed by ISIS. Thirteen years on, questions persist about the role of Saudi funding and support in the planning and execution of the 9/11 attacks. Twenty-eight pages of the House Intelligence Committee findings on 9/11 remain classified, long after the release of the report. While still technically speculative, it has been credibly alleged that these twenty-eight sealed pages contain damming information regarding links between Saudi royalty and the hijackers.[34, 35]

The intention here is not to repeat or rehearse these arguments. The main point to establish here is that in the wake of 9/11 one of the things Bush II sought to do was to establish a line between reacting to the atrocity and maintaining the relationship with Saudi. In his address to Congress on 20 September, Bush II expressed the Bush doctrine which also stated what many saw as a Manichean view of foreign policy:

We will pursue nations that provide aid or safe haven to terrorism. Every nation, in every region, now has a decision to make. Either you are with us, or you are with the terrorists. From this day forward, any nation that continues to harbor or support terrorism will be regarded by the United States as a hostile regime.[36]

He also outlined his vision for strong American leadership in the world and the need to project America's power and influence. In a graduation speech at West Point the following June, Bush II outlined the realities of the new post-Cold War era and a shift in national security strategy, a shift from the Clinton doctrine of containment to the Bush II doctrine of preemption. Bush II stated, "our security will require all Americans to be forward-looking and resolute, to be ready for preemptive action when necessary to defend our liberty and to defend our lives."[37]

One of the frustrations of the time was the Saudi's delayed response to the fact most of the terrorists came from Saudi, and the prevalent ideology of the terrorists was the form of Islam proselytized and paid for globally by Saudi, both officially and unofficially. The Saudis could not accept their subjects would do such a thing. Until it happened to them. On 12 May 2003 terrorists attacked compounds in Riyadh killing 39 people and injuring 160, they were of different nationalities. The king vowed to rid the Kingdom of the perpetrators, their networks and families, and immediately had many terrorist suspects killed or imprisoned, along with any complicit family. However, there remains a body of critics campaigning to establish the money and organizational trail leading back to the highest echelons in Saudi. The release of further documents from the 9/11 commission gave fresh impetus to what these critics see as the battle for truth, which continues.

Then there is Iran. The relationship between Sunnis and Shiites is well known, as is the tension between them within the Kingdom, but in recent years the Saudis have become more insecure in their relationship with Iran. There is heightened fear of what Iran might do, and in meetings between King Abdullah and Condoleezza Rice, he pushed to get Bush II to take "decisive action" on Iran. Rice explained:

The unintended consequences of war with Iran, particularly given the still fragile situation in Iraq, were just too great. In a later meeting with the king, Bob Gates would be considerably blunter about the prospects of a U.S. attack on Iran, saying that the President of the United States would face the wrath of the American people over such a decision. That angered Abdullah, who somehow held out the hope that George W. Bush might be willing to "take care of Iran" before leaving office, despite the fact that the king would periodically meet with the Iranians and even, on one occasion, actually hold hands with Ahmadinejad. Given that fraternization, the Saudis' advocacy for tougher action was a little hard to taken.

The Iranian situation would prove to be pivotal to a change in the Saudi/US relationship during the administration of President Barack Obama and led to a deterioration of the relationship. Before the deal was struck, Prince Turki bin Faisal criticized the president in a Saudi newspaper and addressed Obama directly, stating he had:

> pivoted to Iran so much that you equate the kingdom's 80 years of constant friendship with America to an Iranian leadership that continues to describe America as the biggest enemy, that continues to arm, fund and support sectarian militias in the Arab and Muslim world.[38]

After the United States reached agreement, Saudi cautiously backed the deal for ensuring Iran would be prevented from acquiring nuclear weapons and included a strict and permanent monitoring regime.[39] However, what had been a close historical relationship had now come under deep strain at a time, which coincided with a critical change in Saudi's oil economy.

The Third Era: The Legacy of an Arab Cold War

Is there a reason for the deterioration of the Saudi/US relationship? One might posit it is because President Obama raised a matter of principle, but equally it is no coincidence that it should start deteriorating at the time that everyone recognizes the economic shift in Saudi redraws the political map somewhat. When the Australian prime minister once asked about the relationship with the Saudis, Obama told him "It's complicated."[40] The relationship between the Saudis and Obama created a pivotal moment in US/Saudi relations, but not in the way expected. By the time Obama visited Saudi for the fourth and final time as president in April 2016 the reception was reportedly cool and generated reduced official coverage for such a state visit. Mustafa Alani, a Gulf security analyst who is close to the Saudi establishment, said Obama would find a leadership "that's not ready to believe him" and had little faith in him, adding "The Saudis had disagreements with previous presidents… Here you have deep distrust that the president won't deliver anything."[41] It didn't start out that way. In a meeting between John Brennan, Assistant to the President for Homeland Security and Counterterrorism, and King Abdullah, the king said while he considered both Bushes as friends, Bush II didn't take his advice on dealing with issues in the region, and they found their problems "compounded." The King said, "we are ready to consult, provide guidance and to do whatever is necessary. We are people of the region and we know it well." Brennan responded that Obama would restore credibility to which the king responded, "Thank God for bringing Obama to the presidency" and inspiring "great hope" in the Muslim world. "May God grant him strength and patience," Abdullah continued, "May God protect him. I'm concerned about his personal safety. America and the world need such a president."[42]

Although Obama oversaw the sale $95 billion in arms to the Kingdom and shared in a determined fight against the Islamic State and Al-Qaeda, there were too many issues that made the Saudis feel the relationship was deteriorating. Obama had started his presidency with the aim of getting out of Iraq and Afghanistan, but instead the country remained embroiled in the mess. The eight-year presidency would find the Saudis resenting the president for "preaching" human rights to them, and his failure in not sufficiently supporting Hosni Mubarak and the campaign to oust Assad from Syria. They believed he was not committed nor reliable. The red line speech and its subsequent trajectory signaled America, or at least Obama, lacked backbone in the region. Speaking at the White House in 2012, Obama declared: "We have been very clear to the Assad regime … that a red line for us is we start seeing a whole bunch of chemical weapons moving around or being utilized. That would change my calculus. That would change my equation."[43] The following year, the Assad regime forces shocked the world with his use of chemical weapons in an attack against rebel-controlled areas of Damascus, killing nearly 1500 civilians, including more than 400 children. In a 2017 interview with CBS's "60 Minutes," Obama defended the speech and explained that he had ad-libbed the "red line" phrase, which wasn't in the text of his speech.[44] However, the biggest issue was Iran and the nuclear agreement, which Saudis saw as a case of Obama letting the distrustful Iranians being let back into the international fold. The deal was reached in Lausanne, Switzerland, between China, Russia, France, Great Britain, Germany and the United States and gave

Iran over $110 billion a year in sanctions relief and allowed them to return to the global economy in exchange for halting their nuclear weapons ambitions.[45] The Saudis also feared this was a regional political and economic pivot toward Iran, and certainly did not appreciate Obama stating that Saudi and Iran should "share the region."[46]

Despite the frostiness, a major foreign policy change occurred as a result of what many perceived to be Obama's dithering approach, and this was the Saudi's becoming more self-reliant. In March 2015, Saudi Arabia and regional allies launched military strikes against Iran-backed Houthi rebels in Yemen and began building a new naval base in Jazan near the Yemen border, which started a prolonged engagement in the country.[47] In October 2015, the Saudis then announced a new defense policy "to defend the homeland, protect Saudi citizens, secure national interests, bolster defense of partner states and strengthen inter-agency partnerships."[48] One month later, they announced the formation of a 34-country (mostly Sunni) Islamic Military Alliance to coordinate efforts to fight and defeat terrorism.[49] Saudi Arabia sought to establish its own solution to instability in Yemen, and while the Arab League's decision to form a joint Arab military force are positive signs of increased burden-sharing from the Gulf it does not leave America on the sidelines. The partnership with the United States remained fundamental to the Saudis, as Deputy Crown Prince MbS explained it Saudi Arabia's partnership with the United States is "huge" and "oil is only a small part" of this partnership. He continued "America is the policeman of the world, not just the Middle East… It is the number one country in the world, and we consider ourselves to be the main ally for the US in the Middle East and we see America as our ally."[50]

MbS was speaking some eight months before Donald J. Trump won the presidential election, but he already seemed to be speaking Trump's language by talking up the partnership as "huge." Curiously the man attacked in America for his Muslim heritage was the president distrusted by the Saudis, while the man who insulted Muslims and accused Saudi of being behind terrorism is the president they welcomed with open arms and, at the time of writing, with whom they started a blossoming relationship. President Trump's choice for his first foreign foray in office was an interesting one, visiting first Saudi and then Israel and the Vatican, making a clean sweep of the Abrahamic religions. It is too early at the time of writing to forecast how this will all turn out, but the early signals have been it may well be business as usual for Saudi and America in the region. There are key pressure points, with the Israel question remaining a tension as it always has done. Trump's decision to recognize Jerusalem as the capital was particularly irksome among Islamic states, including Saudi. King Salman stated, "I repeat the Kingdom's condemnation and strong regret over the US decision on Jerusalem, for its relinquishment of the historic rights of the Palestinian people in Jerusalem."[51] The carbon economy will be impacted by greater oil independence and further development of alternatives, making it an economic problem for the Saudis and means Saudis need to become more economically vibrant and self-reliant. The Saudis are already more self-reliant in foreign policy, and we can expect this to continue. Iran and terrorism will be the two biggest pressure points.

It is more than simply "big oil" which explains why the United States and Saudi Arabia have had a long-lasting relationship, often at the cost of not tackling human rights abuses and other concerns critics have about the Kingdom and the relationship. It is a relationship that has fostered a regional dynamic which places Saudi Arabia and the United States at the center. The ending of the Cold War brought the end of Soviet support for aligned Arab states, and American victory made them the only game in town, at least for a while. The legacy of the Cold War relationship has been the outcome of the above policies which have contributed to the problems of the region, most notably in Afghanistan as a theater of Cold War. The Soviet invasion brought the boundaries of communism even closer to Saudi, seen as a threat to the region by both Saudi and America. However, the reality in the early part of the Cold War story was that Stalin had not been as welded to the Arab situation as Eisenhower and Truman had thought he was as they thrashed out new doctrines. Stalin regarded the Arab nationalist leaders as unreliable and bourgeois, and as a result the Middle East was more tangential than the Americans had thought. The Cold War narrative explains much of the regional dynamics and America's role, but with the fall of communism there emerged a new form of Cold War.

The outcome of the end of the Cold War has turned out to be something of a poisoned chalice. The transnational Islamic fighters and radicals who drove out the Soviets had found a new direction, one which led to the so-called War on Terror and the ongoing threat of terrorism and rise of Islamic State. The plethora of Islamic groups today Fred Halliday contended is "not a product of the end of the Cold War, but a pervasive, influential legacy of the Cold War itself."[52] During the Cold War the Arab nations had a habit of using the pretext of Cold War to play regional politics, get arms deals and ease access to the United Nations. To combat this, and the threat of communism, Saudi used Islam as a weapon against the progressive, leftist and nationalist regimes. The Kingdom also supported the spread of Islam outside its borders and brought dissidents into the Kingdom, especially members of the Muslim Brotherhood. The divide went deeper as Khalidi suggests, taking the argument further:

> It may seem hard to believe today, given the current demonization of radical, militant political Islam in American public discourse, but for decades the United States was in fact a major patron, indeed in some respects *the* major patron, of earlier incarnations of just these extreme trends, for reasons that had everything to do with the perceived need to use any and all means to wage the Cold War.[53]

The Soviets backed nationalist regimes and the US absolute monarchies, and thus Khalidi argues the United States was happy to side with ideological Islam while convenient during the Cold War until it was later used against them.

The picture emerging from this brief foray into history is one of a trusted political and economic partnership between the United States and Saudi Arabia. The oil economy, and the relationship with America, formed the backbone of the economic and political position of the Kingdom in the regional and global economy. During the Obama administration there were signs this was being decoupled, and it is not clear whether this decoupling will occur under the Trump administration or in a future administration, but I strongly I suspect there will be a systemic decoupling. This decoupling started with 9/11, and suspicion the Saudis had something to do with it, and deteriorated with the Obama administration stressing human rights and gender, despite continuing to keep the main traditional benefits of the relationship. There are economic consequences to consider as well in this picture. The notion of "oil for security" was found to work both ways, because while Saudi and the United States both had found security in the relationship previously, recent times suggest there is greater security in other relationships, such as Iran, and the underwriting currency of oil is diminishing in importance in defining regional relationships today. This is part of the economic challenge Saudi is facing, because an economically weak or crippled Saudi is of no use to anybody. In this view, the United States is culpable in the emergence of Islamic radicalism, and a weakening Saudi can only exacerbate the threat that the Kingdom will fail. As Kissinger had argued, Saudi had navigated its way thanks to oil and America, but the power of oil and the relationship have been diminished, and we are left to ponder if this is a tipping point toward implosion for a theocracy under threat.

Notes

1. Quoted in Lippman (2012, p. 38).
2. Mitchell (2013) and Vitalis (2009).
3. See, Irvine H. Anderson, Lend-Lease for Saudi Arabia, *Diplomatic History* 3 (Fall 1979), Anderson (1981) and William (1984).
4. For the Truman Administration oil diplomacy, see Miller (1980) and Stoflf (1980).
5. https://www.washingtonpost.com/news/worldviews/wp/2015/02/24/when-some-americans-opposed-the-creation-of-israel/?utm_term=.e06d3fc8af00
6. Judis (2014).
7. Ibid, p. 3.
8. Beisner (2009, p. 536).
9. http://www.politico.com/magazine/story/2016/02/rfk-jr-why-arabs-dont-trust-america-213601
10. https://www.cia.gov/library/readingroom/docs/1945-11-06b.pdf
11. Ibid.
12. Kerr (1965).

13. Speech by Senator John F. Kennedy, Zionists of America Convention, Statler Hilton Hotel, New York, NY, August 26, 1960 ref. Also, see https://www.jfklibrary.org/Research/Research-Aids/JFK-Speeches/United-States-Senate-Military-Power_19580814.aspx, https://www.jfklibrary.org/Asset-Viewer/Archives/JFKCAMP1960-1030-015.aspx

14. Douglas Little (2008, p. 156f.) and Paterson (1989).

15. Khalidi (2009, p. 19).

16. Johnson Library, National Security File, Special Head of State Correspondence File, Saudi Arabia, Presidential Correspondence. Secret. Transmitted to Jidda in telegram 559, April 27. (National Archives and Records Administration, RG 59, Central Files 1964–66, POL 15-1 US/Johnson).

17. DEFCON is the threat level assessment used by the US military. The lower the number, the higher the perceived threat. DEFCON 5 is peacetime, while DEFCON 1 is imminent war. Raising the DEFCON level activates a prescribed set of actions. DEFCON 3 puts military and government on a level of preparedness including evacuation of personnel, and is as close to a war footing without engaging in full combat.

18. Box 4, folder "Saudi Arabia - King Faisal" of the National Security Adviser's Presidential Correspondence with Foreign Leaders Collection at the Gerald R. Ford Presidential Library. https://www.fordlibrarymuseum.gov/library/document/0351/1555849.pdf

19. Ibid.

20. Little (2008).

21. Mattson, Kevin *What the Heck Are You Up To, Mr. President?* (Bloomsbury: New York, 2010) p. 16.

22. By "pursuing a carefully balanced policy of trying not to antagonize any party in the Arab world. For instance, it provides aid to the Palestinians and to the conservative monarchy in Jordan. It maintains influence in most Arab capitals regardless of their ideology or orientation. Joining the peace talks would indicate that the Saudis had taken sides. This would not only anger and alienate such radical regimes as Syria, Iraq, Libya, Algeria and the Palestinians, but might also result in serious military and security problems. Saudi Arabia is no match for countries like Syria or Iraq. In addition, it has a large Palestinian presence in the form of refugees employed in the oil fields and in other positions, both managerial and blue collar. Thus, by joining the peace talks, Saudi Arabia would be taking a considerable risk. Moreover, the immediate benefits in doing so are not yet clear." David Aviel, *Economic Implications of the Peace Treaty*

between Egypt and Israel, 12 Case W. Res. J. Int'l L. 57 (1980) Available at: http://scholarlycommons.law.case.edu/jil/vol12/iss1/4

23. Ronald Reagan: "Toasts at the State Dinner for King Fahd bin 'Abd al-'Aziz Al Sa'ud of Saudi Arabia," February 11, 1985. Online by Gerhard Peters and John T. Woolley, The American Presidency Project. http://www.presidency.ucsb.edu/ws/?pid=38210

24. https://reaganlibrary.archives.gov/archives/speeches/1985/21185a.htm

25. The quotes and narrative is based on a report from the *LA Times*, http://articles.latimes.com/1985-02-11/news/mn-4280_1_king-fahd

26. http://www.cbsnews.com/news/the-tangled-web-of-us-saudi-ties/, http://articles.latimes.com/1994-04-28/business/fi-51537_1_saudi-arabia

27. http://www.nytimes.com/1994/02/17/world/saudi-air-to-buy-6-billion-in-jets-built-in-the-us.html

28. http://www.nytimes.com/1994/05/10/business/at-t-wins-4-billion-saudi-project.html

29. http://articles.latimes.com/1994-04-28/business/fi-51537_1_saudi-arabia

30. https://www.brookings.edu/blog/markaz/2016/04/14/mr-obama-goes-to-riyadh-why-the-united-states-and-saudi-arabia-still-need-each-other/

31. http://www.slate.com/articles/news_and_politics/foreigners/2012/09/benjamin_netanyahu_should_be_careful_about_inserting_himself_too_much_into_the_presidential_race_between_barack_obama_and_mitt_romney_.html

32. https://www.theguardian.com/world/us-embassy-cables-documents/220186 http://www.independent.co.uk/news/world/middle-east/prince-mohammed-bin-salman-naive-arrogant-saudi-prince-is-playing-with-fire-a6804481.html

33. Hegghammer, Thomas *The Failure of jihad in Saudi Arabia*, 2010 https://ctc.usma.edu/posts/the-failure-of-jihad-in-saudi-arabia

34. http://www.brownpoliticalreview.org/2014/12/financing-terrorism-saudi-arabia-and-its-foreign-affairs/

35. These pages were subsequently released by the Obama administration in 2016, and welcomed by Saudi. "This information does not change the assessment of the US government that there's no evidence that the Saudi government or senior Saudi individuals funded al-Qaida," Josh Earnest, the White House press secretary, stated. However, it did not succeed in

ending the speculation. https://www.theguardian.com/us-news/2016/jul/15/911-report-saudi-arabia-28-pages-released
36. https://georgewbush-whitehouse.archives.gov/news/releases/2001/09/20010920-8.html
37. http://www.nytimes.com/2002/06/01/international/text-of-bushs-speech-at-west-point.html
38. http://www.arabnews.com/columns/news/894826
39. https://www.ft.com/content/c740cae0-2644-11e5-bd83-71cb60e8f08c, https://www.theguardian.com/world/2013/nov/24/iran-nuclear-deal-middle-east-reaction-saudi-arabia
40. http://time.com/4408667/911-report-28-pages-classified-saudi-arabia/
41. Ibid.
42. https://wikileaks.org/plusd/cables/09RIYADH447_a.html
43. http://edition.cnn.com/2012/08/20/world/meast/syria-unrest/
44. http://www.worldtribune.com/obama-gives-himself-a-pass-for-red-line-speech-on-syria/
45. http://www.aljazeera.com/indepth/features/2015/04/analysis-iran-nuclear-deal-150403002032133.html
46. https://www.theatlantic.com/magazine/archive/2016/04/the-obama-doctrine/471525/
47. https://www.theguardian.com/world/2015/mar/26/saudi-arabia-begins-airstrikes-against-houthi-in-yemen
48. http://www.arabnews.com/saudi-arabia/news/817166
49. http://www.prnewswire.com/news-releases/islamic-military-alliance-convenes-in-saudi-arabia-vows-to-dry-up-terrorists-resources-300241763.html
50. http://m.gulfnews.com/news/gulf/saudi-arabia/riyadh-upbeat-on-yemen-peace-talks-1.1703531
51. http://www.aljazeera.com/news/2017/12/trump-jerusalem-decision-latest-updates-171212081649751.html
52. Bronson (2006, p. 9).
53. Khalidi (2009, p. 20).

Bibliography

al-Rasheed, Madawi, ed. 2008. *Kingdom Without Borders: Saudi Arabia's Political, Religious and Media Frontiers*. London: Hurst.

Allawai, Ali A. 2009. *The Crisis of Islamic Civilization*. New Haven: Yale University Press.

Aburish, Said K. 2005. *The Rise, Corruption and Coming Fall of the House of Saud*. London: Bloomsbury.

Anderson, Irvine H. 1981. *ARAMCO, the United States and Saudi Arabia: A Study of the Dynamics of Foreign Oil Policy 1933–1950*. Princeton: Princeton University Press.

Axworthy, Michael. 2008. *A History of Iran: Empire of the Mind*. New York: Perseus Books.

Beisner, Robert L. 2009. *Dean Acheson: A Life in the Cold War*. Oxford: Oxford University Press.

Black, Antony. 2001. *The History of Islamic Political Thought: From the Prophet to the Present*. Edinburgh: Edinburgh University Press.

Bronson, Rachel. 2006. *Thicker Than Oil: America's Uneasy Relationship with Saudi Arabia*. New York: Oxford University Press.

Brown, Archie. 2009. *The Rise and Fall of Communism*. New York: Doubleday.

Cook, M.A., ed. 1970. *Studies in the Economic History of the Middle East*. Oxford: Oxford University Press.

Darlow, Michael, and Barbara Ibn Saud Bray. 2012. *The Desert Warrior Who Created the Kingdom of Saudi Arabia*. New York: Skyhorse Publishing.

Fawcett, Louise. 2016. *International Relations of the Middle East*. 4th ed. Oxford: Oxford University Press.

Gause, F., III. 1994. *Gregory Oil Monarchies: Domestic and Security Challenges in the Arab Gulf States*. New York: Council on Foreign Relations.

Halliday, Fred. 2000. *Nation and Religion in the Middle East*. Boulder: Lynne Rienner Publishers.

———. 2002. *Arabia Without Sultans*. London: Saqi Books.

Haykel, Bernard, Thomas Hegghammer, and Stéphane Lacroix. 2015. *Saudi Arabia in Transition: Insights on Social, Political, Economic and Religious Change*. Cambridge: Cambridge University Press.

Hegghammer, Thomas. 2010. *Jihad in Saudi Arabia: Violence and Pan-Islamism Since 1979*. New York: Cambridge University Press.

Hertog, Steffen. 2010. *Princes, Brokers, and Bureaucrats Oil and the State in Saudi Arabia*. Ithaca: Cornell University Press.

Hourani, Albert. 2002. *A History of the Arab Peoples*. Cambridge, MA: Belknap Press.

House, Karen Elliott. 2012. *On Saudi Arabia: Its People, Past, Religion, Fault Lines – And Future*. New York: Vintage Books.

Judis, John B. 2014. *Genesis: Truman, American Jews, and the Origins of the Arab/Israeli Conflict*. New York: Farrar, Straus & Giroux.

Karsh, Effraim. 2006. *Islamic Imperialism: A History*. New Haven: Yale University Press.

Kepel, Gilles. 2004. *The War for Muslim Minds: Islam and the West*. Trans. Pascal Ghazaleh. Cambridge, MA: Belknap Press.

Kerr, Malcolm. 1965. *The Arab Cold War, 1958–1964: A Study of Ideology in Politics*. Oxford: Oxford University Press.

———. 1971. *The Arab Cold War: Gamal 'Abd al-Nasir and His Rivals, 1958–1970*. Oxford: Oxford University Press.

Khalidi, Rashid. 2009. *Sowing Crisis: The Cold War and American Dominance in the Middle East*. Boston: Beacon Press.

Koya, Abdar Rahman, ed. 2010. *Imam Khomeini: Life, Thought and Legacy*. Kuala Lumpur: Islamic Book Trust.

Lacey, Robert. 2009. *Inside the Kingdom: Kings, Clerics, Terrorists, Modernists, and the Struggle for Saudi Arabia*. New York: Viking.

Lackner, Helen. 1978. *A House Built on Sand. A Political Economy of Saudi Arabia*. London: Ithaca Press.

Lewis, Bernard. 2002. *The Arabs in History*. New York: Oxford University Press.

Lippman, Thomas W. 2012. *Saudi Arabia on the Edge: The Uncertain Future of an American Ally*. Dulles: Potomac Books.

Little, Douglas. 2008. *American Orientalism: The United States and the Middle East Since 1945*. 3rd ed. Chapel Hill: The University of North Carolina Press.

Louis, William Roger. 1984. *The British Empire in the Middle East. 1945–1951*. Oxford: Oxford University Press.

Luciani, Giacomo, ed. 1990. *The Arab State*. Berkeley: University of California Press.

Lynch, Timothy J., and Robert S. Singh. 2008. *After Bush: The Case for Continuity in American Foreign Policy*. Cambridge: Cambridge University Press.

Mabon, Simon. 2016. *Saudi Arabia and Iran: Power and Rivalry in the Middle East*. New York: I.B. Tauris.

Mansfield, Peter. 1985. *The Arabs*. London: Penguin Books.

Mattson, Kevin. 2010. *What the Heck Are You Up To, Mr. President?* New York: Bloomsbury.

Miller, David Aaron. 1980. *Search for Security: Saudi Arabian Oil and American Foreign Policy*. Chapel Hill: University of North Carolina Press.

Mitchell, Timothy. 2013. *Carbon Democracy: Political Power in the Age of Oil*. London: Verso.

Patai, Raphael. 1973. *The Arab Mind*. New York: Scribner.

Paterson, Thomas G. 1989. *Kennedy's Quest for Victory: American Foreign Policy, 1961–1963*. New York: Oxford University Press.

Pipes, Richard. 2001. *Communism: A History*. New York: Random House.

Ramazani, R.K., ed. 1990. *Iran's Revolution: The Search for Consensus*. Bloomington: Indiana University Press.

Schwarz, Rolf. 2007. Rule, Revenue, and Representation. Oil and State Formation in the Middle East and North Africa. PhD Thesis, Graduate Institute of International Studies, Geneva

Southern, R.W. 1978. *Western Views of Islam in the Middle Ages*. Cambridge, MA: Harvard University Press.

Stoflf, Michael B. 1980. *Oil, War and American Security: The Search for a National Policy on Foreign Oil. 1941–1947*. New Haven: Yale University Press.

Vitalis, Robert. 2009. *America's Kingdom: Mythmaking on the Saudi Oil Frontier*. London: Verso.

William, Roger Louis. 1984. *The British Empire in the Middle East. 1945–1951*. Oxford: Clarendon Press.

Yahya, Sadowski. 1993. *Scuds or Butter? The Political Economy of Arms Control in the Middle East*. Washington, DC: Brookings Institution.

Yaqub, Salim. 2004. *Containing Arab Nationalism: The Eisenhower Doctrine and the Middle East*. Chapel Hill: The University of North Carolina Press.

Yergin, Daniel. 1993. *The Prize: The Epic Quest for Oil Money & Power*. New York: Touchstone.

6

A Theocracy Under Threat

In the 1970s, oil became the new gold and oil pricing replaced the gold standard in our carbon economy. This power, and the oil economy that facilitated it, is weakening. For Saudi this suggests a very different future and raises the specter of implosion of the Kingdom and its oil-dependent economy if it does not diversify in time. There are many nations that could fail and cause little more than a ripple in geopolitical terms, but Saudi has for so long been pivotal in the Middle East that even a severe weakening, let alone failing, is a problem for all. Already Saudi is in the early stages of changing from being a Cold War partner against godless communism into a less-than-trusted partner. This is a mistake and will not help in dealing with the global political presence of Islamic radicalism. It is also a mistake to demand a reformation in Islam or in Saudi, for the reasons stated earlier. If we are to have a global peace in Islam then the solution for the world may be to have a strong Saudi Arabia and one that is not less Islamic, but more Islamic. Saudi is pivotal in Islam due to its role of custodian, and it should use this as a basis to foster more positive diplomatic relations with all nations, not just by being the "American Islam." What has truly destabilized Saudi's status in international relations is the tipping toward Iran, which is leading to increasing uncertainty in the Kingdom and destabilizing effects. Iran is part of minority

© The Author(s) 2018
D. Cowan, *The Coming Economic Implosion of Saudi Arabia*,
https://doi.org/10.1007/978-3-319-74709-5_6

Islam, but that doesn't stop it from seeking to promote itself as the true home of Islam in opposition to Saudi. A major external pressure in recent years has been the nature of the American relationship, which deteriorated under both President George W. Bush and President Barack Obama. Pressure has been mounting on the United States to forsake its long relationship in part to force Saudi to change its attitude on human rights violations and gender issues, and in part because it is felt the relationship is losing its benefits. The notions that working together would promote internal change and help in regional affairs have been discredited in many quarters. In remarks at the American University in Cairo made on 20 June 2005, the US Secretary of State Condoleezza Rice noted that "for 60 years, my country, the United States, pursued stability at the expense of democracy in this region here in the Middle East – and we achieved neither."[1]

This signaled a change in the US approach to power in the region, which became clear when the Obama administration pushed ahead with the signing of the Iran nuclear deal, signed in July 2015 which meant Tehran agreed to scale back its nuclear capabilities in return for the lifting of most international sanctions. Saudi takes the view the deal makes the regional situation worse, because lifting sanctions has removed Iran's isolation as a rogue state and gives it more revenue, all of which only fuels Iran's ambition to be the regional hegemon and bring down the house of Saud in the process. President Barack Obama sought to refocus the regional issues by focusing on two areas, the Palestinian-Israeli conflict and the American attitude toward Islam. In a much-discussed speech at Cairo University, Obama seemed to be retooling the American approach, stating:

> We seek a new beginning based in mutual interest and mutual respect and based on the truth that America and Islam are not exclusive and need not be in competition.[2]

However, the speech culminated simply in words as far as many in the region were concerned, with as much as 75% of respondents polled in the region, including Saudi Arabia, saying the expectation raised here was never met within a mere two years of him making the statement. Obama turned his attention to Afghanistan, the graveyard of many a national foreign policy and military aspiration, and what he called a "war of necessity" as opposed to the Iraq "war of choice." In his famous speech in Cairo at Cairo University in 2009,[3] President Barack Obama gave a master class in the modern political rhetoric about religion. He attempted to show nuance on the matter in speeches generally and this one was to set the tone for his global handling of Islam. Subsequent events, however, left even staunch supporters concluding his presidency did few favors to the world in practical terms in his handling of the Middle East. An audience member who jumped up emotionally during the speech shouting "Barack Obama, we love you!" has no doubt revisited this outburst of enthusiasm many times since. It is worth dissecting in a little detail this significant speech. First, because of the theology of the speech, and secondly related to this, we can put it in the context of a president who consciously wanted to reach out to Islamic stakeholders but ended up creating more problems and alienating his closest regional ally, namely, Saudi Arabia with its "American Islam."

In an interview with Jeffrey Goldberg of *The Atlantic*, Obama explained that in giving his Cairo speech:

> I was hoping that my speech could trigger a discussion, could create space for Muslims to address the real problems they are confronting – problems of governance, and the fact that some currents of Islam have not gone through a reformation that would help people adapt their religious doctrines to modernity.

At the time of the speech Obama was basking in a wave of global approval, and a Nobel Peace Prize, simply by not being Bush II. Obama explained that America and Islam are not exclusive and don't need to be in competition because they overlap and share common principles. He also stated that throughout history, Islam has demonstrated through words and deeds the possibilities of religious tolerance and racial equality. This is rather stretching the point, since if we are talking about what religions share, they all share a bloody history. In part this can be explained by adherents departing from the faith they profess, but problematically in the case of Islam we have the founder of the faith himself using violence to establish his message. This has to be understood in the light of subsequent history and today, because it is this which essentially validates Islamic violence for those who wish to use such means today. If a Christian is violent it is hard to point to Jesus and say "well, he did it!" To be careful, I am not saying that Islam is a religion of violence; simply that the inconvenient facts here need to be processed.

Another point to tick off on the agenda was the "clash of civilizations" thesis, which Obama did, by stating to much applause, "let there be no doubt: Islam is a part of America." He saw it as part of his responsibility as president of the United States:

> …to fight against negative stereotypes of Islam wherever they appear. But that same principle must apply to Muslim perceptions of America. Just as Muslims do not fit a crude stereotype, America is not the crude stereotype of a self-interested empire.

Turning to the big issue that drives a wedge between the United States and the Arab world, he addressed the Israeli-Palestinian problem. In silence, he clearly stated US support for Israel and the reasons for that support rooted in recognition that Jews had been wronged for centuries culminating the holocaust. However, when he then said America would "not turn our backs on the legitimate Palestinian aspiration for dignity, opportunity, and a state of their own" the applause rang out. For all the attempts to find common ground, the reality is that throughout this speech he was warmly received only when he preached to the choir.

Some of the more theological parts of the speech reveal the problem. To great applause, Obama proclaimed, "I have known Islam on three continents before coming to the region where it was first revealed." Only Muslims believe the Koran was revealed, and revelation is a very specific theological point. Other religions and secular liberalism would declare this was not revelation for different reasons. It was a point he made in the context of the Israel-Palestinian question. He went on to explain:

> Too many tears have been shed. Too much blood has been shed. All of us have a responsibility to work for the day when the mothers of Israelis and Palestinians can see their children grow up without fear; when the Holy

Land of the three great faiths is the place of peace that God intended it to be; when Jerusalem is a secure and lasting home for Jews and Christians and Muslims, and a place for all of the children of Abraham to mingle peacefully together as in the story of Isra, when Moses, Jesus, and Mohammed, peace be upon them, joined in prayer.

Again, we have the reference of "peace be upon him," usually reserved for Muhammad being extended to the "other" prophets. Likewise, we have the positing of an equal claim to Jerusalem. The story of Isra concerns the journey, reported as miraculous that Muhammad undertook from Mecca to Jerusalem, the al-Aqsa mosque to be exact, which sources date at one year before the Hijrah. This journey is believed to have been followed by his ascension into heaven. The Koran 17:1 states:

Holy is He Who carried His servant by night from the Holy Mosque (in Makka) to the farther Mosque (in Jerusalem) – whose surroundings We have blessed – that We might show him some of Our signs. Indeed He alone is All-Hearing, All-Seeing.

There are scant details in the Koran, the more detailed version appears in the Hadith, which Obama was doubtless drawing upon to present a picture of Mohammed with Moses and Jesus. His speech ended with a triumph of liberal hermeneutics over traditional interpretation of religious scripture, when he stated:

The Holy Koran tells us: "O mankind! We have created you male and a female; and we have made you into nations and tribes so that you may know one another." The Talmud tells us: "The whole of the Torah is for the purpose of promoting peace." The Holy Bible tells us: "Blessed are the peacemakers, for they shall be called sons of God." The people of the world can live together in peace. We know that is God's vision. Now that must be our work here on Earth.

The intention here is not to dismiss the Koran or Islamic theory, but to highlight there are differences that exist between faiths that are too easily glossed over by intellectual liberalism and even liberal theology. Nor is my intention here to contest liberal theology. It is necessary to have clarity on these differences, and to assess the underlying worldview and assumptions of statements made in the context of current Middle East politics. What underlies this major speech is Obama's theology, which represents a different tradition to those of his predecessors. Aside from the Roman Catholic John F. Kennedy, Obama's predecessors tended to come from conservative and mainstream Protestant denominations. Obama, as he referenced in his speech, came from a mixed background. In his autobiography *The Audacity of Hope*, Obama [2006:203f] explained:

> In our household the Bible, the Koran, and the Bhagavad Gita sat on the shelf alongside books of Greek and Norse and African mythology. On Easter or Christmas Day my mother might drag me to church, just as she dragged me to the Buddhist temple, the Chinese New Year celebration, the Shinto shrine, and ancient Hawaiian burial sites.

This picture of religious home life is quite normal in Europe, but less common in America and even less common among American presidents. Obama's mother raised him to look at religion anthropologically, and his own faith journey was a mixture of liberalism and liberation theology. In an era of secularism some may take this as a good sign of the times. It certainly equipped Obama to address Muslims in many countries, but the speech did little except to raise fatal expectations and went the way of the Nobel Peace Prize. Obama would have been better served to have had dialogue with the differences, rather than do the liberal secular thing of skating over them. He had the opportunity to have a more authentic dialogue, one that may have made for less of an alienating speech at home and created less expectation in the Islamic world. He had the credibility but did not use it wisely.

Perhaps it is expecting too much of President Obama, after all he had a communication strategy aimed at showing America was different under his presidency while making some specific political points. To this extent the speech was a success in the short-termism of communication strategies. The aim of modern communication is to shape a narrative and influence the narrative sensibilities of others. In his assessment of the speech, David Brooks wrote in the *New York Times*:

In the Obama narrative, each side has been equally victimized by history, each side has legitimate grievances and each side has duties to perform. To construct this new Middle East narrative, Obama strung together some hard truths, historical distortions, eloquent appeals and strained moral equivalencies.[4]

This narrative strategy tends to favor an outcome of ultimately talking past each other. The applause was enthusiastic every time Obama made a concession to the political goals of his audience, and silent where he fired his own salvos. Talking past and not listening in fact. The audience was listening for verbal cues and they got them, but they were so busy at this they were not in fact listening.

Despite such concerns, in an interview with Obama in *The Atlantic* interviewer Jeffrey Goldberg explained:

I have come to believe that, in Obama's mind, August 30, 2013, was his liberation day, the day he defied not only the foreign-policy establishment and its cruise-missile playbook, but also the demands of America's frustrating, high-maintenance allies in the Middle East—countries, he complains privately to friends and advisers, that seek to exploit American "muscle" for their own narrow and sectarian ends.[5]

They were content that day, but by 2015, when Obama famously declared the "red line" in attempt to stop the Assad regime from using chemical weapons, the Saudis and many others in the region were losing their patience. There had been a great expectation that Obama would stick to his line. The Saudi ambassador in Washington at the time, Adel al-Jubeir, told friends, and his superiors in Riyadh, that the president was finally ready to strike. Obama "figured out how important this is," Jubeir, who has been the Saudi foreign minister since 2015, told one interlocutor. "He will definitely strike."[6] When he didn't, there was general disgust in the region. Abdullah II, the king of Jordan, had become deeply disturbed by what he saw as an illogical desire by Obama to distance America from Saudi and its traditional Sunni Arab allies by creating a new alliance with Iran, which he saw as Assad's Shia sponsor. The king ventured in private, "I think I believe in American power more than Obama does."[7] The Saudis, too, were infuriated. Despite the excitement of Obama taking office, they had long held reservations about the president who had long before he became president called Saudi the "so-called ally" of America.[8] "Iran is the new great power of the Middle East, and the U.S. is the old," Jubeir reported back to Riyadh.[9]

Responding to the red line debacle, Gideon Rose, the editor of *Foreign Affairs*, wrote Obama was dithering and casual in making a promise followed by "embarrassingly amateurish improvisation." Shadi Hamid, a scholar at the Brookings Institution wrote that Assad was effectively being rewarded for using chemical weapons rather than punished. Obama had wanted to change the approach to the region, and was a realist rather than a liberal interventionist, like Clinton and Bush before him. He admired the foreign policy realism of President George H. W. Bush and his national security adviser Brent Scowcroft. As David Brooks noted:

> This speech builds an idealistic facade on a realist structure. And this gets to the core Obama foreign-policy perplexity. The president wants to be an inspiring leader who rallies the masses. He also wants be a top-down realist who cuts deals in the palaces.[10]

In many respects, Obama continued much of the Bush policy, and in some respects took stronger and more aggressive action, including the use of drone strikes. He had a limited number of Middle East threats where he was willing to risk US military intervention, namely, opposing Al-Qaeda, ensuring the continued existence of Israel and dealing with a nuclear-armed Iran. In spirit, Obama reversed the policies of the previous two administrations by not wanting to risk American soldiers in order to prevent humanitarian disasters, unless those disasters posed a direct security threat to the United States. In practice, 2479 service men and women lost their lives in the Obama years, more than happened during the Bush II administration.[11]

Obama will be judged by historians, no doubt, but he believed he was right to make the decision not to strike at Syria. However, it led to an outpour of questioning of America's credibility, and his own. The outcome of this Muslim civil war was that Obama let the Middle East slip from America's grasp and into the hands of Russia, Iran and Islamic State.

The US/Saudi relationship became another victim of the Obama regime with the possible future implosion of a once-valued partner, if indeed the relationship is broken irreparably. The global and historical context of the problem was reinterpreted by Obama with a sprinkling of loaded themes such as anti-colonialization, Cold War, proxy wars, modernity, globalization, Muslim identity and Western guilt. This loaded statement reads:

> The relationship between Islam and the West includes centuries of coexistence and cooperation, but also conflict and religious wars. More recently, tension has been fed by colonialism that denied rights and opportunities to many Muslims, and a Cold War in which Muslim-majority countries were too often treated as proxies without regard to their own aspirations. Moreover, the sweeping change brought by modernity and globalization led many Muslims to view the West as hostile to the traditions of Islam. Violent extremists have exploited these tensions in a small but potent minority of Muslims.[12]

Obama attempted rightly, though perhaps clumsily in such a loaded statement, to contextualize the Islamic problem in an historical sense and to demonstrate the Western complicity in creating the tensions in the region. For his part, Obama was hamstrung by the American idealism that supports transition to democracy, and the realist approach which had "to do business," to use Margaret Thatcher's explanation of Gorbachev, with authoritarian regimes. The outcome was that the Obama administration had alienated Saudi as its key partner in the region, which did not have this colonial experience. What Saudi interpreted as a welcoming back of Iran into the international fold, the failure of the so-called Arab Spring and various conflicts in this continuously afflicted region all added up to a situation where there was no clear direction as to where their relationship and the politics of the region was headed. The Trump administration started its foreign policy actions by making Saudi the first foreign visit by President Trump. The "deals" discussed there suggest a more productive relationship, and Saudi certainly did not want Hilary Clinton to be the one stopping off in Air Force One. Saudi believes itself to be under an existential threat politically and economically and that it is more vulnerable because of a less-than-committed America. The Trump administration may well be more sympathetic than the Obama administration, but the inconsistency witnessed hitherto in the new administration does not bode well for any sense of greater security for Saudi. The loss of oil power and the growing strength of Iran are seen as existential threats to Saudi, and there may be less confidence in American support or reliability for the Kingdom. Once you lose your protector then anything can happen, and this is what the Saudis worry about.

Saudis Under Pressure

A realist solution would say it is not up to "the West" to create change in the region, but it does have a critical role in choosing, and influencing, partners in the region. The West has also interfered greatly in the region, and is responsible to a large degree for the contemporary situation in the region. Saudi has been relatively consistent over the decades, remarkably so when one sees the competition for being the top regional partner. From the Saudi perspective, the West is a secular world of both fascination and revulsion. Stories may abound of Saudi businessmen and diplomatic visitors taking in the pleasures of women and alcohol in London, but their youthful graduates on scholarships bring back the ideas they've learned. Saudi tops most lists in terms of users of social media, providing a window into the West for those Saudis who don't travel. Women in Saudi see Western women running businesses, and replicate this from their homes. At the same time, many youthful Saudis remain convinced of family values, respect their elders, love their culture and want to keep their religion. Saudi Arabia is a world of contrasts and perceived contradictions as I have said, which means being cautious in how one interprets the religious dimensions of this Kingdom. Abdullahi Ahmed An-Na'im offers an interesting insight into Islamic identity politics, and there is a great deal to be said for his arguments.[13] However, in essence his answer is still a liberal political one, and this is not the language of those who forge the kind of Islam he finds so problematic. With nationalism came exclusion and protective self-interest, but also uniformity, where the stranger was just that, a stranger. In globalization, which appears in some respects to be receding there are demands being made for a greater encounter with diversity, and this entails the need for greater inclusivity. It is harder in an age of globalization to maintain a monocultural and authoritarian society, but essentially this is what Saudi represents.

Many foreign commentators and political groups take a somewhat prescriptive approach to Saudi, highlighting the wrongs such as human rights and gender issues, calling for radical change in much the same way as change is pressured in the West, which is achieved often dramatically by disruptive and violent means rather than gradualism or even continuity. The Saudi approach appeals to a sense of pragmatism and gradualism, as they seek to change society gradually and gain agreement or deference from across a spectrum of interests in order that the solution will turn out to be a stable and long-lasting one. This is an approach that goes back to the earliest time of the land. The point here is not to defend or attack one position or the other, since critics will simply comment that the gradualism, if they accept the term, is merely the self-serving and authoritarian way the house of Saud protects itself. My task is to delineate the problem we face when we look in depth at Saudi Arabia. Instead, whether we like it or not, we need to grasp that this is in the Saudi behavior and that it is very much opposed to disruption, which has worked as a key tactic in the West to make radical, progressive and other changes in Western society. The state of disruption in the West is exampled most recently in 2016 by Brexit, the 2016–2017 spread of European populism, and the election of President Donald Trump. The theme of disruption has also impacted the Arab world, exampled by the so-called Arab Spring and emergence of Islamic State. For the Saudis, these Western and Arab disruptions serve to reinforce the wisdom of their own gradualist approach. To their critics, it is the mere self-interested continuation of a patriarchal and authoritarian system of power.

This book is coming out in the early phase of a new US administration, and if we look at Donald Trump's foreign policy, we find a candidate who had gone to some considerable lengths to alienate Muslims (among many others), yet was welcomed by many Saudis as a better choice for the Kingdom and the region than his election opponent, the former Secretary of State Hillary Clinton. The opening phases of the new administration suggested a different doctrine from the previous administration, which had alienated Saudi Arabia and ignored to some extent Saudi's historical role as an American ally in the region. The fact that President Trump made his first foreign stop as president a visit to Saudi, followed by Israel and the Vatican, suggested right away, at least in the early days, the desire was to take a different approach to the Kingdom. It is critical that we understand the dynamics of Saudi and Islam together if we are to discern what lies ahead for a nation and a religion that impacts the rest of us, and whose economic implosion may be the catalyst for greater instability in a world that is already under greater stress in the Middle East than has been the case for some time. Losing Saudi as an ally for America is not a good idea—and it appears President Trump does not intend to—especially when the reasons for taking sides seem quite arbitrary.

Saudi faces other external pressures resulting from the reemergence of Iran on the international stage and a protracted war in Yemen, a proxy war with Iran heavily criticized by many international observers. The Campaign Against Arms Trade (CAAT) launched a campaign for a judicial review of the UK/Saudi arms trade, with a spokesman stating, "These arms sales should never have been approved in the first place: Saudi Arabia has an abhorrent human rights record and it has created a humanitarian catastrophe in Yemen."[14] Saudi is concerned about a Shia crescent with Iran creating a transnational arc around Saudi across Syria, Iraq and Yemen. Starting with Syria, Saudi is virulently opposed to President Assad the ruling member of the minority Alawi sect[15] in Syria, whose belief in the divinity of Ali, Muhammad's cousin and son-in-law, separated them from the Shia and marked them as heretical. The Kingdom has been a major provider of military and economic assistance to a number of rebel groups, both secular and Islamist. It called for a no-fly zone to be imposed to protect civilians from bombardment by Syrian government forces. A turning point in the American relationship came in 2013 after a chemical attack blamed on Assad's forces and the Saudis became angered that the Obama administration decided against military intervention. Concerned by Islamic State strength and popularity among Saudis, they later agreed to take part in the US-led coalition air campaign. However, Amnesty International reports that Saudi has been complicit with these groups in torture, abductions and executions.[16]

Moving down to Iraq, Iran remains central to the fighting in Iraq which has been coordinated by Qasem Soleimani, the chief of Iran's elite al-Quds branch of the Revolutionary Guard. Saudi has had a somewhat difficult relationship with Iraq over the decades. In the 1960s and early 1970s, the Saudis suspected Baghdad of supporting political movements opposed to Saudi, but relations improved in the mid-1970s as Iraq foreign policy aims changed and Saudi, apart from some non-military support, remained neutral during the Iran-Iraq War in 1980. Despite making considerable financial investments in creating a political alliance with Iraq, Saudi Arabia has never managed to maintain a consistent relationship. The relationship deteriorated in August 1990, two years after Iraq and Iran had ceased hostilities, when Iraqi forces invaded and occupied Kuwait in a surprising move. The Saudi response was that Iraq's action posed a direct and serious threat to security, and they asked the Americans to provide troops in the Kingdom to combat any threats, which led to Saudi Arabia becoming involved directly in the war against Iraq during January and February 1991.

Finally moving down to Yemen, this small state has some strategic importance because of its position on the Bab al-Mandab strait, a narrow waterway that links the Red Sea with the Gulf of Aden, which is a major passage for the world's oil shipments. At first it seemed at best fanciful, and at worse alarmist, when King Abdullah II of Jordan warned that the legacy of America's toppling of Saddam Hussein in Iraq would be the creation of an Iranian-influenced "Shia crescent" in an expansionist move.[17] Yemen is one of the Arab world's poorest countries overshadowed by its wealthy neighbors, and it has been in deadly conflict since 2011 when the political transition from the authoritarian regime of Ali Abdullah Saleh to President Abdrabbuh Mansour Hadi failed to run smoothly. Saudi has being backing the Hadi government and formed a coalition of Arab, mostly Sunni, supporters and other international forces. The resulting warfare with Houthi rebels since March 2015 has led to more than 40,000 people dead, including large numbers of children. Critics see two major problems with this war, first it is known as a proxy war between Saudi and Iran, and second it has become a humanitarian disaster. Hadi failed to establish a government strong enough to deal with attacks by Al-Qaeda and a separatist movement in the south, as well as corruption, unemployment and food insecurity. Iran has denied they are backing the Houthis financially and militarily, and indeed contend they themselves are backers of President Hadi, and Shia militias claim they are simply defending Shia holy sites.

Historically, the threat from Iran has always been there in various guises, but it came into focus in 1979 when the Ayatollah Khomeini launched a verbal assault on Saudi Arabia as the "American Islam." He was issuing a call to arms for Islam and declaring battle on Western influence, American and otherwise. Saudi was at the nexus of the disconnect between the Islamic world and the West, and the call to arms seemed initially to work as November of that year saw two major acts of revolt. On 20 November the Grand Mosque was seized by Sunni militants on the eve of the new Islamic year and occupied for two weeks, followed by outbreak of rioting on 27 November by Shia Muslims in the Eastern Province. The revolt was beaten down, and Shias beaten down with it. Such verbal assaults have been part of Saudi-Iranian discourse ever since, and it is notable that as recent as the Summer of 2016 the Iranian leadership, perhaps boosted by its new international role and Saudi concerns over its future, has again made strong statements challenging Saudi's role in Islam. Ayatollah Ali Khamenei accused the Saudis of politicizing the annual Hajj pilgrimage, saying Iranians have been effectively barred, for the first time in some three decades, from participating in the 2016 pilgrimage to Mecca due to talks on logistics and security failing. The Ayatollah stated in his annual Hajj address on 5 September:

> Saudi rulers, who have obstructed the path of Allah and Masjid ul-Haraam this year and who have blocked the proud and faithful Iranian pilgrims' path to the Beloved's House, are disgraced and misguided people who think their survival on the throne of oppression is dependent on defending the arrogant powers of the world, on alliances with Zionism and the U.S. and on fulfilling their demands. And on this path, they do not shy away from any treason. … The world of Islam, including Muslim governments and peoples, must familiarize themselves with the Saudi rulers and correctly understand their blasphemous, faithless, dependent and materialistic nature. They must not let those rulers escape responsibility for the crimes they have caused throughout the world of Islam. Because of these rulers' oppressive behavior towards God's guests, the world of Islam must fundamentally reconsider the management of the two holy places and the issue of Hajj. Negligence in this regard will confront the Islamic Ummah with more serious problems in the future.[18]

He was specifically attacking the handling of the 2015 Hajj, when a deadly stampede killed around 2300 foreign pilgrims, including an estimated 464 Iranians, accusing the Saudis of murder. Khamenei stated:

> The heartless and murderous Saudis locked up the injured with the dead in containers, instead of providing medical treatment and helping them or at least quenching their thirst. They murdered them.[19]

His rhetoric is an echo of the 1979 statements and suggests a ratcheting up of the challenge by Iran toward Saudi's leadership role in Islam, and we can only expect more as Iran flexes its muscles with a new global presence and economic strength through investment.

The last year of the Obama administration in 2016 became something of a "vintage" year for Iranian and American relations, ushering in a time when Iran was being embraced by the international community. Iran may have found new love in the world, but it still wanted to weaken its primary rival, and Saudi has been more than usually sensitive about Iran and Shia since 2016. The economic impact in Saudi has coincided with the Iranian rehabilitation in the global community, and Iran is taking full advantage of a very timely pressure on the Saudi economy. Each is a state sponsor of Islam, proselytizing for a sectarian version of Islam, and at the same time has harbored radicalized groups and individuals within their borders. They have also acted within the regional context to promote Islam. Both nations have been critical toward each other and the national leadership. Khomeini said of the house of al Saud it was corrupt and unworthy to be the guardians of Mecca and Medina. If possession is nine-tenths of the law, then Saudi has an inbuilt advantage in its claims against Iran and as guardians, since the two holy sites are within its geographical boundaries. Saudis fear that the change in approach to Iran by America and in the global community will decimate the Saudi relationship, and this will unleash more sectarian forces.

Simon Mabon summarizes the relationship between Saudi and Iran, which has not always been confrontational, as a rivalry that:

> …can be characterised by two areas of competition, namely ideological and geopolitical. The first area of competition is driven by competing identities in particular, ethno-national and religious identities. Historically,

relations between Arab and Persian have been strained, as a consequence of the legacy between both Arab and Persian influence across the region. Religious competition occurs as a consequence of the dominance of Wahhabism within Saudi Arabia... The Iranian revolution of 1979 proved cataclysmic for regional security and was followed by a torrent of rhetoric articulating Iran's desired position within the Islamic world...Particularly damning was Tehran's postulation that the Al Saud was not a legitimate Islamic dynasty and thus could not be accepted as the guardian of the two holy places if Islam... Within the second area of competition, Riyadh and Tehran both lay claim to influence over the Persian Gulf region and the wider Middle East... Additionally, within the geopolitical sphere is an economic rivalry, stemming from Saudi Arabia and Iran's roles as the dominant suppliers of both oil and natural gas, both within the Middle East and the world. This competition has manifested itself within OPEC and has proved to have wide ramifications.[20]

The long-standing antipathy is set against the two nations vying for attention from America, which in turn is in the context of Saudi and Iran competing for the state leadership of Islam. Iran was delighted to welcome the Obama administration and the signing of a nuclear deal. The Saudi perception of the Obama years is that the United States has forged a weaker position in the region, including a diminution of its soft power capability.

The improved position in American relations has allowed Iran to go on something of a global and successful charm offensive. Like Saudi, Iran is opening its business to all who will leave certain principles and sanctions at the front door. Iran has visited many countries, but one that was very much conflicted was Canada and highlights the strange world of diplomacy and being unsure exactly which dog you have in this fight. At the same time as speaking to the Iranians, Prime Minister Justin Trudeau's Liberal government which had just been elected in 2015 was urged not to go ahead with a $15 billion arms sale to Saudi Arabia agreed by the previous Conservative administration of Stephen Harper. The concern was because of human rights abuses, and in a very publicized battle critics stated that Trudeau should be telling Riyadh they must change. In this instance, it is hard to see what is the difference between doing business with Tehran and Riyadh. It was inevitable that Canada would choose to do lucrative business with Iran, and the government went to work repairing damage done attributed to the previous Harper government era. A new government and new prime minister doubtless eases the path of relationship and speeds up the process of rebuilding economic and political ties with Iran. We could argue this is a good thing, since Canada can try and influence Iran to bring in human rights and other reforms. The key word here, however, is "try," because there is little evidence of any likelihood there will be any change in Iranian attitudes. Just as inevitable as the warming of Canadian and Iranian relations was the increasing pressure on the Saudi deal, which never quite built up to a point where Mr. Trudeau felt like going with the flow and stopping that deal. This naturally made the Iranians very happy, and was part of a speeding up of the relationship repair job, no doubt. The Saudi relationship itself is in part based on the pretense that Canada and other Western democracies can have influence on the human rights and other abuses in Saudi. However, there is little evidence that there is ever much influence in Saudi, and no doubt the Iranian trajectory will continue in the same direction.

Around the same time as the Canadian debate, the Saudi human rights question came very much to the fore. While Human Rights Watch in their *World Report 2016* recorded that Saudi Arabia had made positive changes for women and foreign workers in 2015, this is overshadowed by Riyadh conducting 158 executions, 63 of which were for drug crimes. The real outrage followed publication of that report, after the 2 January 2016 execution of 47 men for terrorism-related offenses, most notably the Shia cleric Nimr al-Nimr, and a United Nations report on civilian killings during bombing raids in Yemen. Yet, if we compare the human rights of the two nations, there is little to choose between Saudi and Iran. The same Human Rights Watch report noted that by 1 November 2015, Iran had executed more than 830 prisoners, the majority for drug-related offenses. Other offenses included "insulting the Prophet," apostasy, same-sex relations and adultery. Even adding the shocking January numbers, Riyadh seems to have a little catching up to do with Tehran, which is executing people at three times the rate of the Saudis. In international relations there is always a reason for taking sides, and from the Saudi perspective they believe these events make it look like Canada and other

Western democracies were taking the side of Iran, and this created a feeling of insecurity in Saudi foreign relations since the Obama administration and yet more pressure in the region. The war on Yemen was not just to protect Saudi interests or engage in a proxy war, it is a sign that Saudi is taking a step of independence away from American protection and facing its enemy directly.

Until now, foreign relations for Saudi has been, save for the "hiccup" of the Arab/Israeli war, a steady working in tandem with America. It is critical to understand correctly the relationship between Saudi, along with the rest of the Middle East for that matter, and the United States. Saudi has not, except perhaps in relation to the October War of 1973, used its position of power to influence Western politics. In 1973, King Faisal embargoed oil sales to the United States in response to the US support of Israel. However, Saudi power has been too tied up with the United States to repeat the exercise. The Saudis have tended to use their power more internally within the Arab and Islamic world. To build its global position, critics suggest the Kingdom has promoted its form of Islam among Muslims within Sunni communities globally, which would give it a global support. As Ali Allawi frames it:

> The rise of Saudi Arabia to global status can only take place if the hold of traditional or moderate Sunni Islam on the loyalties of the world's Muslims is reduced.[21]

Egypt and Pakistan, Allawai suggests, could give Saudi a critical mass which could even see a global pact between Saudi Arabia and Iran to recognize each other as the global authority for Sunni and Shia Muslims respectively. It is hard to see such a global pact occurring, and appears to be more in the spirit of wishful thinking than the harsh realities of international relations. The disconnect between Saudi and Iran makes it even more ironic that many in the West treat Islam as monolithic, since it is the diversity and disconnectedness of Islam that prevents it from forming a significant power bloc in the world. It is the cultural, political and economic differences that seem to counterbalance the Islamic sense of unity to prevent any great convergence in this respect.

Commentary in the field of international relations tends to assume Islamic theocratic ideas of state are the opposite of liberal democracy and the Westphalian system. A lack of grasp of the implications or nature of this tension lies behind the naiveté of neoconservatism and liberal interventionist ideas that democracy can be naturally part of the region, along with the misplaced confidence in democracy to triumph in the so-called "Arab Spring." In this approach, the oppositional nature of Islam creates friction in regional affairs, as Hashmi[22] has argued extensively. Islam has been rather more accommodating than this approach supposes, and Islamic rulers and bodies have been more open to embracing Western strategies and diplomacy than critics assume, as Piscatori[23] discusses. The dynamics of politics versus religion has changed over the decades. The political arrangements in the region have come under pressure with the rise of Islamism since the 1967 war, and increasingly so after the Iranian revolution. There has also been a retreat from secularism in parts of Western society, as will be discussed later, which is part of the identity crisis in the West. The Saudi instinct is to avoid such a confrontation and retain the central role of Islam, but how it will evolve is again a matter of debate to be explored in this book.

If we move down to pressures internally at the level of the Kingdom, the social fabric of Saudi is tied together in a powerful and deep-rooted tribal system, united in loyalty and religion rather than through a democratic plebiscite. There are a number of major tribes each numbering around 100,000, joined by traditional bonds such as intermarriages, history and wealth. The principal tribes are the Anayzah, Bani Khalid, Harb, Al Murrah, Mutayr, Qahtan, Shammar and Utaiba. There are also the minor tribes, which include the predominantly urban Quraysh and the ancient Hijaz tribe to which the Prophet Muhammad belonged. In addition, there are the prominent merchant families, including Alireza, Ba Khashab, Bin Ladin, Al Qusaibi, Jamjum, Juffali, Kaki, Nasif, Olayan, Al Rajhi and Sulayman. However, it is not always peaceful and tribes such as the Mutair, the Shammar and the family of al-Aidh have had disputes with the house of Saud resulting in some lingering resentment. There have been reports of splits between the families, largely split over whether they are pro-US or anti-US. In foreign relations, Saudi has been a stable partner with the United States for many decades, especially during the

Cold War. Every US administration since FDR has tended to work closely with the Saudis, though with a few bumps in the road along the way. However, as this relationship deteriorates and loses its attraction as oil dependency lessens, so will there be a weakening of political strength in the region. This may open up tribal divisions further, and undermine the political and social network maintained by the house of Saud. As discussed earlier, in 2017 King Salman implemented changes to shore up the family ties, including changing the line of succession and making MbS the Crown Prince, which represents even more clearly the shift to a younger generation.

This shift in power can be understood within the context of a narrative that has proven popular in critical circles, which is that the outcome of recent events is a new Arab Cold War. This is a narrative that sets conservative and moderate states in the Arab world against the "Shia arc of extremism" supported by the radicals of Iran, Syria, Hizbullah in Lebanon and Hamas in Gaza. This has made the region unstable, but also something of a quagmire for American foreign policy, especially so in the Obama years discussed in this chapter. As the authors of one *Foreign Policy* article explain this view:

> President Barack Obama's attempt to disentangle the United States from the Middle East's many conflicts has only intensified these rivalries. From a particular perspective, Iraq's chaos, Syria's civil war, Libya's accelerating disintegration, and Hosni Mubarak's fall all represent failures of American leadership. As a result, Washington's regional allies have come to the conclusion that they are essentially on their own and have sought to shape the Middle East to their own specific geopolitical needs and benefits. This has stoked the embers of conflict in various arenas — notably Egypt, Syria, Palestine, and now Libya — where this competition is playing out.[24]

As this brief historical excursion demonstrates, for the long years of the Cold War Islam and Saudi were seen as useful, but the end of communism made Islam less useful and now the end of oil power is making Saudi less important. The changing dynamics can be seen in the war in Yemen, which Saudi started. It is controversial, and one that MbS is the figurehead for and success or failure will impact his reputation. Usually

Saudi has waited upon America to act in the region, the Yemen war is a case of Saudi standing on their own two feet. The question is, can they do this militarily at the same time as trying to stand on their own two feet economically? The Arab Cold War is being fought differently. The idea of an Arab Cold War is not a new one. Malcolm Kerr[25] wrote a book on the idea back in 1971, tracing the machinations of inter-Arab politics during an era dominated by Egypt's President Gamal Abdel Nasser. In 1997, Hilal Khashan argued the thesis that Iraq's invasion of Kuwait on 2 August 1990 ushered in a new version of the Arab Cold War.[26] Saudi is emerging from the East/West Cold War itself rather belatedly, but it faces not only this new Arab Cold War but also its own implosion.

This is not simply because of any variant of either Cold War, but for reasons similar to the Soviet Union, namely, for economic reasons. Like the former Soviet Union, Saudi is under pressure externally and internally, and the Kingdom cannot easily afford such wars. This makes a component of the time bomb that could trigger the implosion of the Kingdom. Added to which, Iran has been emboldened by American support, because such support is highly symbolic in the region. Perhaps we will see less talk of Saudi as American Islam by the Iranians, as they seek to become the American Islam. The cost of war, the loss of political authority and the squeeze on trade and the economy are coalescing forces that Saudi, and the house of Saud, may struggle to combat. The current economic and political situation in Saudi thus represents another chapter in the oft-visited narrative of the "fall of the house of Saud." The political challenge for observers and critics has long been the explanation of the ongoing standing of the house of Saud, which many analysts have predicted, with some regularity, would pass at this time or that. Arab nationalism was supposed to lead to its downfall. The so-called Arab Spring was supposed to do likewise. Instead the house of Saud has survived the pressure and adapted and is still very much in situ. It has done so because there were the constants of oil, regional authority and America to offer stability. None of these can now be taken for granted, and there is a scope for a changing political theology.

Notes

1. https://2001-2009.state.gov/secretary/rm/2005/48328.htm
2. https://obamawhitehouse.archives.gov/issues/foreign-policy/presidents-speech-cairo-a-new-beginning
3. https://obamawhitehouse.archives.gov/the-press-office/remarks-president-cairo-university-6-04-09
4. http://www.nytimes.com/2009/06/05/opinion/05brooks.html?ref=opinion&_r=0
5. https://www.theatlantic.com/magazine/archive/2016/04/the-obama-doctrine/471525/
6. Ibid.
7. Ibid.
8. Ibid.
9. Ibid.
10. David Brooks, Obama Tries to Blend Idealism & Realism, *New York Times*, June 5, 2009.
11. http://icasualties.org/OEF/ByMonth.aspx
12. https://obamawhitehouse.archives.gov/the-press-office/remarks-president-cairo-university-6-04-09
13. An-Na'im (2010).
14. https://www.caat.org.uk/campaigns/stop-arming-saudi/judicial-review
15. http://www.joshualandis.com/blog/what-do-sunnis-intend-for-alawis-following-regime-change-by-khudr/, Opposition reported from within the Alawi sect: http://www.telegraph.co.uk/news/2016/04/02/leaders-of-syrian-alawite-sect-threaten-to-abandon-bashar-al-ass/
16. http://www.newsweek.com/syria-rebel-groups-us-torture-amnesty-477858
17. http://www.washingtonpost.com/wp-dyn/articles/A43980-2004Dec7.html See also Moshe Ma'oz *The "Shi' i Crescent": Myth and Reality* Brookings Institution Analysis Report, Number 15, November 2007 https://www.brookings.edu/wp-content/uploads/2016/06/11_middle_east_maoz.pdf This issue is taken up in later by https://www.theguardian.com/world/2007/jan/26/worlddispatch.ianblack
18. http://english.khamenei.ir/news/4121/Hajj-hijacked-by-oppressors-Muslims-should-reconsider-management
19. Ibid.
20. Mabon (2016, pp. 4–5).

21. Allawai (2009, p. 147).
22. Hashmi (2002).
23. Piscatori (1991, pp. 1–27).
24. http://foreignpolicy.com/2014/08/28/the-new-arab-cold-war/
25. Kerr (1971).
26. Hilal Khashan, The New Arab Cold War, *World Affairs*, Vol. 159, No. 4 (SPRING 1997), pp. 158–169.

Bibliography

al-Rasheed, Madawi, ed. 2008. *Kingdom Without Borders: Saudi Arabia's Political, Religious and Media Frontiers*. London: Hurst.

Allawai, Ali A. 2009. *The Crisis of Islamic Civilization*. New Haven: Yale University Press.

An-Na'im, Abdullahi Ahmed. 2010. *Islam and the Secular State: Negotiating the Future of Shari`a*. Cambridge, MA: Harvard University Press.

Axworthy, Michael. 2008. *A History of Iran: Empire of the Mind*. New York: Perseus Books.

Barber, Benjamin R. 2001. *Jihad vs McWorld: Terrorism's Challenge to Democracy*. New York: Ballantine Books.

Bonnefoy, Laurent. 2012. *Salafism in Yemen: Transnationalism and Religious Identity*. New York: Columbia University Press.

Bowering, Gerhard, ed. 2015. *Islamic Political Thought: An Introduction*. Princeton: Princeton University Press.

Champion, Daryl. 2003. *The Paradoxical Kingdom: Saudi Arabia and the Momentum of Reform*. London: Hurst and Company.

Craze, Jonathan, and Mark Huband. 2009. *The Kingdom: Saudi Arabia and the Challenge of the 21st Century*. London: Hurst & Co.

Cunningham, Robert B., and Yasin K. Sarayrah. 1993. *Wasta: The Hidden Force in Middle Eastern Society*. Westport: Praeger.

Delong-Bas, Natana J. 2004. *Wahhabi Islam: From Revival and Reform to Global Jihad*. New York: Oxford University Press.

Esposito, John L. 2002. *Unholy War: Terror in the Name of Islam*. New York: Oxford University Press.

Fawcett, Louise. 2016. *International Relations of the Middle East*. 4th ed. Oxford: Oxford University Press.

Gause, F. Gregory, III. 1994. *Oil Monarchies: Domestic and Security Challenges in the Arab Gulf States*. New York: Council on Foreign Relations.

Halliday, Fred. 2000. *Nation and Religion in the Middle East*. Boulder: Lynne Rienner Publishers.

———. 2002. *Arabia Without Sultans*. London: Saqi Books.

Hamid, Shadi. 2016. *Islamic Exceptionalism: How the Struggle Over Islam Is Reshaping the World*. New York: St. Martin's Press.

Hashmi, Sohail H. 2002. *Islamic Political Ethics: Civil Society, Pluralism and Conflict*, Ethikon Series in Comparative Ethics. Princeton: Princeton University Press.

Haykel, Bernard, Thomas Hegghammer, and Stéphane Lacroix. 2015. *Saudi Arabia in Transition: Insights on Social, Political, Economic and Religious Change*. Cambridge: Cambridge University Press.

Heggenhammer, Thomas. 2010. *Jihad in Saudi Arabia: Violence and Pan-Islamism Since 1979*. New York: Cambridge University Press.

Hertog, Steffen. 2010. *Princes, Brokers, and Bureaucrats Oil and the State in Saudi Arabia*. Ithaca: Cornell University Press.

House, Karen Elliott. 2012. *On Saudi Arabia: Its People, Past, Religion, Fault Lines – And Future*. New York: Vintage Books.

Judis, John B. 2014. *Genesis: Truman, American Jews, and the Origins of the Arab/Israeli Conflict*. New York: Farrar, Straus & Giroux.

Karsh, Effraim. 2006. *Islamic Imperialism: A History*. New Haven: Yale University Press.

Kepel, Gilles. 2004. *The War for Muslim Minds: Islam and the West*. Trans. Pascal Ghazaleh. Cambridge, MA: Belknap Press.

Kerr, Malcolm. 1965. *The Arab Cold War, 1958–1964: A Study of Ideology in Politics*. Oxford: Oxford University Press.

———. 1971. *The Arab Cold War: Gamal 'Abd al-Nasir and His Rivals, 1958–1970*. Oxford: Oxford University Press.

Khalidi, Rashid. 2009. *Sowing Crisis: The Cold War and American Dominance in the Middle East*. Boston: Beacon Press.

Koya, Abdar Rahman, ed. 2010. *Imam Khomeini: Life, Thought and Legacy*. Kuala Lumpur: Islamic Book Trust.

Kuhn, Thomas. 1996. *The Structure of Scientific Revolutions*. Chicago: University of Chicago Press.

Lacey, Robert. 2009. *Inside the Kingdom: Kings, Clerics, Terrorists, Modernists, and the Struggle for Saudi Arabia*. New York: Viking.

Lippman, Thomas W. 2012. *Saudi Arabia on the Edge: The Uncertain Future of an American Ally*. Dulles: Potomac Books.

Lynch, Timothy J., and Robert S. Singh. 2008. *After Bush: The Case for Continuity in American Foreign Policy*. Cambridge: Cambridge University Press.

Mabon, Simon. 2016. *Saudi Arabia and Iran: Power and Rivalry in the Middle East.* New York: I.B. Tauris.

Maher, Shiraz. 2016. *Salafi-Jihadism: The History of an Idea.* London: Hurst & Company.

Matthiesen, Toby. 2015. *The Other Saudis: Shiism, Dissent and Sectarianism.* New York: Cambridge University Press.

Miller, David Aaron. 1980. *Search for Security: Saudi Arabian Oil and American Foreign Policy.* Chapel Hill: University of North Carolina Press.

Mitchell, Timothy. 2013. *Carbon Democracy: Political Power in the Age of Oil.* London: Verso.

Piscatori, J.P. 1991. *Islamic Fundamentalisms and the Gulf Crisis.* Chicago: University of Chicago Press.

Ramazani, R.K., ed. 1990. *Iran's Revolution: The Search for Consensus.* Bloomington: Indiana University Press.

Said, Edward W. 1979. *Orientalism.* Princeton: Princeton University Press.

———. 1981. *Covering Islam: How the Media and the Experts Determine How We See the Rest of the World.* New York: Pantheon Books.

Salame, Ghassan, ed. 1994. *Democracy Without Democrats? The Renewal of Politics in the Muslim World.* London: I.B. Tauris.

Schwarz, Rolf. 2007. *Rule, Revenue, and Representation. Oil and State Formation in the Middle East and North Africa.* PhD thesis. Graduate Institute of International Studies, Geneva

Stoflf, Michael B. 1980. *Oil, War and American Security: The Search for a National Policy on Foreign Oil. 1941–1947.* New Haven: Yale University Press.

Vitalis, Robert. 2009. *America's Kingdom: Mythmaking on the Saudi Oil Frontier.* London: Verso.

Yahya, Sadowski. 1993. *Scuds or Butter? The Political Economy of Arms Control in the Middle East.* Washington, DC: Brookings Institution.

7

A Changing Political Theology

In the year 2000, diary documents were found in Afghanistan that either belonged to Osama bin Laden or to someone very close to him.[1] Included are a number of questions addressed to bin Laden, which focus on oil and the "Jewish-Crusader invasion of the Muslim countries" seeking to control the oil. The questions were posed in the context of there being enough oil to create greater equality in the Muslim world. The maths was made simple. If the Muslim world produces 30 million barrels a day at $150 a barrel, that would create revenue totaling $4.5 billion per day, which when divided among the 1.2 billion estimated number of Muslims globally would lead to giving $3.75 per day to every Muslim and the average Muslim family, averaging 8 in number, an income of $30 daily. This is how the issue was framed in a simple economic calculus between the oil revenue and the social output, and the resentment has been the feeding ground for Muslims around the world. This social disconnect, and the intrusion of hard economic realities drew supporters who felt alienated and lost in the declining welfare theocracy of Saudi and elsewhere. One reporter recorded an assessment on the 9/11 hijackers offered by a Saudi official:

"The hijackers were a direct product of our social failures—a generation with no sense of what work entails, raised in a system that operated as a

© The Author(s) 2018
D. Cowan, *The Coming Economic Implosion of Saudi Arabia*,
https://doi.org/10.1007/978-3-319-74709-5_7

welfare state," a high-ranking government official told me. "We allowed them to grow up in pampered emptiness, until they turned to the bin Laden extremists in an effort to find themselves." Saudis claim that al Qaeda deliberately fills its ranks with the kingdom's alienated young. Bin Laden's goal, they believe, is to topple the Saudi royal family, partly by convincing the West that its principal source of oil is fatally infected with extremism.[2]

Bin Laden took seriously the notion of an Islam which emerged as a force in the seventh century, meeting opposition from Christians and Jews. The Christians had laid claim to the truth and God as a superseding revelation, which is the same claim Islam made in relation to these two older faiths, and it was applied to the emerging doctrine of Jihad. Muslim thought divided the world into the two spheres of the "world of Islam" and the "world of war," the former being a religiopolitical system or theocracy, and the latter being the world where Islam did not rule or was a minority.

Often the conflicts and problems in the Middle East are conflated under the leitmotif of "Islamic threat." Many of the conflicts are historical and have little to do with Islam, and more to do with other cultural and political factors. However, as bin Laden's diaries, the events of 9/11 and the emergence of the Islamic State demonstrate the need for a more nuanced debate and also the need to reassess the means employed to deal with perceived Islamic threats. When Al-Qaeda came into being, the impression was quickly created of a solid organization, which is less the reality of how the network operated. The same happened when the term "Islamic State" was first used and the media struggled with the name to give them, but quickly the brand name settled, and perhaps having realized what they had done the media outlets started to preface their chosen name with "so-called." The problem with the Islamic State is that before media outlets started to call it "so-called" they had already successfully branded this strain of terrorism. In the 24/7 news cycle terms and ideas are rolled out immediately, and there is little time for reflection and nuance as terms are used rapidly and thoughtlessly, only later to be seen as problematic. Islamic State is a product of our media age certainly, but it is also much more than this. Without the publicity, Islamic State would probably have simply been a loose confederation of units and fighters scattered across a range of regional locations. With the aid of 24/7 global media, and politicians on all sides eager to feed the media beast, Islamic State is a loose confederation with a global communication strategy. The Bush II administration may have unleashed the dogs of war, as the media cliché goes, with Al-Qaeda, but the media is instrumental in ensuring Islamic radicalism appeals to individuals in Europe principally, but also elsewhere, by providing a channel for news and image-making.

However, Islamic State is not a state. While the term is not to be equated with Saudi Arabia, the Kingdom does have an Islamic agenda and is a state. The promotion of Islam by Saud before 9/11 is best understood if we understand the fideist category of faith that its Islam belongs to. As we work through this political theology, I ask you to keep in mind there is a great deal of nuance required. Islam is indeed a contested term, and the political prize at stake is the custodianship of the two holy sites, the true symbol of global Islam situated in the Islamic state of Saudi Arabia, which is now facing an existential threat for economic reasons. What has emerged out of the Islamic world is a contradictory picture of the discontent outlined earlier, and the grand narrative of heightened awareness of the faith, history and ideas of Islam, embraced by Muslims around the world. The way this awareness has been translated into the lives of individual Muslims, communities and nations is as diverse as it is misunderstood. We can easily probe the authenticity of these narratives. One sub-narrative, often mistaken for grand narrative, is the emergence of terrorism related to Islam and Islamic ideas. A grand narrative that fails to live up to the facts is the "clash of civilizations" thesis, which sees Islam in irreconcilable conflict with Western standards. What we find in Saudi is a Kingdom seemingly out of sync with the modern world, both economically and politically. The economic problem is one of welfare, which is integral to Islam. The political problem is one of leadership, as the house of Saud seeks to maintain a kingship over democracy. The fear is that Saudi may struggle under the pressure of regional politics and the economy will implode like the Soviet Union did. However, whereas communism all but died Saudi Islam will be scattered even more to the four winds.

If Saudi is American Islam then according to the fundamentalist preachers and the terrorists, what does an Islamic state and political economy actually look like? Does it offer a compelling vision to followers, or is there something else appealing or being manipulated? If we look at the media image often portrayed we get a picture of Islam as one filled with fanatical religionists, waging their war for purity or simply craving for power or some other such reward. Yet, if we consider the 2016 killing of Father Jacques Hamel in Saint-Étienne-du-Rouvray, France, a different picture emerges.[3] It brings to mind the Albert Camus novel *L'etranger*, first translated as "The Outsider," set in French Algiers. The novel starts with the central character learning of his mother's death and ends with him accepting the "gentle indifference of the world." There was more indifference to life itself and the value of others than warfare behind the violent slaughter of Father Hamel. Yet, at the time Pope Francis chose to declare "the world is at war…We don't need to be afraid to say this." He also said it is wrong and untrue to identify Islam with terrorism, and Islam should not be singled out, since the problem is common to religious fundamentalism. He suggested violence is the outcome of social injustice and money idolatry. The problem is not saying all this; the problem is that it is wrong. Taking his last point first, "any connection between poverty, education, and terrorism is indirect, complicated, and probably quite weak," as authors of a 2002 report[4] argued. Second, he should have emphasized Islamic State is not a state actor and has no legitimate claim to authority over a populace or a whole religion. War takes place between state actors with the populace behind it, granted with varying degrees of acquiescence. As we witness destruction and killing by terrorists citing Islam, we can only ponder then what it is they want to achieve and against whom they are waging their war. I think this question is a fascinating one and will be in the background of what proceeds here, but what such a state might look like, and how Saudi may represent such a state in the future, is something I will leave to the concluding chapter. What I want to understand here is the current Islamic state of Saudi Arabia, and as a state actor how it is different in ideology and action compared to the terrorists maiming and murdering in the name of Islam.

I referenced the murder of Father Hamel in France and the pope's response, and as I argued in the *Catholic Herald*,[5] Pope Francis should have said the people who killed Father Hamel are murderers and criminals, plain and simple. This was an act by people with their own complex of motivations and skewed views of reality, inspired by a central idea. The theological source the pope could have gone to as the cause of violence is the same one as down the ages: the broken or sinful nature of humanity. The Church, and Western society, needs to educate society better, and offer theological and moral substance and a vision of faith and belief to confront the godless secularism that makes these individuals feel they are outsiders who are driven in part by the "gentle indifference of the world." The situation for Islam and Saudi is more complex, because there is a different theology and history to engage with in order to face the contemporary situation, and we can all engage with this better. Islam has a theology of broken humanity and Islamic laws for these wrongs, as do other religious, moral and legal systems. There is much common ground here to consider. We can also consider how we understand the terrorists themselves. I think we can accept Louise Richardson's argument in *What Terrorists Want*[6] which is an important one. Simply put, terrorists are not crazy people.[7] They have a sense of moral purpose, however repugnant that may sound to many. They often act on behalf of others, in the Muslim case they act for Palestinians and other Muslims. The idea of dying for a cause, especially a religious cause with heaven as its reward, is a powerful motivator to people, and it is not crazy if one puts it into such an ontological framework. The problem with secular analysis is the arrogance involved, which sought to sideline religion and assume people would grow out of it; this has resulted in two or three generations of social scientists and policy thinkers either ignoring religion or treating it in a narrow sociological sense. Terrorists do not understand themselves as sociological theoretical units or statistics; they understand themselves in this ontological and fideist sense. The terrorist leaders are also highly educated, and so are many of their followers. Islamic terrorists are perhaps the most diverse in sense of class, which should come as no surprise to anyone familiar with the classless attitude of Islam.

Terrorism is most prevalent in countries undergoing change, with economic upheaval reflected in social upheaval and violence. Hence, the social programs terrorist organizations use to build support and dependence, but this too has a theological and legal source in Islam, as Schact explains:

> ...the underlying tendency of the Qur'ānic legislation was to favour the underprivileged; it started with enunciating ethical principles... This feature of Qur'ānic legislation was preserved by Islamic law, and the purely legal attitude, which attaches legal consequences to relevant acts, is often superseded by the tendency to impose ethical standards on the believer.[8]

Islam can share in the struggle over indifference, but it is as much a theological question as a political suggestion. In *Thicker than Oil*, Rachel Bronson argues:

> There is a silver lining to seeing today's challenges as the result of past political decisions. If the problem were Islam or some other basic identity, the situation would be hopeless. A true clash of civilizations would be in the offing, auguring a dark and dangerous future. If, however, the problem is political, then there exists a glimmer of hope. Policies are malleable and can be changed.[9]

It is true that policies are malleable, and Bronson in her book rightly draws on the Cold War to explain a more complex picture than the facile "Big Oil" argument so often made, but she would be wrong to suggest the issue is not about Islam. It is the basic identity in Saudi and elsewhere in the world. It is equally wrong that this being the case inevitably leads to a clash of civilizations. Islam has in the past as a civilization been tolerant of other religions and traditions, though this needs heavily qualified. What is required is not a more malleable politics but a more tolerant Islam today, and an appeal to the better nature of Muslims who in turn need to face the issue of violence more squarely.

This is hard for many to accept, because Islam is often seen narrowly through the lens of terror events. There is also a tendency to understand Islam in the West in terms of a narrative that views Islam as a force that grew, rose and fell and rose again; with the initial rise giving the world intellectual and cultural gifts, and the latter rise giving the world weapons and paranoia. There is, however, a greater nuance to this history that we need to understand better. We also need to think through possible solutions within Islam and Saudi Arabia that are more complicated if we are to understand what is happening today and how we might all approach the future together. We cannot say "this is not Islam," because there is a legitimate ideology in play, even if we find it abhorrent. We cannot say Islam is a religion of peace and keep repeating such a mantra in the hope things will change. It is necessary to face the past and how this has come about. To do this we should look a little more deeply into everyone's history in Saudi, and elsewhere for that matter, and reevaluate the narrative. The root problem, aside from dealing with arms, gender, human rights and a number of other issues of concern, is that Saudi proselytized an Islamic theology and practice that was once useful to the Americans and the West in its fight against communism. With the common enemy gone the teaching, actions and memory remain. This is true both within Saudi as an official Islamic state and within terrorist circles around the world that have grown while it suited a purpose only to become now the enemy itself. We need to take this point seriously if we are ever to find a way out of the religious violence the world faces. After all, Saudi Arabia is a state actor, and its religion is foundational, it also puts people to death for religious reasons. It is an Islamic state and it does engage in violence, as all states do. It is important not to conflate the two, war and religion, since wars such as the war on Yemen is not a religious war per se, but as a proxy war against Iran so there is a religious connection to be considered.

Western perceptions and experience of Islam is inextricably tied with violence. There is continuing violence globally in the name of Islam generally, but also a view that Saudi if not the cause of the violent eruption of Islam certainly fostered an Islamic ideology that created violent Islam. The role of violence in Islam cannot be sidestepped. A violent streak of Islam emerged in the latter part of the twentieth century, breaking onto the international scene in its present political form with the Iranian revolution, and bursting onto the global scene on 9/11 by embracing violent means thanks to the Al-Qaeda and Islamic State networks. There is a great deal of thinking and rhetoric today that assumes we are in a "war" or global conflict with Islam, which is a gross oversimplification, and we require greater subtly if we are to deal with the challenges of political Islam in the twenty-first century. This said, we also have to understand that Islam wasn't invented in 1979 or on 9/11, yet so much discourse plays out as if this were the case. We should also understand Islam is not a monolithic presence, there are many ways that Islam plays out in the world, and there are many points of interaction with politics, culture and other aspects of life. The perception of Saudi as a Kingdom to be blamed for financing terror demands an answer, and as we all know the 9/11 killers were Saudi nationals. This is a narrative we will pursue in detail later. In more recent times, Saudi has been involved in violence in the Yemen and Syria, and its involvement has signaled a different foreign policy approach in the new Arab Cold War, as discussed in the previous chapter.

Terrorism has not been the only security concern of Saudi. Violence has always been a concern from the very inception of the Kingdom. While the numbers are secretive the military spending levels are substantial, and only in part resulting from arms and vehicles purchased from foreign partners. The presence of foreign military advisers and expertise to train the armed forces has been a critical element to military presence with a small and dispersed population making a large presence problematic. There has been a tendency to reject having a large standing army, as other Arab states and nations generally have seen tensions between government and military, as well as military coups. Security of its borders has meant channeling aid into Jordan, Oman and Yemen, as well as into the other Arab nations of Egypt (though less since the Camp David agreement), Iraq and Syria. Much of the aid is aimed at preventing problems. The security of oil supplies led to the building of the pipeline between the Eastern Province and Yanbu to lessen the dependency on the Strait of Hormuz. This is underpinned by a network of underground storage caverns in strategic locations. Another security priority is Mecca and Medina, as the two Islamic holy sites. The symbolism of these two places, and their centrality to Saudi authority, make them obvious targets. As discussed, in 1979 in the wake of the Iranian revolution Mecca was the site of a revolt followed by riots by Iranian pilgrims in 1987. One constant security concern is the influx of illegal immigrants under cover of Haj; in 1987 the Ministry of Labor reported 300,000 expulsions of foreign illegals over the previous two years, and continues to do so periodically.[10]

It is commonplace for different parties to dismiss today's terrorists as un-Islamic or opine that Islam is a fanatical religion of violence, and there is certainly enough stories and statements of violence in the Koran and Hadith, and the Medina constitution, to be taken as resources and justification for battling unbelief in modern Islam. However, to dismiss such groups as being un-Islamic is to ignore the question of legitimacy and authority, which is not so clear-cut in Islam as it might be in parts of Christianity with its built-in hierarchies. Likewise, it is easy to shout "gotcha" at the Saudis because they have proselytized the faith globally and most of the 9/11 bombers came from Saudi. All these concerns and related arguments have their points, but they fall short of being helpful or productive, rather they tend to reinforce incorrect assumptions and stereotypes. Simply denying these people are Islamic doesn't work. Their version of Islam may be out of sync with the tradition, our secular world and the many manifestations of Islam around the world, but whether we like it or not Islamic State can legitimately claim to be Islamic. It expounds a theology. In its fideism it can go back to the Koran and the acts of Muhammad and see justification for violence today, and the only way out is to face up to the difficulties of interpretation, because the supporters of Islamic violence have a strong case in their literalism. Yes, Christians have historically used violence, but if they are fundamentalist or literalist about it they can never go back to Jesus and see justification for that violence, that came later and was borne out of the violence done to Jesus. Not so Muhammad.

Violence and Diversity: A New Constitution of Medina[11]

The attitude toward Islamic violence itself is also a little complicated. If not supporting the violence of Islamic State there is certainly some sympathy with the source and aims of its violence. Many Muslims around the world may show widespread disgust and despair at its means, but even this is a moving target. To look at a specific instance, while many Muslims around the world were horrified by the means of attack on *l'Hebdo* in

Paris, they were not so distant from the reason for the attack. According to the BBC, more than one in four, some 27%, of British Muslims agree with the statement: "I have some sympathy for the motives behind the Charlie Hebdo attacks in Paris."[12] According to a major Turkish newspaper—the *Hürriyet Daily News*—one in five Turks believes Charlie Hebdo's murdered cartoonists "got what they deserved."[13] According to a Gallup poll conducted with Georgetown's John Esposito, 7% of Muslims supported such violence. However, this report is parsed by others as constituting a larger number of 38.6% of Muslims who believe 9/11 attacks were justified (7% "fully," 6.5% "mostly," 23.1% "partially").[14] The Gallup poll contests this reading, stating:

> The evidence refutes this argument. Residents of the Organisation of the Islamic Cooperation (OIC) member states are slightly less likely than residents of non-member states to view military attacks on civilians as sometimes justified, and about as likely as those of non-member states to say the same about individual attacks.[15]

A Policy Exchange report in 2016 stated only 4% of Muslims in Britain believe Al-Qaeda was behind 9/11, though 31% believed it was the United States government.[16]

A key to understanding violence in Islam is the constitution or treaty of Medina, a foundational constitutional document in Islam. Historically attracting little attention, it is now being given a more prominent place in understanding Islamic public law.[17] There is much scholarly debate over its unity, and how it was formed,[18] though it is clear it came from the Prophet Muhammed. The treaty covers relationships within religious diversity, and is written with Muslims as the minority population and Jews as the majority. It also justifies the use of violence and force in Islamic terms, including among its own believers. There has been a long tradition of Muslims battling against Muslims in a battle for religious purity, and often the war is waged more internally than against external forces. In the Constitution of Medina, there are included rules on Muslims cooperating with non-Muslims to kill other Muslims. The Constitution is an insightful place to commence looking at preserving the Islamic way of life. Muhammad was an arbitrator of disputes in the nascent Muslim community, and it was clear that the life of the community was to be judged according to God's law and not human law. The Constitution of Medina was a document drawn up by the Prophet Muhammad to govern the relations between the believers and Muslims of Quraysh and Yathrib, and those who followed them, creating a new *ummah* or community. It is the most significant document surviving from the time of the Prophet, dating from after his arrival at Medina (Yathrib) in the Hijrah (622 CE). The document deals with a range of tribal matters such as the organization and leadership of the participating tribal groups, warfare, blood-wit, the ransoming of captives and war expenditure. There is some debate as to whether the document constitutes a number of treaties concluded at different times. One key aspect of the document deals in matters of pluralism, and as noted the guidance which includes the permission for Muslims to kill other Muslims, and if needs be in alliance with non-Muslims. At the time, there were 10,000 residents in Medina, comprising 45% non-Muslim Arabs, 40% Jews and only 15% Muslims.

The constitution consists of 57 clauses which set forth the formation of a sovereign nation-state with a common citizenship for all communities, protecting fundamental human rights for all citizens, including equality, cooperation, freedom of conscience and freedom of religion. Clause 25 specifically states that Jews and non-Muslim Arabs are entitled to practice their own faith without any restrictions. This was the first document in history to establish religious freedom as a fundamental constitutional right. Some of the clauses[19] dealing with conflict are worth highlighting:

(14) A believer shall not slay a believer for the sake of an unbeliever, nor shall he aid an unbeliever against a believer.

(17) No Jew will be wronged for being a Jew.

(19) The believers must avenge the blood of one another shed in the way of God.

(21) Whoever is convicted of killing a believer without good reason shall be subject to retaliation unless the next of kin is satisfied (with blood-money),

and the believers shall be against him as one man, and they are bound to take action against him.

(24) The Jews shall contribute to the cost of war so long as they are fighting alongside the believers.

(36) None of them shall go out to war save the permission of Muhammad, but he shall not be prevented from taking revenge for a wound. He who slays a man without warning slays himself and his household, unless it be one who has wronged him, for God will accept that.

(37) The Jews must bear their expenses and the Muslims their expenses. Each must help the other against anyone who attacks the people of this document. They must seek mutual advice and consultation, and loyalty is a protection against treachery. A man is not liable for his ally's misdeeds. The wronged must be helped.

(38) The Jews must pay with the believers so long as war lasts.

(44) The contracting parties are bound to help one another against any attack on Yathrib.

(45)(a) If they are called to make peace and maintain it they must do so; and if they make a similar demand on the Muslims it must be carried out except in the case of a holy war.

(45)(b) Every one shall have his portion from the side to which he belongs.

These are clear rules of engagement, though they would receive a mixed reception in today's secular courts.

Between the historical juncture of the Constitution of Medina and contemporary Muslim attitudes, can we say then that Islamic State is alien to Saudi and Islam? Clearly not. Islamic State is a central idea that instrumentalizes violence, not Islam, for an ethereal global media and secular age. Like Mecca itself, it is something individuals in search of meaning can point at, use to claim authority and motivation for their own acts, and, gives them self-importance. It thus has a twofold strategy.

First, to use battalions to attack territories in the region, and to inspire individuals in the West to undertake individual or gang-level attacks. Both approaches play into the notion of global Islam. Likewise, the presence of the 9/11 bombers in Saudi Arabia is a more complex problem than simply identifying them with a nation. The justification of violence in Islam is a very real theological problem for Islam, and a political problem for the rest of the world. We can see here the justification from Mohammad for violence, and we can see a modern-day sympathy for the causes of outrage among Muslims, even if they don't accept the way action is taken. However, the history of Islam is not completely littered with outbreaks of violence persecution or rebellion, it is a modern thing which has traces going back through history. The problem is why has it happened now, and what is the part played by Saudi Arabia in stoking the emotions and this aspect of Islamic theology?

Saudi Links to Terrorism

That there were links to Saudi Arabia and the 9/11 attack is indisputable, but it is contested what links there were and the dominant narrative is that there was no official support for the actions. However, in searching for answers and accountability, relatives have continued to pursue claims and a 9/11 lawsuit. US intelligence had raised suspicions about the hijackers having official connections, but in the original report and when previously classified documents were released in 2016, the 9/11 commission found no evidence that senior Saudi officials or the government had provided funding or backing to the attackers.[20] With 15 of the 19 hijackers that day being Saudi nationals, the focus has always been on Saudi but the Kingdom has always denied any role in the attacks. Saudi lobbied against legislation subsequently passed by Congress the Justice Against Sponsors of Terrorism (Jasta) legislation, after overturning a veto by the president. In a statement following its passage through Congress, the Saudi foreign ministry said, "The erosion of sovereign immunity will have a negative impact on all nations, including the United States." This statement was a mirror of that made by President Obama, who stated it set a "dangerous precedent" that could lead to the United States being opened to "a situation where we're suddenly exposed to liabilities for all the work that we're doing all around the world and suddenly finding ourselves subject to private lawsuits." While not signaling any retaliation, the Saudis called on Congress to reverse the decision. Relatives of those killed in 9/11 welcomed the bill's passing, issuing a statement that "We rejoice in this triumph and look forward to our day in court and a time when we may finally get more answers regarding who was truly behind the attacks."[21]

This event added more fuel to an already ailing relationship between the Saudis and the Americans, but what the 9/11 Commission recommendation had originally stated was:

> The problems in the US-Saudi relationship must be confronted, openly. The United States and Saudi Arabia must determine if they can build a relationship that political leaders on both sides are prepared to publicly defend – a relationship about more than oil. It should include a shared commitment to political and economic reform, as Saudis make common cause with the outside world. It should include a shared interest in greater tolerance and cultural respect, translating into a commitment to fight the violent extremists who foment hatred.[22]

The Saudis feel they have honored this call only to be slapped in the face by its hitherto close allies, though to be more accurate they had become victims of more domestic factors, namely, the American love of their day in court and the political games between Republicans and Democrats in an election year.

As noted, a legacy of the Cold War was that Jihadism as form of terror in Saudi was promoted in Afghanistan as many Saudis went there to fight the foreign enemy, which fitted with the American discourse of anti-communism. Christian America and Islamic Saudi stood side by side in their respective jihad or struggle in repelling the godless Soviet Union. Out of this jihad came the 1990s struggle against America itself, led by Osama bin Laden and harnessing those fighters who had left Afghanistan after the Soviet withdrawal. The new rallying call was for global jihad, this was the doctrine developed by bin Laden and took a path to the World Trade Center (WTC) bombing in 1998 and then 15 Saudis plus others to 9/11, and thus it was we found a changed world that heralded the twenty-first century. The fight in Afghanistan had engendered a transnational Arab network of militants, many of whom were estranged from their home nation and unable to return home. The Afghan rebellion was not the only Islamic struggle of the 1990s, though perhaps the only successful one in this period. This led bin Laden and others, citing also Saudi acquiescence with America, to believe that local struggle was futile and unsuccessful. Instead they urged a global war that posited America as a unifying enemy of Islam. To the outside world this network and doctrine became known as Al-Qaeda, the first transnational jihadi organization and a precursor to the more violent and pervasive Islamic State. The attack on the World Trade Center on 9/11 brought Islam onto the world stage, and started what then President George W. Bush called a War on Terror against an axis of evil, bringing together Iraq and North Korea in an improbable linkage. Osama bin Laden explained:

> They claim that this blessed awakening and the people reverting to Islam are due to economic factors. This is not so. It is rather a grace from Allah, a desire to embrace the religion of Allah. And this is not surprising. When the holy war called thousands of young men from the Arab peninsula and other countries answered the call and they came from wealthy backgrounds.[23]

This raises the question of where these terrorists came from, if Saudi is a successful Islamic state and Islam a religion of peace, where are the problems? Part of this can be answered in a generic sense of understanding terrorism. Louise Richardson, in *What Terrorists Want*, argues there are seven "crucial" characteristics of terrorism:

1. Terrorism is politically inspired
2. It involves violence or the threat of violence
3. It does not aim to defeat the enemy but to send a message
4. The acts and victims have symbolic significance
5. It is an act of sub-state groups and not states
6. The victim of the violence and the audience of the terrorists are not the same
7. Terrorism deliberately targets civilians as culpable

Richardson also draws the distinction that terrorist groups can be assessed on their goals; which may be temporal or transformational; and the proximity to the community they claim to represent, with those most distant from this constituency being the easiest to defeat. Another set of definitions Richardson offers are the defenses given by terrorists for what they do:

1. It is the "last resort."
2. No other strategy is available.
3. Terrorism works.
4. What she calls the teenage defense of "everyone does it."

These defenses may apply in many contexts, but in the current Islamic context, it is primarily the third option that seems to apply. In among this list, Richardson adds two common arguments used by Islamic fundamentalists, namely, the defenses of collective guilt and moral equivalence. As Richardson points out, terrorism was not invented on 11 September 2001. Of course, America had witnessed terrorism in the first World Trade Center bomb, which did not seem to really awaken them to something Richardson and myself had been long used to, though less poignant in my case since I was only evacuated from the Earl's Court bomb attack in 1972. However, American terrorism had certainly been around a long time, the WTC attacks being different in that they resulted from foreign actors. Likewise, religious terrorism was not invented on 9/11. The earliest examples evidenced by Richardson are the religious, Jewish zealots in the first century against Rome, followed much later by the Shia Muslim Assassins in the eleventh to thirteenth centuries, and the Hindu Thugee, the longest lasting some 600 years. Richardson writes that it is difficult to come up with a convincing explanation for terrorism because there are so many terrorists and so few. This is the context in which she writes "If Islam causes terrorism, with 1.2 billion Muslims in the world and, at most, a few thousand Islamic terrorists, why are there not more?"[24]

Richardson has given us a book that is deservedly a classic text for the topic, though in the case of Islam I would question such a distinct separation of politics as primary and religion as a tool when she explains:

…various statements suggests that the political is primary and religion a tool. But we do not know that for sure, and he would certainly deny it. Bin Laden has long listed the American presence in Saudi Arabia as the primary offense.[25]

For Muslims and Saudis, the two are far too intertwined to form the usual Western liberal categorization of a dichotomy that promotes the secular politic above the religious doctrine. However, as Richardson discusses at length, we need to be careful in how we connect terrorism with religion, noting that in 1968, out of 11 terrorist groups, none were religious, they were all secular, which includes the sectarian Irish Republican Army (IRA) in her classification.[26] Since then religious terrorism has undoubtedly grown, and while at the time of writing it is mostly associated with Islam not all Muslims are terrorists. The vast majority of terrorists are Muslim, and Islam the clarion call to action. In this recent history of violence, there is a danger in looking at Saudi Arabia, and indeed Islam, as if Islam only came about as a radicalized force either in the Iranian revolution of 1979 or after 11 September 2001. As Louise Richardson discusses in depth, the relationship between the economic and religious call to arms is a complicated one. A common tactic is to make payments to fighters and terrorist groups who combine social services with ideology,[27] and this is often done by emotive campaigns seen as charitable or helpful giving. It has been a strategy employed by many groups, and was a core activity of Hezbollah in the Lebanon, and a very effective one at that.[28] Terrorists are not always seen as a bad force. However, given this history it is important that Saudi offer an alternative Islam, not an American Islam or an Islamic State Islam. As a mature Islamic state, the Kingdom has the history, stability at present and opportunity to tackle the violence and promote a new pluralism in the Kingdom and in the world. Perhaps, what should be discussed in Saudi now is a new constitution of Medina, a new cooperation for an economic age of uncertainty, where mutuality will rescue Saudi from going on a path toward violence or implosion. To which point, there needs to be a continual retreat from violence and extremism toward a more faithful following of the Islamic path that suits today's world rather than looks backward.

Notes

1. Haykel et al. (2015, p. 138).
2. http://ngm.nationalgeographic.com/features/world/asia/saudi-arabia/saudi-arabia-text/2
3. David Cowan, *Catholic Herald* 8 August 2016, http://catholicherald.co.uk/commentandblogs/2016/08/08/what-pope-francis-should-have-said-in-response-to-fr-hamels-murder/
4. *Education, Poverty, Political Violence and Terrorism: Is There a Causal Connection?* Alan B. Krueger, Jitka Maleckova, NBER Working Paper No. 9074. Issued in July 2002 http://www.nber.org/papers/w9074
5. Ibid.
6. Richardson (2007).
7. http://www.economist.com/node/17730424
8. Lewis et al. (1998, p. 539).
9. Bronson (2006, p. 11).
10. http://regionalmms.org/index.php/component/spsimpleportfolio/item/64-mass-deportations-looming-saudi-arabia-gears-up-to-expe, https://www.hrw.org/report/2015/05/10/detained-beaten-deported/saudi-abuses-against-migrants-during-mass-expulsions
11. This is not the same as saying Saudi has a constitution. A full copy can be read online: http://www.constitution.org/cons/medina/macharter.htm
12. http://www.bbc.com/news/uk-31293196
13. http://www.nationalreview.com/article/427439/muslims-terrorism-and-president-obama-josh-gelernter
14. http://www.washingtoninstitute.org/policy-analysis/view/just-like-us-really
15. http://www.gallup.com/poll/157067/views-violence.aspx
16. http://www.dailymail.co.uk/news/article-3992304/Only-one-25-British-Muslims-believe-Al-Qaeda-carried-9-11-terror-attack-says-think-tank.html
17. S. A. Arjomand refers to the treaty as a "proto-Islamic public law." Arjomand, S. A. "The Constitution of Medina: A Sociolegal Interpretation of Muhammad's Acts of Foundation of the *Umma.*" *International Journal of Middle Eastern Studies* 41 (2009): 555–575.
18. Arjomand, Ibid. Denny, F. M. "*Ummah* in the Constitution of Medina." *Journal of Near Eastern Studies* 36 (1977): 39–47; Gil, Moshe. "The Constitution of Medina: A Reconsideration." *Israel Oriental Studies* 4

(1974): 44–66; Goto, A. "The Constitution of Medina." *Orient: Report of the Society for Near Eastern Studies in Japan* 18 (1982): 1–17; Hallaq (1999, pp. 4–6); Hamidullah, Muhammad. *The First Written Constitution in the World: An Important Document of the Time of the Holy Prophet.* 3d rev. ed. Lahore, Pakistan: Sh. Muhammad Ashraf, 1394/1975; Lecker, Michael. *The Constitution of Medina: Muḥammad's First Legal Document.* Princeton, NJ: Darwin, 2004; Rose, P. L. "Muhammad, the Jews and the Constitution of Medina: Retrieving the Historical Kernel." *Der Islam* 86 (2009); Rubin, Uri. "The 'Constitution of Medina': Some Notes." *Studia Islamica* 62 (1985): 5–23; Serjeant, R. B. "The 'Constitution of Medina.'" *Islamic Quarterly* 8 (1964): 3–16; Wellhausen, Julius. "Muhammads Gemeindeordnung von Medina." In *Skizzen und Vorarbeiten.* Vol. 4. Edited by Julius Wellhausen, 65–83. Berlin: G. Reimer, 1889.

19. This text is taken from Guillaume (1955, pp. 231–233), numbering added.
20. http://www.bbc.com/news/world-us-canada-36811642
21. http://www.bbc.com/news/world-us-canada-37503224
22. 9/11 Report, p. 374.
23. Richardson (2007, p. 59).
24. Richardson (2007, p. 40).
25. Richardson (2007, p. 63).
26. A useful chronology of 1968 to 1974 is accessible here: https://www.rand.org/content/dam/rand/pubs/reports/2007/R1597.pdf
27. Richardson (2007, p. 59).
28. Harik (2004).

Bibliography

al-Rasheed, Madawi, ed. 2008. *Kingdom Without Borders: Saudi Arabia's Political, Religious and Media Frontiers.* London: Hurst.

Allawai, Ali A. 2009. *The Crisis of Islamic Civilization.* New Haven: Yale University Press.

An-Na'im, Abdullahi Ahmed. 2008. *Islam and the Secular State: Negotiating the Future of Shari`a.* Cambridge, MA: Harvard University Press.

Axworthy, Michael. 2008. *A History of Iran: Empire of the Mind.* New York: Perseus Books.

Barber, Benjamin R. 2001. *Jihad vs McWorld: Terrorism's Challenge to Democracy.* New York: Ballantine Books.

Black, Antony. 2001. *The History of Islamic Political Thought: From the Prophet to the Present*. Edinburgh: Edinburgh University Press.

Bowering, Gerhard, ed. 2015. *Islamic Political Thought: An Introduction*. Princeton: Princeton University Press.

Bronson, Rachel. 2006. *Thicker Than Oil: America's Uneasy Relationship with Saudi Arabia*. New York: Oxford University Press.

Cowan, David. 2009. *Economic Parables: The Monetary Teachings of Jesus Christ*. 2nd ed. Downers Grove: IVP.

Craze, Jonathan, and Mark Huband. 2009. *The Kingdom: Saudi Arabia and the Challenge of the 21st Century*. London: Hurst & Co.

Cunningham, Robert B., and Yasin K. Sarayrah. 1993. *Wasta: The Hidden Force in Middle Eastern Society*. Westport: Praeger.

Esposito, John L. 2002. *Unholy War: Terror in the Name of Islam*. New York: Oxford University Press.

Fawcett, Louise. 2016. *International Relations of the Middle East*. 4th ed. Oxford: Oxford University Press.

Gause, F. Gregory, III. 1994. *Oil Monarchies: Domestic and Security Challenges in the Arab Gulf States*. New York: Council on Foreign Relations.

Guillaume, A. 1955. *The Life of Muhammad – A Translation of Ishaq's Sirat Rasul Allah*. Karachi: Oxford University Press.

Hallaq, Wael B. 1999. *Islamic Legal Theories*, 4–6. Cambridge: Cambridge University Press.

Halliday, Fred. 2000. *Nation and Religion in the Middle East*. Boulder: Lynne Rienner Publishers.

———. 2002. *Arabia Without Sultans*. London: Saqi Books.

Hamid, Shadi. 2016. *Islamic Exceptionalism: How the Struggle Over Islam Is Reshaping the World*. New York: St. Martin's Press.

Hamidullah, Muhammad. 1975. *The First Written Constitution in the World: An Important Document of the Time of the Holy Prophet*. 3rd rev ed. Lahore: Sh. Muhammad Ashraf.

Hammond, Andrew. 2012. *The Islamic Utopia: The Illusion of Reform in Saudi Arabia*. London: Pluto Press.

Harik, Judith Palmer. 2004. *Hezbollah: The Changing Face of Terrorism*. London: I.B. Tauris.

Haykel, Bernard, Thomas Hegghammer, and Stéphane Lacroix. 2015. *Saudi Arabia in Transition: Insights on Social, Political, Economic and Religious Change*. Cambridge: Cambridge University Press.

Heggenhammer, Thomas. 2010. *Jihad in Saudi Arabia: Violence and Pan-Islamism Since 1979*. New York: Cambridge University Press.

House, Karen Elliott. 2012. *On Saudi Arabia: Its People, Past, Religion, Fault Lines – And Future.* New York: Vintage Books.

Karsh, Effraim. 2006. *Islamic Imperialism: A History.* New Haven: Yale University Press.

Kepel, Gilles. 2004. *The War for Muslim Minds: Islam and the West.* Trans. Pascal Ghazaleh. Cambridge MA: Belknap Press.

Lacey, Robert. 2009. *Inside the Kingdom: Kings, Clerics, Terrorists, Modernists, and the Struggle for Saudi Arabia.* New York: Viking.

Lackner, Helen. 1978. *A House Built on Sand. A Political Economy of Saudi Arabia.* London: Ithaca Press.

Lecker, Michael. 2004. *The Constitution of Medina: Muḥammad's First Legal Document.* Princeton: Darwin.

Lewis, L., Pellat Ch, and J. Schacht, eds. 1998. *Cambridge Encyclopedia of Islam, Volume II.* Leiden: Brill.

Lippman, Thomas W. 2012. *Saudi Arabia on the Edge: The Uncertain Future of an American Ally.* Dulles: Potomac Books.

Mabon, Simon. 2016. *Saudi Arabia and Iran: Power and Rivalry in the Middle East.* New York: I.B. Tauris.

Matthiesen, Toby. 2015. *The Other Saudis: Shiism, Dissent and Sectarianism.* New York: Cambridge University Press.

Nasr, Vali. 2009. *The Rise of Islamic Capitalism: Why the New Muslim Middle Class is the Key to Defeating Extremism.* New York: Free Press.

Ramazani, R.K., ed. 1990. *Iran's Revolution: The Search for Consensus.* Bloomington: Indiana University Press.

Raphael, Patai. 1973. *The Arab Mind.* New York: Scribner.

Richardson, Louise. 2007. *What Terrorists Want.* New York: Random House.

Said, Edward W. 1981. *Covering Islam: How the Media and the Experts Determine How We See the Rest of the World.* New York: Pantheon Books.

Salame, Ghassan, ed. 1994. *Democracy Without Democrats? The Renewal of Politics in the Muslim World.* London: I.B. Tauris.

Southern, R.W. 1978. *Western Views of Islam in the Middle Ages.* Cambridge, MA: Harvard University Press.

Part III

Religious Implosion

8

No Democracy Please, We're Saudis

At the level of political international relations theorists explore how and why states act and interact, and examine what we mean by sovereignty. The foundation of Western political thought about states is the Westphalian system, which is clearly understood. The Peace of Westphalia in 1648 ended the Thirty Years' War and brought about the modern European nation state system and the system of sovereign states, not just for Europe but the world. While the notions of statehood and sovereignty are applied in the Arab world, the picture is somewhat more complex, for two principal reasons: first, the oft-stated call for Arab unity and second the role of religion in the Arab world. Pan-Arabism is understood to be at the core of regional diplomacy and interactions between the states, which if carried to its logical conclusion would override the Westphalian system of states with their self-interest and conflict, and instead lead to greater unity in the interests of pan-Arab goals. Clearly this is not the case, as pan-Arabism is stymied by the many variances within the Arab world. Likewise religion, which is often taken to be oppositional when it comes to Islam. In the case of Saudi, we have a state that is monarchical and self-interested in maintaining the house of Saud, and one that binds together the leading families with religion as a social thread running throughout the Kingdom. It has many conflicts with other Arab and Islamic states on

© The Author(s) 2018
D. Cowan, *The Coming Economic Implosion of Saudi Arabia*,
https://doi.org/10.1007/978-3-319-74709-5_8

the one hand, and promotes global Islam on the other. In short, Islam overrides nationalism, and Saudi Arabia as a Kingdom understands its role to be custodian of both the two holy sites and the Arabian peninsula as the home of Mohammed's Islam and also globally as a Kingdom that promotes the spirit of global Islam, which in turn eclipses any national identity or interest.

Some of our answers to the current problems can be sourced in this history, as Islam builds on a specific religious history that is connected to the past and influences the future. Like other religions, Islam is alive in the present and is central to understanding or interpreting history. Sadly, history is not central to the political mindset in these troubled times, and is often ignored by policymakers on all sides. We have to understand the history of colonial and American influence if we are to unpick the threads of history in Saudi and the region, bearing in mind that in this respect the Saudi history is quite different from many of the Arab nations. In approaching anywhere in the Arab world or the Middle East, it is thus essential to grasp the past in order to have what historian E.H. Carr called an "unending dialogue" with the past. Sadly, as noted, it is not at the forefront of the political mind to spend much time in the archives and the past, which makes a meeting of Arab and Western minds doubly problematic. Part of a dialogue with the past is understanding the notion of statehood in the Saudi context. Statehood was a creation of the Western Westphalian system, and as such was imposed on the Middle East. The difficulty in assessing Saudi is that it is a religious state, which makes it less easy to fit into categories of international relations thought. The realist approach is to assume an amoral basis on which to view the nation in the context of an anarchic international system.[1] Realism in international relations came to dominance in the 1930s to 1950s, dismissing the earlier utopian liberalism apparent in Wilsonianism and other schools of thought. In looking at states in international relations, the realist approach is very diverse but all realist theories share roots in ideas about human nature and power. Classical realists see the system of nations as primarily anarchic, by which is meant not wild anarchy but the absence of an over-arching authority. They all agree that power, and nations competing for power, lie at the heart of understanding international relations within this anarchic system of nations. However, and this was underplayed in realism just as much as in other disciplines, religion has been unhelpfully dismissed as a critical element. Realists have also underplayed the critical role of sectarianism. The classical realist Hans Morgenthau warned against a utopianism that identifies "the moral aspirations of a particular nation with the moral laws that govern the universe."[2] It is difficult to make such a distinction in the case of Saudi Arabia, which thinks of itself in terms of the moral aspirations ruling the nation, and they extend these inspirationally to the universe, hence its global Islamic education program. In the past pan-Arab nationalism had attempted, and failed, to trump both the Islamic and state-centric models, and a Westphalian approach does not trump the Islamic model either. Saudi Arabia is a nation that seeks to govern by the Islamic laws believed to govern the universe. This is its claim and this is its problem.

Like other Arab monarchies, the house of Saud has used a mixture of Islam and tribalism to legitimize and sustain their rule. Saudi does not strip out Islam from national or Arab identity, hence it could never support the secular pan-Arabism that swept the region in the 1950s and 1960s. This is because these movements were more ideological and geographical than cultural and geographical. The Islamic way of life, national security and the house of Saud are all parts of a piece in Saudi, which is set in the context of a world divided in a bipolar sense, not in terms of capitalist West versus communist East as in the Cold War years, but in terms of believers versus nonbelievers. The leadership of the house of Saud is tied to its role of being custodian of the holy sites, so their objectives are part of the custodial duties by extension and vice versa. The Kingdom may have established itself in part by battle and sword, and not just with the tribes of the peninsula, but Saudi has also built strong tribal and regional alliances as well as global ones. The Western alliances and relationships are conducted on the basis that Saudi Arabia is a kingship and opposed to democracy, despite a few nods and winks to democracy and women in recent times, such as expanded education opportunities and the dropping of the driving ban.

Saudi opposition to democracy is not simply because of a self-serving interest in royalty. It is based on Islam, which is theocratic in its political understanding. Thus how power is exercised, and what role the people play in an Islamic society, is not to be dismissed lightly. A criticism made by Tariq Ramadan in *Islam and the Arab Awakening* is that Islamism is in fact the problem, it is about political interests and power. He elaborates that the Western relationship with Saudi is a prime example of Western hypocrisy:

> ...the alliance with the Kingdom of Saudi Arabia, where Islam is the state religion and where the ruling monarchy claims that Islam is, by its essence, opposed to democracy, offers proof positive that the West has no problem with political Islam as such, as long as Islamist leaders promise to protect its economic and political interests.[3]

The customs and practice of Islam are made universal by way of the *sunnah* and creation of the *umma*, those people who confessed one God and accepted the Koran and Hadith as normative for behavior, and they abide by the law or *Sharia*. The source of authority is God and its expression in society is clearly demarcated. Historically, ruling families have based their legitimacy in being linked to a particular Islamic "grouping" which comprises a loose confederation of political and religious notables.[4] This elite of royal rulers appears prima facie to be in contradiction to a core component of Islam, which is its universality and sense of equality, a denial of elitism. The fact that there is a form of elitism in Saudi is what the Meccan rebels in 1979 and other groups since have played on in their own propaganda war. There may be elitism, but Saudi society has traditionally been bound by *'asabiyya*,[5] which is the sense of solidarity with the Sunnah of the Prophet, the people who submit to the path and live according to sharia.

The Anglo-Lebanese scholar Albert Hourani, author of *History of the Arab Peoples*, explained it is important to see *'asabiyya* or "Clannism" as the lens through which to understand the intricacies of Arab relations. Hourani explained the economic and social processes in rural areas tended to produce what can best be termed a tribal society. He looked at various levels of society, the nuclear family of three generations (grand-parents, parents and children), and larger units of which there were two kinds: kinship and common interest. The latter may comprise a claim to blood relations or other claims to common ancestral links, but these were not necessarily known and a particular genealogy may have tended to be fictitious. Hourani explained the tribe "was first of all a name which existed in the mind of those who claimed to be linked with each other… It could have a corporate spirit (*'asabiyya*) which would lead its members to help each other in time of need."[6]Saudi "used the language of Islam spontaneously and continuously" and had "been created by a movement for the reassertion of God's Will in human societies. Others, however appeared to have been driven into it." However, "even in Saudi Arabia, the principles of Hanbali jurisprudence were invoked in order to justify the new laws and regulations made necessary by the new economic order."[7] The fourteenth-century Muslim philosopher of history Ibn Khaldun (1332–1406 AD), whose major work was *Kitab al-'Ibar*, links *'asabiyya* to power in society, which is based on family lineage and connections, and was common in nomadic and savage peoples. Each *'asabiyya* evolves through four generations, with the emergence of a generation rising to power culminating in the fourth generation that wastes the legacy of the first three generations. The cycle then renews itself.

Authority is rooted in this paradigm and this is how Saudis theoretically understand authority, which is different from secular liberalism and Western democracy. The political philosophy of Saudi is in fact a political theology, and it underpins a theocratic state. Historically, there has been a tendency in political literature to assess Saudi Arabia, and other Arab states, though the lens of secular ideas without really seeing clearly the religious dimension. Since 9/11, social scientists and others have been scrambling to learn about religion, having assumed the Weber secularization thesis.[8] As Capitalism and Western liberal society developed, received wisdom assumed the secularization thesis which suggested that religion was a private affair, largely irrelevant to public life. The rise of a number of religious movements globally, but chiefly Islam, has forced many in the various fields of intellectual endeavor to play catch-up in the last decade or so, seeking a greater understanding of religion. However, talk of a "clash of civilizations" and other fanciful notions has not been helpful, but unfortunately has been influential in both intellectual circles and the *vox populi*. The secular worldview of the West is very much a part of global capitalism and underpins economic values and ethics. For a long time, it has been almost alien to consider the influence of religion on politics and politics. However, in the Islamic context[9] it is essential to explore this conflict of values, which is not the same as saying there is a clash of values. We can explore more constructively and creatively than talking about clashes and cultural conflict, which is not to dismiss these elements that also exist. All religions and the politics of society have historically had demarcation disputes. In Christianity there have been times when society was run by the church, but today we have societies that have quite different church and state arrangements, though usually either on the fringes or on the outside of the mainstream. It can be unclear to what extent Christianity is privatized or should be privatized, but if there is no clear boundary between the two in Christianity then it is even more difficult to determine the question in Islam. As Antony Black rightly points out in *The History of Islamic Political Thought*, "under Islam even more than under Christianity, a great deal of political ideology was conducted in terms of *Religonspolitik*."[10]

It is a mistake to look at Islam in Saudi Arabia, and elsewhere, simply through the political lens of Western religion, secularism and political philosophies. Islam is more integral to Saudi politics than the state religion of Western Europe. It is more community and kinship-based than the Protestant individualism of America and elsewhere. It is also distinct from Roman Catholicism and the Anglican communion, as it lacks a fully institutionalized hierarchy a Pope or Archbishop, and for the most part, its clergy do not have the extensive formal training that most Christian churches have traditionally demanded, though the stringency of such training in Christian churches has become less formal than in times past. To assess the role of religion in political thought in Western discourse is to understand a quite different experience from Islam. To understand the political thought of Islam requires understanding the theology and the history and also requires understanding that perhaps Western political orthodoxy is inadequate to answer all the global questions faced in Saudi and the region. As noted above, at the very outset, unlike the United Kingdom for instance religion is at the very base of the constitution of the Kingdom. Religion in the West is largely instrumental or utilitarian, and the state religion meant adherence to social mores of society more than any evangelical sense of belonging to the Christian religion. I think it was Geroge Orwell who suggested the English don't really like religion, as it seems too enthusiastic for them to them to be take it to heart. The religion of the English is more English than religious is the implication. In Saudi, it would be constructive to draw such a distinction and see Islam as an integral part of the identity and personality of the Kingdom and the people, and the state and public life reflects this religious faith. The presence of mosques within the hearing distance of all Muslims and observance of prayer times makes the faith very present to people, every day and in the workplaces and malls, unlike the one-hour Sunday inoculation we increasingly witness in the Christian West, if there is religion practiced at all. Indeed, it is curious sometimes to hear evangelicals in America complain about the loss of religion and they call for a certain presence of faith in public spaces, yet they can only be jealous of the role and acceptance of Islam in Saudi Arabia.

Thus, to understand Saudi Arabia we have to dig deeper than is usually done in Christianity into the faith as doctrine and as practice, if we are to see how central its role is in forming the worldview of the average Saudi, not just as an instrument of state rule. The State and the house of Saud can make use of Islam because the people are Muslim, rather than using religion to manipulate people. The populace is too well-versed in Islam to be taken easily for fools, which is the essence of the Weberian and sociological attack on Christianity. However, just as there is not a monolithic Islam in the world, there is some diversity in Islam practiced within the Kingdom, principally the tension between the Sunni majority and the Shias, who are mainly in the Eastern Province. The presence of a significant Shia population within the Kingdom undermines primarily the religious cohesion of Saudi, though Shias are not the only Islamic sects in the Kingdom. There are also Sufis and Ismalis, though the latter have enjoyed relatively cordial relations with the elite Saudis, especially the Yam tribe which has allied with Saud in the sensitive southern areas close to Yemen. The Shias, however, are the most significant grouping, and during the so-called Arab Spring they were the one group who did demonstrate and seek advantage from the mood sweeping the region.

Attempts have been made to bring the Sunni and Shia traditions together, including the 1940s creation of a formal body at al-Azhar University for just such an objective, and later the Amman Message in 2005,[11] whereby the King of Jordan initiated an attempt to clarify some of the common ground. This attempt was supported by the Saudis, with encouragement of the *ulama* organizations to attend. The conference issued various resolutions, supported by the Saudis, that amounted to a call for Muslim unity, and condemned terrorism along with a curb on fatwas issued by a multitude of groups without true claim to legitimacy. Most notably, the Saudis formally acknowledged the legitimacy of Shia Islam.[12] However, while the Saudi state representatives gave full support to these resolutions, they were not signed by many of the Wahhabi clerics present. After the Arab Spring protests, and with the emergence of a more internationalist Iran, the Saudis have backtracked on what little dialogue they have had with the Shias. The problem is more deeply rooted, because Shias have been excluded from the top echelons of society and positions of government and in the private sector. Toby Matthiesen explains:

> Saudi Shia have sought to redress this situation and embraced various revolutionary ideologies throughout the twentieth century. From communism to Khomeinism, Shia have tried most political ideologies in the Middle East but to no avail; the opposition movements failed to change the inferior status of Saudi Shia fundamentally.[13]

As Matthiesen suggests, the Shias have been too few to make an impact and too many to be ignored. It also made possible the rise of Islamist movements, since all the secular ones have failed.

The modern form of political Islam in Saudi is rooted in the influx of Muslim Brotherhood leaders in the 1960s and 1970s, as they inserted themselves into the education system. The Brotherhood was founded in Egypt in 1928 by Hassan al-Banna, a schoolteacher, and it sought to combine past and present. They took aspects of Islamic understanding and history, seeing Islam and sharia as central to political challenges of today, and tried to work within the existing, largely secular, institutions and framework rather than trying to overhaul them. This approach has been surpassed by modern and more radical movements. In many, secular and liberal eyes, this is a battle for the soul of the "real" Islam, but this assumes there is something akin to a "real" Islam. We need to stop thinking in these terms. There are many Islamic voices and identities in play here, and they blend differently depending on the culture, and whether the host culture is Muslim or where the Muslim communities are a minority presence. Radical groups prey on the notion there is an Islam and there is a globalized Islam, a central focus for appealing to individuals and groups around the world to begin about a new Islamic age. It appeals to idealism, to conservatism and to disengaged secular youth in different measures. Islamic State is not remotely interested in the subtler approaches of the Muslim Brotherhood or Saudi Arabia. They want to establish a new caliphate. From their vantage point, Saudi is failing in its duty. Riyadh offers retail therapy, while Islamic State offers a road to salvation. Riyadh's moderation will only lead the people toward the boredom of secularism, whereas Islamic State can recapture the excitement of the Islamic and Arab way of being and living. This is an attack from within.

Saudi is a Sunni state, Islamic State is a Sunni variant and the Shia a sect, which calls for a different analysis than the Christian sects more commonly known in the West. Christian sects are from more modern roots and are outsiders split by more recent doctrinal and practical differences, while the Shia are outsiders who have been in existence from the beginning and see themselves as the continuation of Islam from the Prophet. This point illustrates the inadequacy of sociology in treating the subject. The theology is important, but the Shia problem is due in part to the differences over the historical sources of their faith and partly in the religious discrimination that has excluded Shias politically and socially from more secular concerns, such as the distributive benefits of the oil. This gives the Shias a different outlook to their Sunni counterparts, apart from resentments toward Saudi hierarchy. As they feel related to transnational themes, such as the influence of Iran and the plight of Shias elsewhere. Little wonder that Matthiesen calls them the "Other Saudis."

An Evolving Theocracy

The external attack is that Saudi is not a democracy, and the Shia and others, especially women, are excluded from participation despite having some made small steps toward representation in the Shura Council. The system of royal power, religious constitution and lack of democracy make Islam generally and Saudi Arabia specifically appear to the West as a nation needing to be enlightened in the same way. It also appears to critics that neither Islam nor Saudi has produced a political theory of any real sophistication. As Ali Alawi, former Defense and Finance Minister in the Iraqi postwar governments, explains:

> Of course, what all these critics really mean is that Islam has not produced a political theory or practice that fits with the western liberal democratic tradition. While this may be literally true, the conclusion that Islam has not produced a logically consistent and relevant political theory is patently false.[14]

This is not to say nothing changes or the Saudis are stubbornly clinging to the past. Especially under King Abdullah and King Salman, Saudi has been going through a process of gradual change and development which cannot be ignored. As Abdullah F. Ansary explains:

> The process of change and development in Saudi Arabia has affected the country both socially and politically. The political reforms of the 1990s indicated that progressive changes were being officially promoted in the Kingdom of Saudi Arabia, which has opened the door to more participatory values in areas such as shared decision-making and checks and balances. The recent leadership transition occurred smoothly, which is viewed as a sign of stability in the Kingdom. The constitutional evolution indicates that the Kingdom will continue to flourish, as it has since the founding of the modern State. It is evident from the characteristics of this progressive evolution that the recent reforms in the Saudi constitutional system will not be the last but, on the contrary, will be followed by other developments as and when the need arises.[15]

This gradual change may not be fast enough for many women and the Saudi youth, and it is far from the pace demanded by international critics. The main problem is religion, but the discourse, as noted, has been less nuanced about religion than needs to be the case if there is to be change. There has been a popular narrative in the West that Islam needs a reformation, but as Ali Allawi puts it "On closer inspection, however, the utility of the analogy falls apart; the parallels are absurd." To frame the question in terms of reformation is to show both an ignorance of Christianity and Islam, and in fact what critics really mean is that Islam should be neutered in much the same way as Christian conservatives believe Christianity has been. Sharia law has already been subjugated or abandoned in most Islamic states, apart most notably from Saudi Arabia and Iran. The Christian reformation was an institutional rebellion focused on a theological question of indulgences and an ecclesiological question of power. Martin Luther did not seek to schism the church indeed he wrote perhaps naively to address the pope in the expectation that the practice of indulgences would cease. This religious revolt was usurped by the secular as royalties sought to use religion to gain political power and independence from the church. It was enlightenment thinking that drove forward the theological and structural changes in a renaissance of the humanities, and the queen of sciences became increasingly sidelined. Islam never had such a structure or a papacy in need of reform. The lack of organization is what has made it more disparate, as in many cases an Imam is a popular or respected person in the community without a truly in-depth training, having perhaps read and memorized the verses of the Koran but not versed in the way Christian clergy have been traditionally.

The basic fallacy in the call to a reformation is that it has already happened. The development of Wahhabism was a religious reformation, which the 1979 occupation of the holy site at Mecca led to a reassertion of conservative Wahhabi clerical influence in Saudi, to stem the modernization being advanced by the royal rulers. This drove global efforts to promote Wahhabi Islam, and an ideological buttressing against Shia Islam and for the Afghan resistance movement. What had been a minority interest in Islam had now become a dominant ideology in one of the largest and richest Islamic states, raising both its status and influence, and in turn overshadowing other more classical schools of Islam and giving rise perhaps to a mistaken perception in the West that there is a monolithic Islam. The oil gave an economic underpinning to this reformation, if that is what it can be called, thus we find in Saudi a theocratic state and not a democracy. The Saudi state is, in the phrase *al-islam din wa dawla*, a belief that Islam is both religion and state. This is why it can be defined as an Islamic state, one that is political and theocratic. Saudi styles itself an Islamic state, as does Iran, but the two nations are quite different in many ways, with the most distinct division being between the Sunni and

Shia forms of Islam. Saudi, of course, holds a preeminent position as custodian of the two holy sites, giving it a distinct self-understanding and image to the outside world. The distinctive way in which Saudi is an Islamic state is its role in promoting the welfare of believer-citizens. From the beginning with King ʿAbd al-ʿAzīz there has been a strong presence of paternalism creating a quite different social contract and welfare state from that borne out of the European renaissance.

The geopolitical, theological and historical problems of Islam and Arab culture can be approached in many ways, and can fill library shelves many times over, and they do. It is important, however, to offer some definition around these terms. One term to be cautious with is Pan-Islamism. While the Saudi experience is different historically from its Arab neighbors, it does share a central idea in the Arab world, an idea that crosses boundaries and creates a shared set of interests and relationships. The historical pan-Arab concerns have been replaced to an extent by a concern for the objective of pan-Islam, which is a global and not a regional phenomenon. Thus, for instance, in conversation with young Saudis I have found them more moved by concern for faithful Muslims on the other side of the globe more than they are for secular Arabs geographically closer to them. As a result of Pan-Islamism, we need to explore cultural nuances, and this means we need to understand Arab and Islamic identity. Raymond Hinnebusch introduced the helpful notion of "identity incongruence,"[16] which defines the incongruence between identity and territory. In the Arab world the draw of Islamic identity takes us beyond the national boundaries, but it also suggests we have to look more closely at what the national boundaries are in the first place, given that they were drawn up somewhat arbitrarily by colonial and American powers and by committee. Saudi's experience of drawing boundaries is again different from most of its Arab neighbors. We ought to consider how they defined their territory, it is defined as the Arab peninsula by the words of Mohammed. Because pan-Arabism has been in decline as an ideology in the region, replaced with political Islam, more attention needs to be paid to how Saudi, along with Iran, represents the most highly defined state approaches to an Islamic society. This is not just about Sunni against Shia, it is also about leadership in pan-Islam. Familism is another critically important definition in understanding Saudi identity. The role of prominent families has already been raised, and deserves a framing note here as well. Saudi was formed by founder King ʿAbd al-ʿAzīz in a similar way to how Mohammad first brought Islam together, through uniting families or tribes by agreement, preferably, or violence, lamentably. The family network in Saudi is rooted in the monarchy and reaches all parts of the society. This network maintains social cohesion and stability in the Kingdom and provides a means of communication that ensures a level of consensus. It is the network that sustains the Kingdom, and any attempt to assess the future will have to understand how the families will react to events, either in concert with the house of Saud or in opposition to it.

Recent years have seen Western liberal democracies witnessing an eruption of identity politics related to nationalism, religion, gender, sexuality and specific political causes such as environmentalism and "conservatives versus liberals." Movements like Occupy Wall Street and Black Lives Matter have manufactured new levels of dissent. Brexit and the 2016 American presidential election raised questions about identity and immigration, with the former leading to a redrawing of the European map. In this ever-changing picture, we also need to consider the role of protest and dissent in relation to Saudi, itself a target of some of these political causes. The so-called Arab Spring in 2011 was a seemingly momentous time where people across the Arab world appeared to oppose the existing regimes and demand a political change, a cry for democracy. The problem is there was little sense of what they wanted in its place, and in contrast to the Western expectations they certainly did not want Western-style democracy. They didn't get it either. Saudi experienced little disturbance from these events, it was more of a Spring day out, dramatized as a "Day of Rage," and religious authorities had already effectively spiked it by stating it was forbidden to protest. On March 11, a document authored by Shia intellectuals was presented to King Abdullah, with a number of points outlined relating to civil rights and imprisonment of Shias in Saudi. The day saw several dozen arrests from a crowd of 800 protesters, hardly the stuff of frenzied 24/7 television coverage. The other outcome which made the Day of Rage one largely of quietude was a package of stimulus measures announced by the king, amounting to $66.7 billion for jobs, housing and medical facilities. Much of the Arab world reverted essentially to a status quo, and certainly in Saudi there was barely a ripple of effect to be felt or reported. Likewise the drive to recognize gender rights, which has sparked a handful of protest against driving and women removing the hijab, but we are not about to see Saudi women baring their breasts in protest any time soon.[17]

The Salman Rushdie affair perhaps did more than anything to raise the profile of Islamic protest in the West and brought the *fatwa* onto the cultural and political landscape. Discussion of Islamic law and *Sharia* courts has long since become common fare at the best of dinner parties and on television chat shows. I discussed the affair in a book review:

> The author Salman Rushdie, famously sent into hiding due to a fatwa, once quipped 'No, I don't think it's fair to label Islam "violent." But I will say that to my knowledge, no writer has ever gone into hiding for criticizing the Amish.' Rushdie's comment is another iteration of the long-running boundary dispute between religion and state and it is easy to think of Rushdie as the poster child for religious toleration before 9/11; but equally, could his statement imply that the Amish are simply being good American Lockeans, faithful to the founding fathers' sense of Lockean toleration?[18]

To the key point, there is a difference in legal philosophy, Muslims and Saudis are not Lockeans. The difference in legal approach is critical to understanding the difference between Islamic societies and liberal democracies, and it is important to note that religious law and theology in Islam is quite different from the understanding of law and theology in the Amish tradition, or indeed Christianity. For Muslims, Islamic law is central to interpreting society and welfare and we should be careful that we do not see religion simply as instrumental to, or in the service of, politics and the welfare of society. In Saudi the Islamic religion and law is in the DNA of the culture, not dissimilar to the role Christianity had in the past in Europe, but with a distinctive difference. Christianity has a long tradition of being divided between private and public. There are those who see faith as ultimately individual and private, seen most starkly in the quietism of the Lutheran Church in Nazi Germany. There are then those who promote a more public and political role for the faith, a prime example being Liberation theology. Most of the time the churches and faithful manage a mixture of the two views in a complex way. Martin Luther's "two kingdoms" theology is one attempt that has been made to distinguish the sense of boundaries, though it is often misunderstood and misinterpreted. It is an often-thought view that Luther was arguing for two separate kingdoms, and never the twain should meet. Luther's thought was more complex. The fundamental idea is that we have a left- and right-handed kingdom, the kingdom of the world and the kingdom of God. The latter is ruled by divine law alone, while the former is ruled by human or natural law ultimately derived from God but in the hands of humanity. The law, as Paul wrote, was not laid down for the just. The natural law discernible by our everyday human law is a necessary evil, because of the fallen nature of humanity.

The question is more settled in Islam, but it is also framed differently. Islam has always regarded the two kingdoms, if we can use such a term, as being a whole. Islam asserts that the Islamic religion applies to the society as a whole, and also the person as a whole. Sura al-Maidah 5.3 states "This day those who disbelieve have despaired of [defeating] your religion; so fear them not, but fear me. This day I have perfected for you your religion and completed my favor upon you and have approved for you Islam as religion." The word "religion" here does not convey the original Arabic *Din*, which means the whole code that governs the whole life of the individual, and cannot be defeated by the disbelievers. In a secular context such an holistic explanation is jarring to the ear, but it takes us to the heart of the problem Islam faces. Christian societies have become more secular since the Renaissance, and the religion more subjugated if not regarded as largely irrelevant, resulting in the evolution of a liberal faith. Islam has not had to face a triumphal liberalism or a fully secular society, except for those Muslims who lived in such Christian societies. The talk of a reformation for Islam springs from this historical change in Christianity, suggesting that Islam likewise needs to go through the same evolution, requiring in short order that Islam conform to the liberal Western agenda. We will return to this discussion later, suffice to note at this stage that Islam places holistic demands on the individual and the society, with society embracing individuals rather than individuals contesting what a good society should be for them. The model of society is different to liberal democracy, and as a result how we are to understand its approach to the welfare of individuals and society is also different. In respect to Saudi Arabia, to delve into understanding this difference requires us to consider what I call the "Saudi mind."

There has long been a tradition of speaking about the "American mind," sometimes distilled to a mixture of Calvinist and Lockean philosophy. We can undertake a similar quest by examining the "Saudi mind." This is quite a different discussion from that which erupted from the publication of the Arab Mind, which tried to integrate a set of behaviors that are far too diverse to be shoehorned into a single description. The "American Mind" involves focusing primarily on the *idea* of America. The American historian Richard Hofstadter noted "It has been our fate as a nation, not to have ideologies but to be one."[19] What Madeleine Albright called the "indispensable nation"[20] has found its relationship with Saudi indispensable over years, and it has been both a pragmatic and ideological relationship, with a pragmatism that has worked both ways in a meeting of minds. If we try to discern the "Saudi Mind" we will need to take a different tact. The Saudi mind is more about religion, community, personality and behavior than ideas. There is a high level of pride in their Arab and family identity, more than in terms of power and money in Saudi society. The sense of *Inshallah* can give the appearance of a certain degree of fatalism among Saudis, but it is more of a sense of reliance on God, since it means if God wills it, otherwise nothing happens. Saudis are very relationship-based, get that wrong and you get the whole deal wrong. Saudis highly value trust, and they believe where there is trust then there is relationship, but once you lose that trust you lose the relationship forever. Hence, the Western attention to problem-solving is of less interest than the need to keep the relationship, and not "lose face." Problems tend to be addressed in relation to specific contexts, rather than being multi-dimensional as in Western problem-solving. Behavior is thus less-compartmentalized than in Western society. Hence, there is a lot of personal behavior expressed in the business context. A business conversation is thus interspersed by much personal discussion and silence, both of which may be regarded as disruptive to the more defined, and arguably impatient, engagement in a Western context.

While a great deal of commentary on Saudi and the United States has tended to focus on the oil, the relationship is so much more than that, and because the focus has been on oil, much has been missed and hence there has been a failure in some policy quarters to come to terms with the Saudi mindset. To understand truly the mindset we have to start with the fact that Saudi is Islamic, and this drives its choices. So yes, oil was a major factor, but so too has been the joint ideological opposition during the Cold War to the Soviet Union and Communism. While much of the Arab world, dealing with the aftermath of European colonialism, took secular socialism as the basis for asserting Arab nationalism and economic independence, Saudi had a quite difference experience. The colonial relationship was different for Saudi, and socialism did not appeal to Saudis in the same way. Equally, claiming the custodianship of the two holy sites of Islam gave Saudi a strong religious identity that put it in natural opposition to what they saw, in line with the Americans, as godless communism and opposition to God's law. This relationship certainly worked well for the Americans, but across the Arab world, there was a shockwave that brought religion to the fore in 1979, which gave rise to what everyone was calling "Islamic fundamentalism," indicating a certain mindset that is religiously simplistic in the extreme, and used in Western commentary as an inadequate heuristic to interpret Saudi and Islamic behaviors.

Notes

1. Morgenthau (1954, p. 10), "Realism maintains that universal moral principles cannot be applied to the actions of states in their abstract universal formulation." In Williams (2008), Anthony F. Lang, Jr., writes "Realists are either amoral analysts of the international system who focus only on power or immoral Machiavellians who see nothing wrong with using violence and deception to advance the national interest." p. 18, explaining at least this is the caricature.
2. Morgenthau (1954, p. 11).
3. Ramadan (2012, p. 15).
4. Hopkins and Ibrahimed (1998) and Gause III (1994).
5. "Social solidarity with an emphasis on group consciousness, cohesiveness, and unity. Familiar in the pre-Islamic era, the term became popularized in Ibn Khaldun 's (d. 1406) Muqaddimah. Asabiyyah is neither necessarily nomadic nor based on blood relations. In the modern period, the term is analogous to solidarity." Oxford Islamic Studies Online, http://www.oxfordislamicstudies.com/article/opr/t125/e202

6. Hourani (2002, p. 107).
7. Ibid, p. 453.
8. The secularization thesis argued that modernity and progress would make society free of religion. Building on the work of Max Weber, the thesis was chiefly advanced by sociologists Bryan Wilson (1966) and Peter Berger (1973). We have to question whether secularization is a case of excluding religion altogether or making religion independent, and thus all religions being equal in a secular society; while this is an intriguing question, it lies beyond the scope of this chapter.
9. The same might be argued in the Christian context. There is not room here to discuss this, but I have looked at some of these conflicts in Cowan (2009).
10. Black (2001, p. 5).
11. See Allawai (2009, p. 122ff.). A website exists for the Amman Message http://ammanmessage.com/
12. Ibid, p. 122.
13. Matthiesen (2015, p. 10).
14. Allawai (2009, p. 160).
15. Update: A Brief Overview of the Saudi Arabian Legal System, *Dr. Abdullah F. Ansary* http://www.nyulawglobal.org/globalex/Saudi_Arabia1.html
16. Hinnebusch (2003, pp. 54–72).
17. In the West, two Femen protesters disrupted a conference in Paris, with the activists, aged 25 and 31, ripping off their Arab-style cloaks and jumped on to the stage on Saturday evening. One had the slogan "No one subjugates me" inked across her torso. The other bore the words "I am my own prophet." The point is referenced not to trivialize feminist protest, but to highlight such protests generally aim to shock the morals and religion and in Saudi any protest is more likely to confirm to the religion rather than reject some basic precepts, such as modesty, that is subject to debates of degree rather than the binary protests so common in the West. http://www.telegraph.co.uk/news/worldnews/europe/france/11862220/Topless-protesters-disrupt-Muslim-conference-on-women.html
18. http://jts.oxfordjournals.org/content/early/2013/07/12/jts.flt081. As an aside, the Rushdie quote was subsequently tweeted as a meme, prompting him to tweet "I don't believe I ever said that. But it's funny...."
19. Lynch and Singh (2008, p. 25).
20. Lynch and Singh (2008, p. 53).

Bibliography

al-Rasheed, Madawi, ed. 2008. *Kingdom Without Borders: Saudi Arabia's Political, Religious and Media Frontiers*. London: Hurst.

Allawai, Ali A. 2009. *The Crisis of Islamic Civilization*. New Haven: Yale University Press.

Barber, Benjamin R. 2001. *Jihad vs McWorld: Terrorism's Challenge to Democracy*. New York: Ballantine Books.

Berger, Peter. 1973. *The Social Reality of Religion*. Middlesex: Penguin.

Black, Antony. 2001. *The History of Islamic Political Thought: From the Prophet to the Present*. Edinburgh: Edinburgh University Press.

Bowering, Gerhard, ed. 2015. *Islamic Political Thought: An Introduction*. Princeton: Princeton University Press.

Champion, Daryl. 2003. *The Paradoxical Kingdom: Saudi Arabia and the Momentum of Reform*. London: Hurst and Company.

Cowan, David. 2009. *Economic Parables: The Monetary Teachings of Jesus Christ*. 2nd ed. Downers Grove: IVP.

Craze, Jonathan, and Mark Huband. 2009. *The Kingdom: Saudi Arabia and the Challenge of the 21st Century*. London: Hurst & Co.

Cunningham, Robert B., and Yasin K. Sarayrah. 1993. *Wasta: The Hidden Force in Middle Eastern Society*. Westport: Praeger.

Esposito, John L. 2002. *Unholy War: Terror in the Name of Islam*. New York: Oxford University Press.

Fawcett, Louise. 2016. *International Relations of the Middle East*. 4th ed. Oxford: Oxford University Press.

Gause, F. Gregory, III. 1994. *Oil Monarchies: Domestic and Security Challenges in the Arab Gulf States*. New York: Council on Foreign Relations.

Halliday, Fred. 2000. *Nation and Religion in the Middle East*. Boulder: Lynne Rienner Publishers.

Hamid, Shadi. 2016. *Islamic Exceptionalism: How the Struggle Over Islam Is Reshaping the World*. New York: St. Martin's Press.

Haykel, Bernard, Thomas Hegghammer, and Stéphane Lacroix. 2015. *Saudi Arabia in Transition: Insights on Social, Political, Economic and Religious Change*. Cambridge: Cambridge University Press.

Hegghammer, Thomas. 2010. *Jihad in Saudi Arabia: Violence and Pan-Islamism since 1979*. New York: Cambridge University Press.

Hinnebusch, Raymond. 2003. *The International Politics of the Middle East*. Manchester: Manchester University Press.

Hopkins, Nicholas S., and Saad Eddin Ibrahimed, eds. 1998. *Arab Society: Class, Gender, Power & Development*. Cairo: The American University in Cairo Press.

Hourani, Albert. 2002. *A History of the Arab Peoples*. Cambridge, MA: Belknap Press.

House, Karen Elliott. 2012. *On Saudi Arabia: Its People, Past, Religion, Fault Lines – And Future*. New York: Vintage Books.

Karsh, Effraim. 2006. *Islamic Imperialism: A History*. New Haven: Yale University Press.

Kepel, Gilles. 2004. *The War for Muslim Minds: Islam and the West*. Trans. Pascal Ghazaleh. Cambridge, MA: Belknap Press.

Kerr, Malcolm. 1965. *The Arab Cold War, 1958–1964: A Study of Ideology in Politics*. Oxford: Oxford University Press.

Khaldun, Ibn. 1967. *The Muqaddimah: An Introduction to History*. Princeton: Princeton University Press.

Lacey, Robert. 2009. *Inside the Kingdom: Kings, Clerics, Terrorists, Modernists, and the Struggle for Saudi Arabia*. New York: Viking.

Lewis, Bernard. 2002. *The Arabs in History*. New York: Oxford University Press.

Lippman, Thomas W. 2012. *Saudi Arabia on the Edge: The Uncertain Future of an American Ally*. Dulles: Potomac Books.

Luciani, Giacomo, ed. 1990. *The Arab State*. Berkeley: University of California Press.

Lynch, Timothy J., and Robert S. Singh. 2008. *After Bush: The Case for Continuity in American Foreign Policy*. Cambridge: Cambridge University Press.

Mabon, Simon. 2016. *Saudi Arabia and Iran: Power and Rivalry in the Middle East*. New York: I.B. Tauris.

Mansfield, Peter. 1985. *The Arabs*. London: Penguin Books.

Matthiesen, Toby. 2015. *The Other Saudis: Shiism, Dissent and Sectarianism*. New York: Cambridge University Press.

Miller, David Aaron. 1980. *Search for Security: Saudi Arabian Oil and American Foreign Policy*. Chapel Hill: University of North Carolina Press.

Morgenthau, Hans J. 1954. *Politics Among Nations: The Struggle for Power and Peace*. 2nd ed. New York: Alfred A. Knopf.

Nasr, Vali. 2009. *The Rise of Islamic Capitalism: Why the New Muslim Middle Class Is the Key to Defeating Extremism*. New York: Free Press.

Ramadan, Tariq. 2012. *Islam and the Arab Awakening*. New York: Oxford University Press.

Raphael, Patai. 1973. *The Arab Mind*. New York: Scribner.

Said, Edward W. 1979. *Orientalism*. Princeton: Princeton University Press.

————. 1981. *Covering Islam: How the Media and the Experts Determine How We See the Rest of the World.* New York: Pantheon Books.

Salame, Ghassan, ed. 1994. *Democracy Without Democrats? The Renewal of Politics in the Muslim World.* London: I.B. Tauris.

Shabbir, Akhtar. 1985. In *Philosophy Bridging the World Religions,* ed. P. Koslowski. Dordrecht: Kluwer.

Vitalis, Robert. 2009. *America's Kingdom: Mythmaking on the Saudi Oil Frontier.* London: Verso.

Williams, Michael C. 2008. *Realism Reconsidered: The Legacy of Hans J. Morgenthau in International Relations.* Oxford: Oxford University Press.

Wilson, Bryan. 1966. *Religion in a Secular Society.* London: Watts.

9

Fideism I

When Islam came to prominence due to the Iranian revolution, the term that was used then and for much of the following years was "fundamentalism." The terminological difficulties critics and commenters face have led to the explosion of terms mentioned and seem to have rendered the term fundamentalist almost a quaint artifact of recent political debate. The term is still used, especially in polemics, and Salafism and Wahhabism are usually condensed into the broader term of fundamentalism in an attempt to narrow the understanding of Islamism, which in turn reduces the understanding of diversity and dissonance in the Islamic world. Fundamentalism is a problematic term that originated in early twentieth-century American Christianity. The term was derived from the major work at the heart of American fundamentalism, a multi-volume set of some 100 essays in 12 volumes published from 1910 to 1915 called "The Fundamentals" authored by leading scholars at the time, including James Orr, Charles Erdman, H.C.G. Moule and Bishop Ryle. The roots go deeper into the late nineteenth century, with the building opposition to an emerging liberal theology and the new higher biblical criticism; though "higher than what?" Canon Dyson Hague, one of the authors, asked. Matters came to an historical nexus during the 1925 Scopes Monkey

© The Author(s) 2018
D. Cowan, *The Coming Economic Implosion of Saudi Arabia*,
https://doi.org/10.1007/978-3-319-74709-5_9

Trial in Dayton, Tennessee, when conservative evangelical Christians became labeled as fundamentalists and derided as anti-scientific and set against the modern world. The fundamentalists won the trial battle, maintaining a legal ban on teaching of evolution in schools, but lost the public opinion war. Chided by the experience, fundamentalists retreated from the public square, and remained apart from it until the 1980s, when Jerry Falwell, a fundamentalist who broadened the message, created the Moral Majority.[1]

Ernest Sandeen explains the situation in which "fundamentalists" found themselves:

> Fundamentalism lives in symbiotic relationship with other forms of religion and with cultural trends, leading the Fundamentalist, paradoxically, to affirm both his despair over the world and his identification with much of the world's culture. He has resolved this tension through the creation of innumerable parallel institutions which, though completely Fundamentalist, affirm essentially worldly values. Fundamentalism represents a relatively rare example of an authentic conservative tradition in American history.[2]

There are elements in common with American conservatism, but while historical memory is important to conservatism and certain periods are highlighted, they are not merely selective as Sandeen argues. Besides this objection, it might be said that all political debates operate on the basis of selective memory, and all movements are built from grass roots, from Marxist base communities to Falwell's Moral Majority. Certainly fundamentalists have articulated their case well, but this is not on the basis of slick spin but on the basis of fundamental beliefs and an attendant fideism, which does give it a confidence that seems to thrive from age to age. This is the group that formed the major part of those who stayed out of the public square in the wake of the Scopes trial and who became resistant to any political drift leftward.

It is not within the remit of this book to go deeper into the fundamentalism of American Christianity, the aim has been to offer some insight to the term that emerged in response to the reemergence of Islam in Western discourse. Intellectuals scrabbled around in their somewhat religiously bare intellectual tool bags to find a way to address the emergence of Islam in contradiction to the Weberian secularization thesis and the sensitivities of Western modernity. This has overshadowed much academic discussion of Islam and modernity, but worse still it has muddied the waters of popular discourse as people uncritically accepted the "fundamentalist" naming, without understanding the roots of that term and the forces the word was being applied to in any meaningful or engaging way. One may consider that the rise of fundamentalism, if that is what it is, came as far as it did as much as a result of its opponents' assault as it did from the activists promoting certain Islamic ideals. As Shaykh Muhammad Husayn Fadlallah writes:

> We Islamists are not fundamentalist in the way Westerners see us. We refuse to be called fundamentalists. We are Islamic activists. As for the etymological sense of *usuliyya* meaning returning to one's roots and origins [*usul*], our roots are the Qur'an and the true *sunna* of the Prophet, not the historical period in which the Prophet lived or the periods that followed – we are not fundamentalists [*usuliyyin*]in the sense of wanting to live like people at the time of the Prophet or the first Caliphs or the time of the Umayyads.

In the face of Western liberalism and secularism, for many Muslims this activism held up a mirror to our age and offered an appealing vision. The inadequate dismissal of this Islamic activism through intellectual laziness and ignorance of religion may well have contributed to the appeal to many Muslims, and certainly did little to help in the dialogue between a newly confident Islam and a postmodern Western discourse. The irony being that Western liberalism was performing intellectual summersaults to celebrate cultural diversity and understanding, but failed to recognize the most powerful of alternative cultures, perhaps because this culture did not look like the multiculturalism that liberalism had fallen in love with. The liberalism that sneered at colonial naming of "aborigines" or "red Indians" as an imposition of Western power on indigenous peoples was simply doing the same, by imposing on Muslims their own, hopelessly inadequate, terminology to name a culture intellectually foreign to them. The same argument can be made about the term "conservative" in Islam, which again is a Western assessment of a certain approach.

Other terms have emerged as Western liberalism has sought to come to terms with this religious force: Islamism, radical Islam, Islamofascism, Jihadism, Islamic terrorism, political Islam, the list seems to grow. The terminological confusion is significant. Both the average Saudi and religious leader would simply call it Islam, and suggest many of these manifestations are not real Islam. Advancing the term "Islamism" as perhaps the best of an inadequate bunch, Roxanne Euben offers a useful approach, that given this disagreement over terminology:

> …it is particularly useful to approach Islamism as an interpretative framework rather than a set of propositions and strategies to which every Islamist subscribes in the same way or to the same degree. Understood as an interpretative framework, Islamism does not simply reflect or obscure a set of material conditions and socioeconomic grievances but instead constitutes a lens on the world that determines how and in what terms such conditions and constraints are understood. Such an approach enables observers to attend to the differences and diversity of what travels under the rubric of "Islamism" without losing sight of it as a complex system of representation that articulates and defines a range of identities, categories, and norms; organizes human experience into narratives that assemble past, present, and future into a compelling interpretive frame; and specifies the range and meaning of acceptable and desirable practices. In short, this approach makes it possible to define Islamism without essentializing or instrumentalizing it.[3]

For Euben, the term Islamism captures something in the Islamic world that goes back to the 1920s and has changed and evolved over time, mixed with other variables. Islamism is thus a group of believers, thinkers and groups seeking to regain the foundations of Islam and reinterpret them for the modern world and restore a normative Islam in the present. Euben usefully notes Islamists have a diagnosis and cure response, so we can see the diagnosis is secularization and corruption of the truth, and the cure is a recovered Islam for a people they see who have rejected the normative Islam. Euben notes:

> As Islamist exhortations to change collective life require words and deeds, they may be further defined not only as political but also as activist, thus

distinguishing them from the quietism characteristic of some Saudi Salafis, whose acquiescence to established power is no less political than Islamist intransigence.[4]

The difficulty, and Euben does highlight this, is that the Islamist seeks to speak for God and becomes political in defining how people should respond to their assertion of God, to the point of stating who is in and who is out. Indeed, the same holds true for other movements, including Christian groups. This is a common response, and generally leads us to liberal arguments about tolerance and a postmodern acceptance of difference, which from the Islamist point of view is itself a fundamentalism. This is where we have to take an extra step that is all too often avoided, and that is to see that from within the faith system, whether it is Islam, Christianity or anything else. Islam believes that what was conveyed to the Prophet and the world is revelation and an exhortation to live according to God's path. Having embraced this revelation and submitted to this path then one immediately deems all else to be at best wrong and at worse profane. From such a view the liberal approach is simply disingenuous and misleading.

It seems the real struggle people are having is not so much "political Islam" but "violent Islam," especially in the West because it has been visiting them, and we do need to come to terms with this. Patricia Crone rightly points out a problem in looking at the foundations, which we can put in the context of the fundamentals of faith by contrasting Jesus and Muhammad:

To the Christians, jihad has always been a stumbling block. Jesus did not use force to establish, or even to defend, himself but rather died as the victim of coercive power; the early Christians also preferred martyrdom to the use of arms. By contrast, Muhammad waged war to establish his message and died as the leader of a polity. Whereupon his followers set out to conquer the world.[5]

In the context of discussing these Christian terms of "fundamentalism" and "reformation," if we take the reformation cry *ad fontes*! then it is easy to see where it leads to violence, and so it becomes hardly surprising that one element of Islamism is the use of force. Christians have used violence, but they can never go back to Jesus and see any justification for that violence, not so Muhammad. The reformation was an attempt to recover the original Christianity and to return to biblical authority, so by parallel we can see that Islam has already been undergoing a reformation. What people really mean is they want to see a renaissance effect, whereby Islam can copy Christianity and be absorbed by the humanities and liberalism, which in the eyes of conservatives and evangelicals allowed theology and biblical authority to be usurped by human critical thinking and will. Islamic fundamentalism is often treated as a recent aspect of Islam as if it appeared in 1979 or on 9/11, whereas it has been an emerging force over a period of decades. The roots, however, run historically deeper, because there has long been debate over the nature of prophecy and revelation in Islam, and the role of reason, which has been contested by Wahhabi and Salafi groups for a very long time.

A Threat to Saudi Religious Life?

In the wake of 9/11, Samuel Huntingdon's thesis of a clash of civilizations came into vogue, along with Francis Fukuyama's "end of history." Both books heralded the end of the last millennium in the most dramatic terms. Huntingdon discussed a clash of religions as the problem, pointing to the rise of Islam with its opposition to the individualism and perceived arrogance of Western civilization. He argued that Muslims viewed Western secularism to be more problematic and concerning than the Christianity of the West. While Cold War America had seen itself in conflict with godless communism, Muslims came to see themselves in conflict with "the godless West." However, to understand whether we have a clash of civilizations or religions, we have to go deeper into understanding the religion than the often superficial sociological treatments of Huntingdon and others who are getting hysterical about Islam, starting with definitions. As in so many matters, the nomenclature of Saudi's form of Islam presents us with some challenges. At its broadest it is Sunni, and there was much self-congratulation in foreign policy circles when people started to talk about the binary dissection of Islam as Sunni and

Shia, rather than a monolithic Islam, as if it were job done and terminology mastered. This is not enough. The majority rule in Saudi is indeed Sunni, though with a Shia minority chiefly in the Eastern Province and a significant, if limited, number of Shia individuals in senior positions in government and industry, but still few and far between. As familiarity grew with the challenges posed by the emergence of Islam in geopolitics, experts found themselves able to talk about Saudi's Wahhabism, due to its links to the doctrines of Muhammad ibn 'Abd al-Wahhab. More recently, like tourists shifting for a more exclusive deal, the commentary has moved on to referencing the Salafi school. The more deeply diving analysis of Islam in Saudi will thus discuss a conservative strain of Sunni-Wahhabi-Salafi Islam in the Kingdom.[6]

Saudi's Islam has occasionally been contested, though the dominance of the house of Saud has kept disruption to a minimum. This is because opposition to the house of Saud has essentially been on religious grounds, not political ones, with allegations made that it deviated from the true Islamic path. There were opposing parties which challenged al Saud and the religious establishment in September 1965, when a small group led by Prince Khalid Ibn Mus'ad Ibn Abd al-Aziz attacked the newly erected television studio in Riyadh. Again, in November 1979 an opposition group led by Juhayman al-Utaybi captured the Grand Mosque in Mecca and held it for a number of weeks. Further opposition movements erupted in the 1980s and the 1990s, comprising many young middle-class urbanites who feared that Western culture and technology would undermine the Saudi Islamic culture. Public protests in 1991 and in 1992 included demands for religious reforms, social justice, legal equality and an end to government corruption. The protests ended with many protesters losing their freedom or committing suicide.[7] The government and Saudi scholars promoted arguments to demonstrate that the Kingdom was ruled according to the strictest Islamic principles, which included public participation and social justice. However, Helen Lackner argues this is an instrumental use of religion:

> the Al Saud have good reason to retain Wahhabism as the base of their political control as it prevents the development of independent thinking, dangerous to their rule, and has given them the opportunity to develop

their ascendancy in the Muslim world. Here Wahhabism has been the product, and financial power the means.[8]

This religious dimension is a problem for many Western analysts, because for many a decade social scientists in particular have been trained to ignore and privatize religion. Even if they analyze what they see as a theocracy, they have treated religion at best sociologically rather than theologically or in any deep cultural sense. For this reason, we end with conversations and recommendations that do not fully grasp the reality of what is truly happening. If we are to understand Islam fully we have to understand it from within its own hermeneutical circle, seeing how believers understand Islam and act upon this belief. History has not helped us in this respect, and equally our Western hermeneutic tools are to be used with great care. Tearing down the edifice of biblical literalism and a conservative hermeneutic in Christianity took decades and it is still ongoing, but it is a different task from understanding the Koran and Islamic ideas in our contemporary context. On the other hand, we cannot be idealist about this and assume the faithful in Islam are all terribly religious. Just as people in England used to say they were "CofE," so too many Arabs are Muslim but they don't necessarily follow the faith closely. They may go on Hajj for the experience, community respect or any number of reasons, but it is akin to the many people in England who attend church on Christmas Eve, though the latter requires considerably less effort. Religious identity is complex and multi-faceted, and it goes deep into the life of the individual and the nation.

However, from the earliest form of Islam, there have been apologetical attacks in the Western tradition made on Islam and the Koran. Where the Christian saw a tradition building on Judaism, Islam saw a tradition building on Judaism and Christianity. In religious identity disputes, including exclusive claims to God, each has rejected the others in making a supreme claim. Christianity is pivotal in the sense that it sees a new covenant in Israel while rejecting Islamic claims, whereas Islam claims a change in relationship between humanity and God by, in part, limiting the truth claims of the two older religions. In short, the discourse has often taken place in terms of exclusivity and rejection while limiting the claims of those outside of the religion. In even shorter terms, they have been in contest and competition. In recent decades both scholarship and faith groups have sought to find common understanding and shared discourse to address this contest. In parallel, faith groups have also sought to triumph their truth claims, ranging from attempts to proselytize through to converting people forcibly. In the *polis*, faith groups have sought to impose their moral vision, again ranging from being special interests through to attempts to "reclaim" what they see as a faithful nation. Many historical assessments have set out Judaism, Christianity and Islam as a one, two, three step process. It is not quite understood in this way by adherents, who see the history of the world as His-Story, in other words God's story, and traditionally this has been hailed in male terms.

While the economy may be argued to be a reasonably neutral space or *topos* allowing people with different interests, beliefs, values, backgrounds, identities and so on to engage with each other for material purposes, religion does not create such a neutral space or *topos*. Unlike the market, religion trades in truth claims and asserts the truth of one religion over all other forms of knowledge, because God is to be placed above all else. Within faiths there are people who do not make such assertions, but for the most part, this is of little consequence in dealing with the reality of a religion in the world today. Though such "liberal" believers may well influence the future and even control some religious institutions today, they don't really impact the problem we face in this study. For our purposes, we know that Saudi is Islamically conservative, and the question we have to confront is whether Saudi will succumb to a form of radical Islam, or whether it will through economic and political change become a renewed Islamic state, by which I do not mean 'Islamic State' or any permutation of this group. From the Iranian perspective, and in a negative sense, Saudi has already reformed or renewed because it has become American Islam. In this book, I will examine whether what Saudi may need is more, not less, Islam.

The economic problems Saudi is facing if not effectively dealt with will be the catalyst for setting off many political and religious challenges that lie ahead. Already the economic problems are causing a questioning of the underlying economic philosophy of Saudi, and questions are asked as to what Saudis needs to do to have a global mindset or to choose a Saudi route through the problems the Kingdom faces. To understand fully the complexity of the economic problem in Saudi it is essential to put religion at the heart of economic discussion, not simply as an aside or afterthought. Which is exactly where the Kingdom itself places religion. Saudi's constitution is unwritten, but clear in defining the basis of the Kingdom and its economy with the "Basic Law of Governance"[9] setting out the legal basis of the Kingdom, stating in Article 1:

> The Kingdom of Saudi Arabia is a sovereign Arab Islamic State. Its religion is Islam. Its constitution is Almighty God's Book, The Holy Qur'an, and the Sunna (Traditions) of the Prophet (PBUH). Arabic is the language of the Kingdom. The City of Riyadh is the capital.

In this respect, there is a high regard for law in the form of Sharia. This is not necessarily the same as respect for the rule of law,[10] which is widely accepted as the international litmus test for a country's legal system. In the West, the rule of law is seen as only truly possible in tandem with democracy. The Saudi legal and political system is based on traditional Islam in the form of the Hanbali School of Law and the Wahhabi doctrine, the organization of power through the monarchy and a tribal network, and finally the various and modern institutions which have emerged over the years. The monarchic rule of Saudi and concerns about human rights, meaning the operation and content of the law in Saudi, are cited as reasons to doubt the role Saudi plays in the international community. This said, from the Saudi point of view crime rates are low, and the process for finding oneself losing life or limb in the colloquial "Chop Chop Square" is well-defined. Yet, when it comes to activities such as drug smuggling and terrorism, and activities directed against the state or the royal household, one can quickly find law and process overridden by state action.

For our purposes specifically, the interesting part of the Basic Law at this juncture is how it defines the economy. Article 22 of the Basic Law states "Economic and social development shall be carried out according to a fair, wise plan." What the weekend change demonstrated was that a fair and wise plan is not always the reality. It also highlighted what is often criticized by businesses working with the Kingdom as the Corinthian nature of Saudi business and economic life. Yes, the change of the weekend was an economic decision to make the Kingdom more aligned with the rest of the Arab world, but it shows a lack of planning and consultation that economies elsewhere would take for granted. Despite this, the economic and business benefits were certainly welcome. The change gave an extra business day on the *Tadawul* stock exchange in preparation for opening up the exchange to international investors. The change did away with a three-day business week with international investors, which was as inconvenient for investors as it was for expats working in or with the Kingdom. Outside observers may ponder that surely such changes really ought not to be done in such a cavalier, or Corinthian, manner, but the reality was it was done quickly, effectively and with no negative fallout from the change. The Corinthian spirit is one of the signs that it can be hard to see how the Kingdom can survive the economic challenges ahead in its present form. Change is needed, but it cannot effect change in the way the weekend was changed. Certainly, the weekend change demonstrated the power of the house of Saud to effect a major economic change, and to have it embraced with barely a whimper from the people. After all, critics would say, if you have that level of power then you can pretty much do as you want.

The Role of Sharia: Orthodoxy and Expectations[11]

A central element to the Saudi behavior is the assumption of custodianship and a strong religious orthodoxy. Religious orthodoxy means the Koran, hadith and sunnah, which defines the life of the individual and the society. As noted, Saudi lives by a strong sense of the "rule of law," though different in how the term is used in the West to define essentially the benchmark of liberal democratic doctrine.[12] From an Islamic perspective, the *Sharia* is the rule of law, and it is in this sense that all Muslims and Islamic societies respect the rule of law. The *Sharia* is for the most part incompatible or at the very least contradictory to Western law, in general jurisprudential terms, because the two legal systems rest on very different assumptions. If a community within Britain decides to live by

Sharia law then that is akin to a club or organization setting its own rules of membership. For the most part it may not create problems, and people of the community could go to a Sharia court to determine if their actions or relationships are contrary to God's law, which is ultimately more important than human law. However, the problem lies in areas where there is a conflict of laws, and where *Sharia* rulings may not conflict but the punishment to be meted out is contrary to local law in non-Muslim societies. In this respect, we have to consider the *Sharia* in the context of an Islamic society, specifically in our case Saudi Arabia, and also consider the relationship between *Sharia* and Muslims in the context of non-Islamic societies. Most of my discussion will be on Saudi, though the latter remains very topical, and like certain parts of Christianity, Islam is most in conflict today with matters of sexual and family laws and norms. To study this fully means in the first instance grasping there are many varieties of Islamic society and history to consider, and in the latter case teasing out the many aspects and controversies about the relationship between the law and such social issues. However, these matters lie beyond the scope of this book, but to address the Saudi situation there are some common matters of *Sharia* law to cover.

This is not to see Saudi and Saudis as ritualistically pure or even the best example of Islamic practice, although they are often perceived this way by many Muslims in other parts of the world. All religious orthodoxy tends to be more consistent in its teachings than in the belief and practice of its adherents. The same holds for Islam, which covers vast geographical areas, civilizations, cultures, societies, polities and economies, and has done so since its founding. Like other religions, Islam has assimilated many ideas and practices that do not always appear to conform to the Koran and hadith, owing more to culture than orthodoxy, though often still rooted in the teachings. A good example is the wearing of the *hijab* and *niqab* by women, which has some roots in the Koran and Islamic teachings, in terms of modesty, but how it is worn largely comes down to a cultural interpretation. These are points that apply to Saudi and the Saudi adherence to Islam. Since the creation of the Kingdom of Saudi Arabia on 23 September 1932, the Kingdom has been governed by Islamic law, *Sharia*. This was enacted by the Basic Law of Rule, Royal Order No. A/90 of 27th Sha'ban 1412 Hejra corresponding to 1 March 1992, and is essentially the country's constitutional basis. *Sharia*, like Islam itself, is not a monolithic legal approach. There are a number of schools of Islamic law and a variety of *Sharia* boards in existence, and they may express different opinions on any specific issues of law. The four recognized Sunni schools (s. *madhhab*, pl. *madhhahib*) are Hanafi, Shafa'i, Maliki and Hanbali, while the three Shi'a schools are *Ja'fari*, *Zaydi* and *Isma'ili*.

The basic rule of the Saudi state states the monarch is custodian of the faith in a way quite different to the reigning British monarch, for instance, as the British monarch is head of the state church, but the Bible is not the constitution, though some of the roots are there. Article 1 of the Basic Law of Government, issued by King Fahd in March 1992, states:

> The Saudi Arabian Kingdom is a sovereign Arab Islamic state with Islam as its religion; God's book and the Sunna are its constitution; Arabic is its language; and Riyadh is its capital.

Defined by the Basic Law, the role of the state is to protect the principles of Islam and enforce the *Sharia*. Islamic law governs the administrative actions and the relationships between government, the ruler and the ruled, and these relationships are based on principles of brotherhood, consultation, friendship and cooperation. The Basic Law contains nine chapters:

1. General Principles
2. Law of Governance
3. Saudi Social Values
4. Economic Principles
5. Rights and Obligations
6. State Authorities
7. Financial Affairs
8. Audit Institutions
9. General Provisions

The Basic Law sets out the monarchical basis of the law of property, and its economic principles, rights and obligations, which emphasize that the State must protect human rights in conformity with the *Sharia*, safeguard the Kingdom's public funds, ensure the inviolability of private homes and private communications and guarantee the protection of private property and individual freedom from arbitrary arrest and punishment, except in cases of due process of law. In matters of welfare, the Basic Law places the State under an obligation to provide healthcare for all citizens; support those "in situations of emergency, sickness and old age"; and protect workers and employers.[13] In recent years, the Saudi legislature has undertaken a series of steps toward modernizing the Saudi judicial system. For the first time in the Kingdom's history, a High Court has been established in Riyadh as the Kingdom's highest judicial authority, assuming the responsibilities previously held by the Supreme Judicial Council. The new structure exercises authority over criminal and other specialized circuits and gives the Supreme Judicial Council oversight of the administrative role of the judiciary, including the selection of judges, judges' personnel affairs and the establishment of specialized courts. The 2007 Law of the Judiciary established courts of appeal in the 13 provinces, speeding up the resolution of disputes and improving the delivery of appellate rulings by making them more efficient by distributing their caseload among specialized civil, commercial, criminal, labor and personal status circuits. Lastly, the Law of Procedure has been consolidated to ensure the two pillars of right and justice are upheld for all claimants, giving claimants legal redress to an independent court of law.

However, while this glacial change in the Saudi judicial system is moving ahead and is seen positively as improving the social and economic infrastructure of Saudi, for some there is a more fundamental issue. The courts may improve what exists in Saudi today, but the essential rights and obligations of state and individuals are still seen as oppressive by international commentators and Saudi liberals, especially for women and low-paid immigrant workers. The rights of anyone in the Kingdom, native or foreign, are not treated as inherent rights by virtue of being a human person. Rights derive from the king underpinned by a claim to Koranic truth. The state law and rights exist to promote Islam, family and monarchy. Thus, homosexuality is regarded as wrong by traditional Islam, and is therefore outlawed, whether the homosexual is a Muslim or not. It is the law of Islam, thus it is the law of the land, and it applies to the whole person. This is part of why Islamic law is so central to the Saudi mind, which seeks to present God's law and is to be embraced in its totality by the believer. As Joseph Schacht, in the opening of his classic work *An Introduction to Islamic Law*, explained:

> The sacred law of Islam is an all-embracing body of religious duties, the totality of Allah's commands that regulate the life of every Muslim in all its aspects; it comprises on an equal footing ordinances regarding worship and ritual as well as political and (in the narrow sense) legal rules…Islamic law is the epitome of Islamic thought, the most typical manifestation of the Islamic way of life, the core and kernel of Islam itself.[14]

This legal approach means that theology, as Schacht points out, has never been on the same level as Islamic law, the reverse of protestant Christianity but also different from Jewish law and Canon law, in that it is less codified. It also differs from secular law, because the legal system is not something one goes to in order to adjudicate a problem or is simply accepted because it is the law of the land. Those outside of religion tend to miss the fullness of what law means within a faith, something shared by the Abrahamic religions. It is not simply about "do's" and "don'ts," nor is it simply about God commanding the believer to do this or do that. There are over 500 verses of legal import in the Koran, and there is a strong leaning toward law in the book as a whole, which demonstrates a strong desire to create a robust legal structure. In the Koran, many of the laws are specific to certain areas of life, in particular applied to economic and commercial matters. Within each of the Abrahamic faiths there are various schools of law, interpreting differently and offering a distinctive way to live according to religious law. However, what they all share is that religious law is about being in a right relationship with God, responding to God's will and acting out one's life accordingly. Thus law is something which resonates deeply with the believer, and breaking the law does not merely mean one will be punished, it means that one has broken with God and needs to do something in order to repair the relationship. One does not just accept one has broken a rule, the believer feels what they have done deeply and knows, depending upon how deep one's faith runs, that what one has done has put one's very soul in jeopardy. No prison sentence or punishment is going to be greater than the ultimate sense that an action has potentially an outcome for eternity. The pain of a whipping will wear off or a prison sentence will be finished, but in religious terms there is forever a questioning of what the damage is beyond these physical inconveniences. The law positively instructs the Saudi on how to live their life, which in other words means that for the Saudi the law is the rule and not the exception.

Early on, the problem arose of whether to restrict legal thought to the Koran and the example of the prophet, or whether it may be extended in some way. One of the confusions about the role of *Sharia* law is that it is often assumed by some believers and disbelievers alike that *Sharia* is in the same category as the Koran. The Koran contains much of the source material of *Sharia*, but it is still a human interpretation that bridges the Koranic text and the context of society. The question is how is this bridge constructed? As Schact explained:

> By their decisions, the earliest Islamic *qāḍīs*, did indeed lay the basic foundations of what was to become Islamic law. They gave judgment according to their own discretion or 'sound opinion' (*rāyy*), basing themselves on customary practice which in the nature of things incorporated administrative regulations, and taking the letter and the spirit of the Qur'ānic regulations and other recognized Islamic religious norms into account as much as they thought fit.[15]

Sharia comprises four principle sources. The first two are considered revelatory, meaning they come from God, and they are the Koran and the Sunnah, which means the practice and teachings of the Prophet Muhammad. The other two are based on rational endeavor, and they are formed by consensus (*ijma*) and analogical jurisprudential reasoning (*qiyās*). How this translates into a holistic legal approach in Saudi means looking into two specific aspects of Saudi Islam: the Hanbali school of jurisprudence and the Wahhabi and Salafi teaching of Islam, the latter two terms often being used interchangeably. As Thomas Hegghammer explains, religious and theological language do not necessarily help us with the political actions of terrorist war. Washington mouthpieces and media commentators may self-congratulate on delving deeper into these terms, but it is not as clever as it sounds. Hegghammer comments:

> …many of the theological descriptors commonly used in the literature on Islamism, such as *salafi*, *wahhabi*, *jihadi salafi* and *takfiri*, do not correspond to discrete and observable patterns of political behaviour among Islamists…It make no sense to speak of a 'salafi social movement,' for the simple reason that actors labeled salafi have wildly different, often diametrically opposing, political agendas.[16]

These terms are important to understanding the religious dimensions of our problem, but they are not helpful when bandied about as political labels. We can go on to explore a tripartite appellation used to discuss Saudi Islam in the current debate: Hanbali-Wahhabi-Salafi Islam; which is not the term I am using, but describes how critics and commentators are describing Saudi Islam.

Hanbali Legalism

In Saudi Arabia, the dominant school of Islamic law is the Hanbali school. This is stated in a Royal edict of 1928, which set down that judges have to apply the principles set out in specified Islamic law texts of the Hanbali school. The Basic Law of Rule in 1992 varies this somewhat, stating that the Saudi Arabian courts must issue rulings in accordance with the Qur'an and the Sunnah as the basic sources of Islamic law, without specifying any particular school of law whose rules are binding, but it can arguably be taken as implied because it has been the historic practice of Islamic law in the Kingdom. Thus in effect the Saudi legal system remains largely based on the Hanbali interpretation of law, taken here to be implied rather than explicitly stated. *The Oxford Dictionary of Islam* defines Hanbalism as an:

> Islamic school of legal thought (madhhab) whose origins are attributed to Ahmad ibn Hanbal in ninth-century Baghdad. The official school in Saudi Arabia and Qatar, with many adherents in Palestine, Syria, and Iraq.

Recognizes as sources of law: the *Quran*, hadith, fatwas of Muhammad's Companions, sayings of a single Companion, traditions with weaker chains of transmission or lacking the name of a transmitter in the chain, and reasoning by analogy (*qiyas*) when absolutely necessary. Encourages the practice of independent reasoning (*ijtihad*) through study of the *Quran* and *hadith*. Rejects *taqlid*, or blind adherence to the opinions of other scholars, and advocates a literal interpretation of textual sources. Ritualistically, the Hanbali school is the most conservative of the Sunni law schools, but it is the most liberal in most commercial matters.[17]

Hanbalism is arguably the most consistent and rigorist form of Islamic jurisprudence, defining clearly the sacred and profane with doctrinal purity, resulting in claims it is fundamentalist. However, it may be more productive to see Hanbalism in terms of fideism rather than fundamentalism. While Hanbalism has been dogmatically and ritually minimalist, it has also given some scope for interpretation in legal and political matters, resulting in a degree of realism in Hanbalite political theory.[18] Aziz Al-Azmeh explains Hanbalism in fideist terms, which we will return to shortly:

The title under which the doctrinal minimalism of the Hanbalites was officiated was fideism (*tafwid, tawqff, irj*), the affirmation of dogmatic articles without a qualification that would discursively carry them beyond the bounds of their given textuality, on the assumption that the sense of the divine statement is *sui generis* and comprehensible to us only within the terms of this very statement, and that any qualification of the divine statement, in the form of explication or otherwise, is tantamount to imputing to the Divinity and to the Prophet utterances they did not make. This is the sense of the statement attributed to Ibn Hanbal and repeated with many variations by countless followers, that religion as such is the Book of God and veracious narratives about the Prophet and his associates, that religion is imitation, and that the substance of scriptural statements is textually incontrovertible while being intellectually ineffable. In antithesis stands *ta'wil*, interpretation, execrated by the Hanbalites for its venture beyond the letter of the sacred text, and most often identified by them with the allegorical interpretation of the scriptures which they said added to them what was not in them, and consequently presumed on their behalf in a manner which can only lead to perdition.[19]

Such fideism is interpretive, not simply literalist or opaque. It interprets through the lens of the basic belief of Islam that there is one God
who is Allah and Mohammad is his prophet, and the Koran is the work
of God. It also means God comes to us, not the other way around.
However, the interpretations are grounded in the historical situation and
it is this history that doesn't change rather, than the Koran or Sharia as a
discipline. As Christopher Houston asserts:

> Indeed, the logic of the Shari'a, with its minimal number of clear interdic-
> tions, and maximal scope for the interpretative extension of key precepts to
> particular situations, means that any freezing of the ulama's 'arbitrary' deci-
> sions arises not so much from the essential characteristics of the Shari'a, but
> from the historic institutionalizing of a particular legal tradition or method
> of exegesis or from the hegemony of a particular interpretation. Whether
> this lack of institutional and conceptual closure ironically encourages mod-
> ern Islamist states (Saudi Arabia?) or groups to force such closure is another
> question. Paradoxically, the provisionality of law-making allows some
> Islamist groups to interpret the Qur'ān as affirming a radical negation of
> human autonomy.[20]

Thus, it is this freezing or the encrustation of an historical decision that
needs to be examined more carefully in the light of today's context and
how the original decision was understood at the time. Thus, rather than
a "reformation" Islam requires a review of its legal decisions and current
day practices in the light of change in the human situation and society.
This will preserve the integrity of the Islamic tradition while applying it
to the modern day, instead of yielding to fundamentalism. Bernard Lewis
explains how religious fundamentalism, which he admits is an unfortu-
nate term partly along the lines I have discussed, enjoys the advantage
over other ideologies of having a readily intelligible message and themes,
and concludes that broadly speaking,

> Muslim fundamentalists are those who feel that the troubles of the Muslim
> world at the present time are the result not of insufficient modernization
> but of excessive modernization, which they see as a betrayal of authentic
> Islamic values. For them the remedy is a return to true Islam, including the
> abolition of all laws and other social borrowings from the West and the

restoration of the Islamic Holy Law, the shari'a, as the effective law of the land. From their point of view, the ultimate struggle is not against the Western intruder but against the Westernizing traitor at home. Their most dangerous enemies, as they see it, are the false and renegade Muslims who rule the countries of the Islamic world and who have imported and imposed infidel ways on Muslim peoples.[21]

There is an element of fear here, a fear that to be faithful means trying to recover the past, a kind of religious nostalgia that becomes potent when fused with a fundamentalist mindset. With such a mindset it is a short step to justifying today's murders of believers and unbelievers unlike in terms of the Koran and the life of Muhammed. This is a thorny question, and a difficult conversation to be had, but in the context of today's Islamic-inspired violence it is essential and we will return to the subject later. For the time being, it is enough to suggest that the fideist approach discussed here may be a more productive avenue to explore, because it would not require dialogue partners to "go back" as the fundamentalist does, but to go forward according to the timeless principles held up by believers in dialogue with the modern world. Such an approach may be closer to the Saudi mindset rather than fundamentalist, and to treat Saudis as fundamentalist rather than fideist merely leads to critics talking past their audience.

The difficulty for the Saudi lies in facing Western ideas of modernity and postmodernity, understanding democracy and pluralism. In discussions of the Western liberal system it is customary to talk of capitalism and democracy together, and there is growing literature looking at the relationship between law and economics. If we apply this to the Saudi situation then we need to look at a different system of law, and a different political arrangement. Conventional law and economic reasoning assumes people hold a set of beliefs and choose rationally, and this in turn assumes a certain type of legal reasoning. What of Islamic legal thought? Islamic law and belief lays claim to a specific set of truths. The pragmatism and liberalism which are hallmarks of capitalism and democracy provide for a world of difference and plurality. The capitalist system of choices does not depend on establishing an agreed moral foundation, nor does it dictate answers to reality or personal conduct.[22] This is not to say morality plays no role, though there are those who might argue a distinct separation. Islam rejects this argument, the faith dictates a set of beliefs, a basic welfare system, and prescribes specific law for economic behaviors, covering areas such as interest payments, contracts and futures trading. Saudi has compromised much of Islamic economic law, and the question arises as to how much further does the Kingdom go to promote a capitalist economy, or can it move more toward an Islamic political economy? To answer this, we should go deeper into the theological questions.

Notes

1. Denominations which house fundamentalists include Apostolic Christian Church of America, Baptist Bible Fellowship International, Christian Israelite Church, Fellowship of Fundamental Bible Churches, Fundamental Baptist Fellowship Association, Fundamental Baptist Fellowship International, Gloriavale Christian Community, Independent Baptist, Independent Baptist Fellowship International, Independent Baptist Fellowship of North America, Independent Fundamental Churches of America, International Churches of Christ, Southwide Baptist Fellowship, Wealthy Street Baptist Church, Wisconsin Fellowship of Baptist Churches and World Baptist Fellowship; and again, may be found in other broader denominations. An authoritative view is provided by George M. Marsden, *Fundamentalism and American Culture* (Oxford: Oxford University Press, 2006). Steve Bruce, Modernity and fundamentalism: the new Christian right in America, *British Journal of Sociology* (41:4, 1990) 477–496, argues fundamentalism fails in its engagement and remains sectarian. James Barr probed theologically, and controversially, into fundamentalism in his two major works *Fundamentalism* (London: SCM Press, 2nd Revised edition, 1981) and *Escaping Fundamentalism* (London: SCM Press, 1984). Martin E. Marty led the Fundamentalism Project from 1987 to 1995, culminating in five volumes published by the University of Chicago Press from 1994 to 2003; see http://www.press.uchicago.edu/ucp/books/series/FP.html, last accessed 28 April 2012.
2. Ernest R. Sandeen, Fundamentalism and American Identity, *Annals of the American Academy of Political and Social Science*, Vol. 387, The Sixties:

Radical Change in American Religion (January 1970), pp. 56–65. Sandeen, Ibid, pp. 56–65.

3. Bowering (2013, p. 55).
4. Ibid, p. 57.
5. Bowering (2013, p. 249).
6. David Commins offers a very useful overview of this question beyond this quote, and the changing dynamics which need not detain us further at this point, and I will return to his discussion later.
7. See R. Hrair Dekmejian, The Rise of Political Islamism in Saudi Arabia, *Middle zournal*, Vol. 48, No. 4 (Autumn, 1994), pp. 627–643. On the organized opposition groups, particularly the Committee for the Defense of Legitimate Rights (CDLR: founded in May 1993) and the Committee for Advice and Reform (CAR: founded in April 1994), see Madawi al-Rasheed, Saudi Arabia's Islamic Opposition, *Current History*, Vol. 95, No. 957 (January 1996), pp. 16–22; Middle East Contemporary Survey (MECS), Vol. 17, 1993 (Boulder, CO, 1995), pp. 575, 577–578; Economist Intelligence Unit (EIU), Country Report, Saudi Arabia, 1st quarter, 1996, pp. 9–10; 2nd quarter, 1996, pp. 8–9; 3rd quarter, 1996, pp. 8–9. 20.
8. Lackner (1978, p. 217).
9. http://www.saudiembassy.net/about/country-information/laws/The_Basic_Law_Of_Governance.aspx
10. http://arizonajournal.org/wp-content/uploads/2015/10/Esmaeili.pdf
11. http://www.islamicsupremecouncil.org/understanding-islam/legal-rulings/52-understanding-islamic-law.html
12. An interesting discussion can be read here on Sharia and rule of law: http://www.nytimes.com/2008/03/16/news/16iht-16shari-aht.11119704.html?pagewanted=all
13. http://www.nyulawglobal.org/globalex/Saudi_Arabia1.html sets out the Basic Law very usefully.
14. Schact (1964, p.1).
15. Lewis, L., C. Pellat, and J. Schacht, eds (1998, p. 544).
16. Hegghammer (2010, p. 5).
17. http://www.oxfordislamicstudies.com/article/opr/t125/e799
18. For review of the literature, see Aziz Al-Azmeh, Orthodoxy and Hanbalite Fideism, *Arabica* T. 35, Fasc. 3 (November 1988), pp. 253–266. Also, see Ibn Qudama, text in H. Daiber, 'The Creed (CAqfda) of the Hanbalite Ibn Qudama al-Maqdisi. A Newly Discovered Text', in

Studia Arabica et Islamica, Festschrift for Ihsan Abbas, ed. W. Al-Qadi, Beirut, Qadi, Beirut (1981) p. 111.
19. Aziz Al-Azmeh, *Orthodoxy and Hanbalite Fideism*, Arabics, T.35, Fasc.3 (November 1988) p. 265.
20. Houston, Christopher, *Islamism, Castoriadia and Autonomy*, Thesis Eleven, Number 76, February 2004, p. 56.
21. Lewis (2002, p. 132).
22. Renowned work has been pioneered by legal theorists John Rawls and Richard Posner.

Bibliography

al-Rasheed, Madawi, ed. 2008. *Kingdom Without Borders: Saudi Arabia's Political, Religious and Media Frontiers*. London: Hurst.
al-wadi'i, Muqbil. 2005. *Mushahadaiî iî al-Mamlaka al-'Arabiyya al-Sa'udiyya*. Sanaa: Dar al-athar.
Allawai, Ali A. 2009. *The Crisis of Islamic Civilization*. New Haven: Yale University Press.
An-Na'im, Abdullahi Ahmed. 2008. *Islam and the Secular State: Negotiating the Future of Shari`a*. Cambridge, MA: Harvard University Press.
Black, Antony. 2001. *The History of Islamic Political Thought: From the Prophet to the Present*. Edinburgh: Edinburgh University Press.
Bonnefoy, Laurent. 2012. *Salafism in Yemen: Transnationalism and Religious Identity*. New York: Columbia University Press.
Bowering, Gerhard, ed. 2013. *Islamic Political Thought: An Introduction*. Princeton: Princeton University Press.
Craze, Jonathan, and Mark Huband. 2009. *The Kingdom: Saudi Arabia and the Challenge of the 21st Century*. London: Hurst & Co.
Delong-Bas, Natana J. 2004. *Wahhabi Islam: From Revival and Reform to Global Jihad*. New York: Oxford University Press.
Hallaq, Wael B. 1999. *Islamic Legal Theories*. Cambridge: Cambridge University Press.
Hamid, Shadi. 2016. *Islamic Exceptionalism: How the Struggle Over Islam Is Reshaping the World*. New York: St. Martin's Press.
Hamidullah, Muhammad. 1975. *The First Written Constitution in the World: An Important Document of the Time of the Holy Prophet*. 3rd rev ed. Lahore: Sh. Muhammad Ashraf.

Haykel, Bernard, Thomas Hegghammer, and Stéphane Lacroix. 2015. *Saudi Arabia in Transition: Insights on Social, Political, Economic and Religious Change.* Cambridge: Cambridge University Press.

Hegghammer, Thomas. 2010. *Jihad in Saudi Arabia: Violence and Pan-Islamism since 1979.* New York: Cambridge University Press.

———. 2015. *Saudi Arabia in Transition: Insights on Social, Political, Economic and Religious Change.* New York: Cambridge University Press.

Hourani, Albert. 2002. *A History of the Arab Peoples.* Cambridge, MA: Belknap Press.

Karsh, Effraim. 2006. *Islamic Imperialism: A History.* New Haven: Yale University Press.

Kepel, Gilles. 2004. *The War for Muslim Minds: Islam and the West.* Trans. Pascal Ghazaleh. Cambridge, MA: Belknap Press.

Lackner, Helen. 1978. *A House Built on Sand. A Political Economy of Saudi Arabia.* London: Ithaca Press.

Lecker, Michael. 2004. *The Constitution of Medina: Muḥammad's First Legal Document.* Princeton: Darwin.

Lewis, Bernard. 2002. *The Arabs in History.* New York: Oxford University Press.

Lewis, L., C. Pellat, and J. Schacht, eds. 1998. *Cambridge Encyclopedia of Islam, Volume II.* Leiden: Brill.

Luciani, Giacomo, ed. 1990. *The Arab State.* Berkeley: University of California Press.

Lynch, Timothy J., and Robert S. Singh. 2008. *After Bush: The Case for Continuity in American Foreign Policy.* Cambridge: Cambridge University Press.

Maher, Shiraz. 2016. *Salafi-Jihadism: The History of an Idea.* London: Hurst & Company.

Mansfield, Peter. 1985. *The Arabs.* London: Penguin Books.

Matthiesen, Toby. 2015. *The Other Saudis: Shiism, Dissent and Sectarianism.* New York: Cambridge University Press.

Nasr, Vali. 2009. *The Rise of Islamic Capitalism: Why the New Muslim Middle Class is the Key to Defeating Extremism.* New York: Free Press.

Quaesem, Muhammad Abdul. 1983. *The Jewels of the Qur'an: Al-Ghazali's Theory.* London: Islamic Book Trust.

Raphael, Patai. 1973. *The Arab Mind.* New York: Scribner.

Said, Edward W. 1979. *Orientalism.* Princeton: Princeton University Press.

———. 1981. *Covering Islam: How the Media and the Experts Determine How We See the Rest of the World.* New York: Pantheon Books.

Salame, Ghassan, ed. 1994. *Democracy Without Democrats? The Renewal of Politics in the Muslim World.* London: I.B. Tauris.

Schact, J. 1964. *An Introduction to Islamic Law*. New York: Oxford University Press.

Shabbir, Akhtar. 1985. In *Philosophy Bridging the World Religions*, ed. P. Koslowski. Dordrecht: Kluwer.

Southern, R.W. 1978. *Western Views of Islam in the Middle Ages*. Cambridge, MA: Harvard University Press.

Watt, W. Montgomery. 1953. *The Faith and Practice of Al-Ghazali*. London: George Allen and Unwin.

Wilson, Bryan. 1966. *Religion in a Secular Society*. London: Watts.

10

Fideism II

The underlying theology of Saudi Arabia is Wahhabism, which refers to the eighteenth-century teachings and doctrines introduced in the central Arabian region of Najd by religious reformer Muhammad ibn Abd al-Wahhab (c. 1702–91), which dates back to the middle of the eighteenth century. He was schooled in the Hanbali tradition and to a lesser extent in Sufism. As a scholar of the Hanbali school, he was greatly influenced by the earlier Hanbali scholar, Taqi al-Din ibn Taymiyya (1263–1328). Ibn Taymiyya preached unwavering adherence to the Hanbali view that the only true Islamic doctrine was based on two of the recognized sources of Islamic law, the Quran and Hadith.[1] Delong-Bas argues that the hadith, in al-Wahhab's view, were to be assessed according to their content, rather than the chain of transmission, which had become the way of scholars in examining them for authenticity. The aim was to reform Islam, which al-Wahhab believed had strayed from the strict demands and guidance of the Koran and Hadith, with Muslims incorporating un-Islamic sources and practices. Delong-Bas explains the reform aims of the era:

> The desire of eighteenth-century reformers to embrace and study scripture directly was not simply a matter of religious purity or theological quibbling.

© The Author(s) 2018
D. Cowan, *The Coming Economic Implosion of Saudi Arabia*,
https://doi.org/10.1007/978-3-319-74709-5_10

These reformers were concerned not only by the fact that their fellow Muslims were not paying sufficient attention to Islamic values and ethical considerations but also by the fact that their fellow Muslims did not distinguish between the scriptures and their interpretations. In their experience, many Muslims of their time considered the scriptures and their interpretations to be equally authoritative.[2]

Al-Wahhab contended that the core texts needed to be understood in the context of their times, and how the text applies to other eras had to be seen in the context of their time, but certainly does not involve making the text in our own image. This would fit in with the fideist view I propose.

He was taking his message into the community, which already had its beliefs, religious leaders and power structures in place, and his message was set out in contradiction to this existing order. This created tensions with some believers and *ulama*, or religious scholars. It should be noted that today's calls for reform seem to neglect Wahhabism was a reform movement, which took place just over a century after the reformation and counter-reformation of the Christian church. This Islamic reform had not dissimilar concerns, such as the intercession of saints as an unnecessary barrier between God and the believer. Like the reformation cry of *ad fontes!* the Wahabbis attempted to recover the faith of the early founding, and demanded that Muslims return *ad fontes* to the Koran and hadith and to be faithful to God, with an emphasis on *tawhid*. A major precept of Wahhabism, therefore, was rejection of any religious belief or practice not based on those two sources, which al-Wahhab considered an heretical "innovation" (*bid'a*). Which is why he condemned intercessional prayers (*tawassul*) to Muslim saints and viewed pilgrimages to their tombs as heresy. He preached that the only valid intercession was to the one true God (*tawhid*), and that Muslims needed to return to the teachings of Islam as followed by Ibn Hanbal with strict obedience to the Koran and Hadith, weeding out those innovations considered as distortions, primarily intercessions with saints, ritual excess and aspects of Sufism.

Like the Christian Reformation Wahhabism was a reform movement that came from within the faith, and the audience for the call for change comprised Muslims. The change demanded involved both the individual and society, because the reform of the individual would be the way to reform society, rather than the other way round. This echoes Luther's statement that you can rule the world with the Gospel, but you better fill it with real Christians first. Al-Wahhab also emphasized the communal nature of Islam and Islamic society, and this permeates his writings, which makes his reform necessarily political. However, such reform was not to be achieved by coercion, rather he favored dialogue and persuasion to effect change, though he was not shy of violence when the occasion seemed to call for it. Despite the modern view of Wahhabism, Delong-Bas[3] explains jihad as holy war was not the argument of al-Wahhab, and furthermore this was a reform movement led by scholars (*ulama*) not politicians. Wahhabism has been likened to Puritanism in Christianity, and his reputation for doctrinal purity was turned against him and his followers by opponents, who characterized his teachings and actions as forms of fanaticism and violence. His arguments were dismissed from the very outset by opponents, particularly the Ottomans, as a Kharijite sectarian heresy, and the term Wahhabism was coined to identify the teachings and the followers of al-Wahhab and his perceived heresy. The Wahhabis identified themselves as Sunni, but David Commins highlights that apart from a couple of twentieth-century exceptions, "nobody wanted to be called a Wahhabi. The connotations of fanaticism and heresy associated with that name had staying power."[4] The portrayals of opponents back in the time of al-Wahhab retain resonance today, but Delong-Bas offers a sustained case that in truth today's portrayals are somewhat of a distortion.

The movement itself has had staying power because it has evolved in tandem with Saudi Arabia. Bernard Lewis in giving a very potted history of Saudi and Wahhabism offered the following observation:

> Wahabbism was now the official, state-enforced doctrine of one of the most influential governments in all Islam – the custodian of the two holiest places of Islam, the host of the annual pilgrimage, which brings millions of Muslims from every part of the world to share in its rites and rituals. At the same time, the teachers and preachers of Wahabbism had at their disposal immense financial resources, which they used to promote and spread their version of Islam.[5]

Saudi embraced Wahhabism in an alliance between the religious and political leadership on the Arab peninsula, though there were, and continue to be, tensions between the two leadership domains. Initially it was King ʿAbd al-ʿAzīz's wife who accepted al-Wahhab, followed by two of his brothers, Thunayan and Mashari. However, in 1744 the Saudi *amir* and the *imam* agreed an alliance and swore a mutual oath of loyalty. While they struck an alliance between religious and political domains, there was some friction from time to time. The final outcome Delong-Bas notes was "Ibn Abd al-Wahhab's goal of reforming Islam was overshadowed and ultimately overwhelmed by King ʿAbd al-ʿAzīz's quest for state consolidation."[6] To undermine al-Wahhab further, the *ulama* supported military opposition to the reform and accused him of ignorance, sorcery and lies, all of which are legitimate reasons for conflict based on the Koran, the outcome of which was a declaration of jihad by al-Wahhab as self-defense. After the conquest of Riyadh al-Wahhab withdrew from the fray, and Delong-Bas offers an interesting summary of what followed after al-Wahhab handed over the reins to Abdulaziz, who "proceeded to expand his vision beyond the confines of Najd into the rest of Arabia, Iraq, and Syria. His actions made clear that the Al Saud family had as its ultimate goal the expansion of its territories and power, with or without religious legitimation. In fact, Saudi-Wahhabi power reached its height between 1792 and 1814, long after Ibn al-Wahhab withdrew from public life." This again suggests a parallel with the Christian reformation, in that the political use of religion on the European continent ultimately trumped the religious reform. This was because modernity meant people ultimately rejected a religious worldview, and ceased to be fideists.

Followers of Wahhabi movement view Islam materially more than spiritually. This has led to an emphasis on approaching many areas of criminal law in a way that results in physical punishment for wrongful acts. There is less scope for reform or forgiveness in this legal approach as a way to tackle the wrongdoer. The outcome is a legal approach that is essentially negative, emphasizing the wrong, the wrongdoer and the punishment of wrong. The Egyptian Islamic legal scholar Abū Zahrā of Al-Azhar University went further when he explained there is a dogmatism about Muḥammad ibn Abd al-Wahhab that became increasingly extreme and then "his followers went to even further extremes surpassing all bounds of jurisprudence, declaring countless acceptable matters 'forbidden.' The Wahhabi movement, never content to promulgate its beliefs by tongue or pen, wielded a sword to fight whoever differed from its ideology."[7] This makes protecting human rights somewhat fraught, though the 2016 sentencing and execution of a Saudi prince was seen as a sign of greater equality in Saudi law. As Prince Faisal bin Farhan Al Saud, a member of the Saudi Arabian royal family and the chairman of Saudi-based Shamal Investments, wrote in an opinion piece for *Newsweek*:

> The case of the late Prince Turki will serve as an important reminder to members of the royal family, especially the younger ones, that no one in the Kingdom is immune from the law, and it will also give the Saudi public increased confidence that justice will continue to be applied equally to all in practice and not just in theory. In Saudi Arabia, unlike in other monarchies, the royal family is not set above the people. Rather, it is first among equals and the deference and respect its members receive is based on the family's role as a unifying force not some perception of noble lineage. The Kingdom has come a long way since the third Saudi state was established in 1932, and it continues to evolve at growing rate and I expect that this evolution will continue.[8]

Today the image of Wahhabism is one of fundamentalism and extremism, a typical portrayal being that of Lewis, who offered what he saw as a parallel image of the Ku Klux Klan taking control of Texas, and then concluded:

> Organized Muslim public life, education, and even worship are, to an alarming extent, funded and therefore directed by Wahhabis, and the version of Islam that they practice and preach is dominated by Wahhabi principles and attitudes. The custodianship of the holy places and the revenues of oil have given worldwide impact to what would otherwise have been an extremist fringe in a marginal country.[9]

This image has been further enhanced, though not in the Saudi view, by employing another term that of Salafi. As Commins explains Wahhabism, "the tendency to refer to it as Salafi is a recent development that first emerged among Wahhabism's defenders outside Arabia and well before Wahhabi's themselves adopted the term."[10] It is to Salafi we now turn, which we will do in dialogue with Wahhabism.

Political Salafism

The term Salafi has been embraced by Sunnis to represent loyalty to a form of Islam which lays claim to the origins and early times of Islam as the only correct understanding of Islam. Salafist modern-day adherents claim to emulate "the pious predecessors," the *al-salaf al-ṣāliḥ* who are understood to be the first three generations of Muslims. In discussions around Salafism there is often a great deal of confusion, in part because commentators come at the issue from different angles. Thus, one has to be cautious in using the term Salafi as it is used to refer to modern movements but does not mean that the Salafis of today are identical to the Salafis of the earlier period, or at any other time. This highlights the fact there are some nuances to consider between modernist Salafism and classical Salafism. What these two strands share is their challenge to the mainstream of Islamic thought, whether it is Sunni or Shiʿite orthodoxy. Shiraz Maher suggests the modern movement relates to what he calls "a reactionary soteriology"[11] which practically can be divided into three branches:

1) Quietist Salafism, focused on "cleansing" and teaching Islamic "purity" rather than political ideology
2) Political Salafism, focused on direct political commitment as an holistic part of Islam, but eschews revolution
3) Jihadi-Salafism, focused on overthrowing through violent jihad what they see as apostate regimes in the Islamic world

Despite these variances the term "Salafi" is on many occasions used more broadly as a synonym for, or interchangeably with, the term "Wahhabism." The added difficulty is that there is some scholarly disagreement over the term Salafism and whether it truly represents a unified tradition. The simplest way to understand the relationship is that Wahhabism is part of the larger phenomenon of Salafism. Salafist thought has challenged the authority and legitimacy of various developments in Islam down the centuries to the present day, and turn to the Koran and the hadith in a literalist sense to undermine or delegitimize these developments. In contrast, there is a large body of Muslim scholars who, while agreeing the Salaf are effective role models, argue that the history of the Islamic communities and the institutions they have produced also represent legitimate expressions of Islam. This includes many elements, including the various schools of law (*madhhab*), the adoption of Greek logic and speculative theology, and the Sufis, whose legitimacy has generally been accepted by mainstream Sunni and Shi'ite scholars, though not whole-heartedly. David Commins further offers a useful distinction between following the way of Salaf, which is a position on theology and worship, and claims to an identity distinct from other Sunnis which impacts views on public institutions and social identity. To draw this distinction more fully, he offers a contrast between living according to classical Islamic thought and religion as a way of life.

The popular narrative is that Salafism has exported its extremist ideas from Saudi Arabia to the rest of the Muslim world, linked to the promotional activities of the Saudi state to spread conservative Islam to combat the perceived threat of Shi'ism in Iran, Iraq and Lebanon. However, Salafism is not a unified or organized movement. Instead there are various branches emerging in many countries, with interest in Salafism gathering pace since the Arab uprisings and Salafi participation in political elections in Egypt and Tunisia. The appropriation of Salafi and Wahhabism by Saudi religious scholars is part of a larger Wahhabi Salafi "turn" in Islam; it is also part of the struggle over who has authority in Islam. Commins explains:

The modernist Salafis sought general principles in authoritative texts that permit flexible adaptation to novel forms of governance, law, and education. By contrast, Wahhabis focused on fidelity to what they construed as the creed and cult of the Pious Fathers. For those who regard the modernists as the true Salafis, Wahhabis' claim to be Salafis is spurious. According to this view, Salafism stood for a modernist outlook until Saudi religious scholars decided to appropriate the Salafi mantle to validate their teachings, reducing Salafism to dogmatism.[12]

Commins goes on to elaborate:

the Wahhabi establishment embraced the Salafi label. The underlying
political context was Al Saud's decision in the 1960s to open the kingdom
to foreign Muslims to develop public institutions, especially in the field of
education. With the influx of Muslims came independent Salafi scholars
and Islamic revivalist organizations. The cosmopolitan Salafi world was
transplanted to Saudi soil.[13]

In the 1970s, this found further outlet through various publications,
and took hold in education and was used a way to rebut the Muslim
Brotherhood and Arab socialism.

The view that Saudi was an exporter of Salafism, Commins suggests,
overlooks three factors. First, it was the modernist themselves who first
classified Wahhabis as Salafis. Second, setting these two terms as distinct
camps does not resolve the terminological problem outlined above.
Third, this naming debate is part of a broader discourse on how Saudi is
part of the Muslim world. Commins draws the interesting conclusion
that:

Without suggesting that Salafi is an infinitely elastic term, we might interpret its permutations as an instance of the ways political context shapes
arguments over religious rectitude…religious scholars looked to the Pious
Fathers for principles that harmonized with the impulse to adapt to new
conditions. Salafi shifted from a term in theological debates to a modernist
temperament seeking a foundation for remaking education, law, and politics. In the emergent culture of nationalism, the call to return to the way of
the Pious Fathers filled two purposes. It anchored a narrative of the community's rebirth…and it affirmed the community's special place in the
world…as a bearer of a universal divine mission. The latest twist in the
meaning of Salafi, its association with armed struggle (jihad) against the
Muslim world's enemies, resulting in the "Salafi-Jihadi" neologism, also
reflects the impact of political context on religious discourse.

Another challenge to this notion is offered in the case study of Saudi
and Yemen, which merits spending a little time on. Laurent Bonnefoy's
book *Salafism in Yemen* provides a case study of Yemen to contest the

notion of models of foreign ideologies being aggressively exported as the explanation for the spread of Al-Qaeda influence in parts of Yemen, and finds them to be wrong. A common global criticism of Saudi is that it exported its own brand of Wahhabism and promoted terrorism and other activities. A typical narrative was published in a review of Bonnefoy's book:

> Since Salafism has its origins in—and is widely acknowledged as—the official creed of Saudi Arabia, conventional wisdom has tended to associate it with Saudi state power. In this view, Saudi officials actively promote and fund Salafism abroad to increase Saudi soft power and to gain leverage in regional politics. Indeed, several wealthy Saudis have financed Salafi sheikhs and religious centers all over the world. Moreover, Salafis outside Saudi Arabia are easily identified by their distinctive Saudi style of dress.[14]

Bonnefoy contests this dominant narrative of Salafism as a Saudi state export to promote its own agenda, explaining that Yemen had its own Salafi traditions and norms while admitting that Yemeni Salafism is shaped by its relationships with Saudi Arabia, which tend to be more grassroots based than at the higher levels of national engagement. Salafism emerged in Yemen around three decades ago and since then the country's Salafi movement has maintained complex, if not tense links with Saudi Arabia.[15] The roots of the current issues with modern Yemeni Salafism can be found in the activities of Muqbil al-Wadi'i, who died in 2001. He was a tribesman from the highlands of Sa'ada in the north of Yemen, but was educated in Saudi during the 1960s and 1970s in the top centers of religious education, including the Islamic University of Medina. Significantly, while in Saudi al-Wadi'i was involved in the *Jama'a al-Salafiyya al-Muhtasiba* movement, which was the movement that spawned the group leading the 1979 Mecca Great Mosque occupation. He was seen to have influenced the ringleader Juhayman al-'Utaybi, who challenged the legitimacy of the monarchy, and as a result al-Wadi'i was expelled from Saudi a matter of months ahead of the rebellion. He established the Dar al-Hadith school in Sa'ada city, attracting students from Yemen and abroad, including Europe and America.[16] There was a final reconciliation between al-Wadi'i and the Saudis, when shortly before his death he returned to Saudi Arabia to receive medical treatment, and the opportunity was taken to reconcile with the Saudi rulers, much to the surprise of many because it seemed to contradict the Saudi position as stated by al-Wadiʻi. As a mark of this reconciliation, al-Wadiʻi was buried in Mecca close to the graves of the Saudi *ʻulama* ʻAbd al-ʻAziz bin Baz and Muhammad al-ʻUthaymin.[17]

Echoing Maher's tripartite classification of Salafism, Bonnefoy splits Yemeni Salafism into three, a mainstream missionary or "quietist" Salafism (*salafiyya daʻwiyya*), a more violent jihadi-Salafism (*salafiyya jihādiyya*) and politicized activist Salafism (*salafiyya munazzama* or *harakiyya*). He argues Yemeni Salafism aspires to be apolitical and universalist in nature. The relationship between Saudi and Yemen he examines by positing "Transnational Salafism," by which he means the development of Salafism in Yemen through transnational connections and migrations between Yemen and Saudi Arabia, in particular the 1990/1991 expulsions. Bonnefoy rejects the notion of a "Saudization" of Yemeni Salafism, arguing the need to understand it as a "transnationalization," though direct connections remain and a number of Saudi organizations and actors support Yemeni Salafism. Bonnefoy makes use of Edward Said's "travelling theory" to explain how these transformations occur during relocation and argues there is a "Yemenization" of quietist Salafism based in the "ordinariness" of the Yemeni religious landscape. The death of al-Wadiʻi, his reconciliation with the Saudi authorities and the political dynamics of the "global war on terror" led to a new level of normalization of the Salafi movement in Yemen. Most of its leading figures, such as Yahya al-Hajuri, Muhammad al-Imam and Abu al-Hasan al-Maribi, appear to have abandoned some aspects of this "muqbilian"-style Salafism, either by adopting a more conventional apolitical stance reminiscent of the doctrine of the *ulama* of the Saudi religious establishment or by growing more political and being influenced by the Sahwa movement and the Muslim Brotherhood. Bonnefoy observed "In a way, this whole and complex normalization process meant abandoning much of the heritage of Juhayman al-ʻUtaybi, therefore ending a cycle and obliterating the indirect influence that the *Ikhwan* movement has had on Yemeni Salafism."[18] Bonnefoy's book was the outcome of a painstaking four years of field research and review of the literature of Yemeni Salafism in Yemen, and though critics have pointed to concerns about his hard division between the quietists and jihadis, he has as reviewer Jillian Schwedler notes done a useful job of demonstrating "that efforts to characterize Salafism as an ideology that has spread like a disease entirely miss the mark."[19]

Faith and Fideism: Opening Up Dialogue

What people really mean by their calls for a reformation of Islam is a secularization or liberalization akin to the Christian church. For Christian traditionalists the modern outcome of reformation has resulted in the mainstream churches capitulating to most major secular social change, hence the normalization of abortion, ordination of gay priests and acceptance of same-sex marriage in many mainstream traditional churches. There has been a conservative resistance to this by the Roman Catholic Church, Lutheran Church Missouri Synod and others on doctrinal and ecclesiological terms, while other opponents have taken a different biblical approach which has led to the growth of non-traditional and Pentecostal churches. There is a popular demarcation dispute between conservatives who look to maintain historical, biblical and doctrinal norms, and liberals and progressives who use these norms to reinterpret and change the Christian experience in a more contingent sense. Islam faces similar challenges to the modern world, but it seems for the most part Islam as a whole remains conservative and there is not the same dissonance in Islam that we find in Christian circles. It is hard to see Saudi Muslims going down any liberalizing or progressive road at this point, and if it were to go in that direction then it will be a very slow journey, as the Saudi way of things is much more gradualist.

To understand the place of Islam in the Saudi mind, it is important to understand the various terms of Islamic reference, and some of the work has been done in these last two chapters. In order to proceed to think through these practical questions, we should be clear on the hermeneutical foundation of Saudi thinking. To do this, I propose we start with a foundational description of fideism, rather than the term fundamentalist and the various subsets of this fideist mindset. I suggest this will lead us all into a

more productive dialogue. Aziz Al-Azmeh captures some of the intricacies of the term in reference to the Hanbali thinking and practice:

> Fideist dogma is hence quintessentially and thoroughly technical, and
> therefore constitutes a quarry of authority, that of the Hanbalite leaders in
> whatever context they had been active. Fideism can only be rigorously
> maintained by administrative means… The arbitrariness of fideism indi-
> cates it not as a form of knowledge or of apprehension, but as a form for
> the expression of a particular authority that decrees and disseminates it. It
> indicates, furthermore, a form of religious knowledge and for the transmis-
> sion of such knowledge that is appropriate for preachers, and it is a fact that
> Hanbalites were very active at this level of communication… Fideism thus
> appears a form of knowledge appropriate for a religious party with a keen
> interest in the populace at large, and hence with a decided tendency
> towards proselytism.[20]

The first part of his comment suggests the connection between this
fideism and the maintenance of Islamic power as a "quarry of authority"
by the house of Saud, and also that this fideism is integral to the Saudi
mindset which draws on a sense of authority and administrative support.

Let me offer then a way to assess the term "fideism" further to see if we
can get to the heart of the matter in a more constructive way. The Stanford
Encyclopedia of Philosophy defines fideism as follows:

> "Fideism" is the name given to that school of thought—to which Tertullian
> himself is frequently said to have subscribed—which answers that faith is
> in some sense independent of, if not outright adversarial toward, reason. In
> contrast to the more rationalistic tradition of natural theology, with its
> arguments for the existence of God, fideism holds—or at any rate appears
> to hold (…)—that reason is unnecessary and inappropriate for the exercise
> and justification of religious belief. The term itself derives from fides, the
> Latin word for faith, and can be rendered literally as faith-ism. "Fideism" is
> thus to be understood not as a synonym for "religious belief," but as denot-
> ing a particular philosophical account of faith's appropriate jurisdiction
> vis-a-vis that of reason.

As the reference to Tertullian suggests, although much discussed in
Christian theology, and rejected by Roman Catholic theology but present

in much conservative Protestant theology, the term is not essentially a Christian term. In short, it means a reliance on faith rather than reason in the pursuit of religious and ultimate truth. Thus, the believer tests all findings in the world against faith, because the world does not contradict God. Instead, the fideist believes that truth in religion is ultimately based on faith rather than on the use of reasoning or based on the evidence. Christian theologians and believers have stated that the fundamental tenets of religion cannot themselves be established by proofs or by empirical evidence and hence need to be accepted on the basis of faith. The famous formulation by Saint Anselm *fides quaerens intellectum*, "faith seeking understanding," is used to explain this relationship between faith and our capacity for reasoning, since we cannot reason or factually prove faith to ourselves. The earlier Augustinian expression of *credo ut intelligam*, "I believe in order to know," is in the same line of thinking in placing the primary emphasis on the role of faith in thought. What our reasoning can do is take us to a deeper understanding of faith and God, indeed it is the only true path of understanding in these terms. Nothing is truly knowable if God is absent from our thought, and our thought processes are a process of discovering what God has given to us or has revealed.

Fideism has a long tradition in the Christian and Western philosophical tradition to reflect on as well. Blaise Pascal, famous for Pascal's wager, explanation in the Pensées is also a form of fideism, when he argued that the natural capacities of people are inadequate to lead them to any completely certain truth. There are other variations on the theme, and we need to be careful to capture these if we are to find the term useful for our purposes. Some treatments of fideism simply denigrate or deny the value of reason and science at all, and such fideist accounts amount to a form of irrationalism. This fideism was perhaps best explained by David Hume in his ironic statement at the end of his essay "Of Miracles":

[The] Christian Religion not only was at first attended with miracles, but even to this day cannot be believed by any reasonable person without them. Mere reason is not sufficient to convince us of its veracity; and whoever is moved by Faith to assent to it, is conscious of a continued miracle in his own person, which subverts all the principles of his understanding, and gives him a determination to believe what is most contrary to custom and experience.[21]

A more recent formulation of fideism is Wittgensteinian Fideism. Ludwig Wittgenstein posited that religion is a self-contained and primarily expressive system which is governed by its own internal logic or "grammar." Indeed, religion is logically cut off from other aspects of life, and religious discourse is essentially self-referential, which means the religious believer is not allowing us to talk about reality. The outcome is that religious beliefs can be understood only by religious believers, on the one hand, and religion cannot be criticized, on the other. These last two points tend to be the ones that cause problems in dialogue. The first aspect of Wittgensteinian Fideism is fine because people can simply remain outside of the system, in other words it appeals to a privatized or quietest religion. The problem is when in dialogue with other systems, or the liberal system of thinking, there is an intransigence and failure to communicate, with the religious person measuring all aspects of life against the norms of the faith.

We find this Wittgensteinian Fideism in the major Islamic thinker Abu Hamid Muhammad Al-Ghazali (1058–1111), who explained all branches of all Islamic learning stem from the Koran. His position is similar to Tertullian's fideism in his *Tahafut al-falasifa* [1095], the "Incoherence of the Philosophers," in which Al-Ghazali was mainly concerned with the negative aspects of faith and those Muslims who thought some un-Islamic things to be Islamic. Where the claims of reason come into conflict with revelation, reason must yield to revelation. Al-Ghazali explains:

The highest and noblest knowledge is the knowledge of God (may he be exalted!), because all other forms of knowledge are sought for the sake of it and it is not sought for anything else.[22]

All the sciences, including those outside of the Koran, "are drawn out of one of the seas of knowledge of God."[23] Thus, all knowledge is self-referential in liberal terms, but put Islamically all knowledge comes from God, and we cannot know all things and so we cannot make sense of everything. This is not to say we live by blind faith, as noted in Tertullian and Augustine we seek to understand more, but in understanding more we are moving toward God and not toward human knowledge for its own sake. Discussing the knowledge revealed by the Prophet, Al-Ghazali explains:

> This knowledge is not attained by means of the various special branches of knowledge to which most people devote their attention. As a result, most people's knowledge only makes them bolder in disobeying God most high. Genuine knowledge, however, increases a man's reverence and fear and hope; and these come between him and sins (in the strict sense) as distinct from the unintentional faults which are inseparable from man in his times of weakness.[24]

There was a different response to this from another great Islamic thinker, known as Abu al-Walid Muhammad ibn Ahmad ibn Rushd, better known in the West as Averroes (1126–1198). Shabbir Akhtar suggests Averroes was inspired more by Aristotle than the Koran, and was a philosopher who saw religion as "metaphysics for the masses."[25] Akhtar explains causation and meaning of events in this world are contingent for Averroes, and the true knowledge which is the meaning of the Koran is hidden from the people, with only the philosophers able to penetrate and explain its meaning.[26] Averroes was influential in Thomist and other medieval Christian thinking, bringing translations of Aristotle to the West, and he was more influential in the Islamic world. It was Al-Ghazali's explanation of knowledge, authority and divine revelation that became normative for Islamic orthodoxy up to the present day. We should be cautious, and the foregoing discussion shows there is a great deal of intellectual discussion, that the fideism of Islam is not simply blind faith or irrational. In this respect we should consider, however unpalatable people may find this point, that Islamic State and Al-Qaeda have a theological and legal basis to their beliefs and actions. They are pursuing a soteriological aim and pursue this through their claim to be a caliphate as a source of worldly power and proselytism to draw others into the pursuit of salvation.

Fideism provides a very powerful hermeneutic tool, and one I suggest is at the heart of the Saudi Islamic mindset which is common to

Hanbalism, Wahhabism and Salafism. The followers of religion and critics from other disciplines, believer and unbeliever unlike, can easily fall into the trap of talking past each other. To help connect the dialogue, I propose we use this common term "fideism" as a more useful way of speaking than the terms in current use to describe the "Islamic problem." It is less familiar than the other terms discussed, hence I suggest it gives us a better grasp and a less contentious foundation on which to examine, understand and explain Islam and the relationship between Islam and the contemporary world, whether we are talking about Saudi, Islamic State or Islam in other parts of the world. There is certainly a fideist streak running through Islam, common to those who support jihadism as much as those who have thought through the world today in faith and resisted the option to choose violence or confrontation to deal with the secularism of the modern world. Saudi Arabia has proselytized Islam, named by the West as conservative and fundamentalist, but speak to many a Saudi they do not necessarily recognize the terminologies outlined above. Hence, younger Saudi generations of men and women are not simply accepting or rebelling, as the West would have it. They are questioning their society, wanting some freedoms while welcoming what the West determines to be restrictions. We cannot assume that the younger generations want the freedoms of Western secularism or even international norms. Many, and perhaps most, want Islamic freedom.

There are conflicts between a number of international norms, in particular in areas of human rights, gender and sexuality. Saudi is changing on some of these matters, but what change there is fails to impress Western critics who want to see faster and more radical change. This is, however, the problem. How does one effect radical change in a Kingdom where things do not happen in the often disruptive way that change happens in the West? We can ponder whether rather than having dialogue based on Western progressive notions of rights, gender and so forth, there are ways to have a discussion on the role of rights based on engaging the Islamic foundations and how changes are implemented in Saudi, indeed in any twenty-first-century Islamic country. The Western agenda is based on secular norms, and when I suggest people talk past each other it is because they are working from different foundations. This is not to say every dialogue partner on these issues behave this way, but in the knockabout world of politics we end up retreating into these foundational positions. The Koran supports caution as a dialogue principle:

> If a group of people from every tribe stayed behind to study (and ponder on) the religion, (they would be able) to warn and admonish their people when they return to them so that they are cautious. (Al-Tawbah. v.122)

Thus, more thoughtful and reflective engagement is needed with Sharia and Fiqh in order to have such a dialogue in the Islamic public square. Is it possible that there can be a dialogue derived from an understanding, and reinterpretation, of this tradition rather than the importing of Western rights-based and political thinking? The problem with the fideism of Islam is that it is not other-worldly, to use Max Weber's term, rather it demands that believers recognize and change the world in conformity with Islam. Are we then in a position where Saudi and other Islamic societies can only draw a straight line between the fideism of Islam and the political actions currently tormenting the world?

Notes

1. There are four recognized Sunni schools (s. *madhhab,* pl. *madhhahib*), Hanafi, Shafa'i, Maliki and Hanbali, and three Shi'a schools, Ja'fari, Zaydi and Isma'ili. See also http://www.mei.edu/content/tawhid-or-jihad-what-wahhabism-and-not#edn
2. Delong-Bas (2004, p. 11).
3. Ibid.
4. Haykel et al. (2015, p. 186).
5. Lewis (2002, p. 128).
6. Delong-Bas (2004, p. 38).
7. See quote from Zahra, Muhammed Abu *History of Islamic Schools of Thought,* Cairo, 1997, p. 208 http://www.islamicsupremecouncil.org/understanding-islam/legal-rulings/52-understanding-islamic-law.html#_ftn6
8. http://europe.newsweek.com/saudi-royal-execution-my-distant-cousin-shows-nobody-above-law-512574?rm=eu
9. Lewis (2002, pp. 129–130).

10. Haykel et al. (2015, p. 151).
11. Maher (2016).
12. Haykel et al. (2015, p. 152).
13. Haykel et al. (2015, p. 162).
14. https://newrepublic.com/article/103071/salafism-yemen-laurent-bonnefoy
15. Laurent Bonnefoy, "Salafism in Yemen: A Saudisation?" in Madawi (2008), pp. 245–262.
16. Thomas Hegghammer and Stephane Lacroix, "Rejectionist Islamism in Saudi Arabia: The Story of Juhayman al-'Utaybi Revisited," *The International Journal of Middle East Studies*, Vol. 39, No. 1 (2007), pp. 97–116.
17. Muqbil al-Wadi'i, *Mushahadaî iî al-Mamlaka al-'Arabiyya al-Sa'udiyya* (Sanaa: Dar al-athar, 2005).
18. http://www.mei.edu/content/how-salafism-came-yemen-unknown-legacy-juhayman-al-utaybi-30-years#edn3
19. Ibid, Bonnefoy (2012).
20. Aziz Al-Azmeh, *Orthodoxy and Hanbalite Fideism*, Arabica, T. 35, Fasc. 3 (Nov, 1988, p. 265).
21. Hume (2007, p. 95).
22. Quaesem (1983, p. 43).
23. Ibid, p. 46.
24. Watt, W. Montgomery, The Faith and Practice of Al-Ghazali (George Allen and Unwin), https://www.ghazali.org/works/watt3.htm
25. Koslowski (1985, p. 26).
26. Koslowski (1985, p. 27).

Bibliography

al-Rasheed, Madawi. 2008. *Kingdom Without Borders: Saudi Arabia's Political, Religious and Media Frontiers*. London: Hurst.
Allawai, Ali A. 2009. *The Crisis of Islamic Civilization*. New Haven: Yale University Press.
An-Na'im, Abdullahi Ahmed. 2008. *Islam and the Secular State: Negotiating the Future of Shari'a*. Cambridge, MA: Harvard University Press.
Berger, Peter L. 1967. *The Sacred Canopy: Elements of a Sociological Theory of Religion*. New York: Anchor Books.
———. 1973. *The Social Reality of Religion*. London: Penguin.

————., ed. 1999. *The Desecularization of the World: Resurgent Religion and World Politics*. Grand Rapids: Eerdmans.

Black, Antony. 2001. *The History of Islamic Political Thought: From the Prophet to the Present*. Edinburgh: Edinburgh University Press.

Bonnefoy, Laurent. 2012. *Salafism in Yemen: Transnationalism and Religious Identity*. New York: Columbia University Press.

Bowering, Gerhard, ed. 2015. *Islamic Political Thought: An Introduction*. Princeton: Princeton University Press.

Craze, Jonathan, and Mark Huband. 2009. *The Kingdom: Saudi Arabia and the Challenge of the Twenty-First Century*. London: Hurst & Co.

Delong-Bas, Natana J. 2004. *Wahhabi Islam: From Revival and Reform to Global Jihad*. New York: Oxford University Press.

Esposito, John L. 2002. *Unholy War: Terror in the Name of Islam*. New York: Oxford University Press.

Fawcett, Louise. 2016. *International Relations of the Middle East*. 4th ed. Oxford: Oxford University Press.

Hallaq, Wael B. 1999. *Islamic Legal Theories*. Cambridge: Cambridge University Press.

Hamid, Shadi. 2016. *Islamic Exceptionalism: How the Struggle Over Islam Is Reshaping the World*. New York: St. Martin's Press.

Hamidullah, Muhammad. 1975. *The First Written Constitution in the World: An Important Document of the Time of the Holy Prophet*. (3rd Rev. ed.). Lahore: Sh. Muhammad Ashraf.

Haykel, Bernard, Thomas Hegghammer, and Stéphane Lacroix. 2015. *Saudi Arabia in Transition: Insights on Social, Political, Economic and Religious Change*. Cambridge: Cambridge University Press.

Heggenhammer, Thomas. 2010. *Jihad in Saudi Arabia: Violence and Pan-Islamism Since 1979*. New York: Cambridge University Press.

————. 2015. *Saudi Arabia in Transition: Insights on Social, Political, Economic and Religious Change*. New York: Cambridge University Press.

Hourani, Albert A. 2002. *History of the Arab Peoples*. Cambridge, MA: Belknap Press.

Hume, David. 2007. *An Enquiry Concerning Human Understanding*. Oxford: Oxford University Press.

Karsh, Effraim. 2006. *Islamic Imperialism: A History*. New Haven: Yale University Press.

Kepel, Gilles. 2004. *The War for Muslim Minds: Islam and the West*. Trans. Pascal Ghazaleh. Cambridge MA: Belknap Press.

Kerr, Malcolm. 1965. *The Arab Cold War, 1958–1964: A Study of Ideology in Politics*. Oxford: Oxford University Press.

Koslowsk, P., ed. 1985. *Philosophy Bridging the World Religions*. Dordrecht: Kluwer.

Lecker, Michael. 2004. *The Constitution of Medina: Muḥammad's First Legal Document*. Princeton: Darwin.

Lewis, Bernard. 2002. *The Arabs in History*. New York: Oxford University Press.

Lewis, L., C. Pellat, and J. Schacht, eds. 1998. *Cambridge Encyclopedia of Islam, Volume II*. Leiden: Brill.

Luciani, Giacomo, ed. 1990. *The Arab State*. Berkeley: University of California Press.

Maher, Shiraz. 2016. *Salafi-Jihadism: The History of an Idea*. London: Hurst & Company.

Mansfield, Peter. 1985. *The Arabs*. London: Penguin Books.

Patai, Raphael. 1973. *The Arab Mind*. New York: Scribner.

Plantinga, Alvin, and Nicholas Wolterstorff, eds. 1983. *Faith and Rationality: Reason and Belief in God*. Notre Dame: University of Notre Dame Press.

Quaesem, Muhammad Abdul. 1983. *The Jewels of the Qur'an: Al-Ghazali's Theory*. London: Islamic Book Trust.

Said, Edward W. 1979. *Orientalism*. Princeton: Princeton University Press.

———. 1981. *Covering Islam: How the Media and the Experts Determine How We See the Rest of the World*. New York: Pantheon Books.

Schact, J. 1964. *An Introduction to Islamic Law*. New York: Oxford University Press.

Shabbir, Akhtar. 1985. In *Philosophy Bridging the World Religions*, ed. P. Koslowski. Dordrecht: Kluwer.

Southern, R.W. 1978. *Western Views of Islam in the Middle Ages*. Cambridge, MA: Harvard University Press.

Taylor, Charles. 2007. *A Secular Age*. Cambridge, MA: Belknap Press.

Watt, W. Montgomery. 1953. *The Faith and Practice of Al-Ghazali*. London: George Allen and Unwin.

Weber, Max. 2010. *The Protestant Ethic and the Spirit of Capitalism*. Oxford: Oxford University Press.

Wilson, Bryan. 1966. *Religion in a Secular Society*. London: Watts.

Part IV

Conclusion

11

Theocracy and Secularization

Saudi is not a secular society, but it is partly capitalist. The spirit of modern capitalism is secular, and indeed secularization has gone hand-in-hand with capitalism. Secularization theory[1] is a term that was used in the 1950s and 1960s by a number of social scientists and historians to describe social and economic change, and diagnosed that modernity inevitably produces a decline of religion. If we take this point seriously, then we can perhaps understand the resistance from within Islam and Saudi toward aspects of modern capitalism. If the product is secularization then the inevitability is social change, and for many believers the damaging of Islam and the Saudi way of life. As discussed in the previous chapter, Islam is not anti-economic or anti-capitalism as such, but there is much in the modern form of capitalism that is of concern and is also the basis of much anti-Americanism. When some Christians express fear that Islam is a threat to their faith, they might want to reflect on the argument that in some respects Christianity has been much more "damaged" by American capitalism and secularization than it has by Islam. In the secular West, capitalism has generated a consumer culture which holds up a mirror to society. The easy availability and disposability of goods has impacted values, while social media and communications have distracted society. There is a greater materialist culture, though no shortage of spiritual ideas and pursuits, many produced by the materialist state of affairs.

© The Author(s) 2018   **253**
D. Cowan, *The Coming Economic Implosion of Saudi Arabia*,
https://doi.org/10.1007/978-3-319-74709-5_11

It seems that the richer a society gets the more spiritually impoverished it is; but this need not be the case. It is hard to see how Western society can reverse this trend, if indeed it should, but Saudi as an Islamic country has the potential to show how a society can evolve in a spiritual way and at the same time be economically successful. The question is one of whether economic development and success is necessarily secular and needs a secular spirit. To understand this, we need to look at what we mean by the term secular.

Secularism as a Western construct has a long history, but I will start with a contemporary definition by Charles Taylor who defined secular in three senses. First, it is the absence of God from public spaces. Second, it is the absence of God from our discourse in terms of norms and principles. In these first two senses, we can encounter the world entirely without mention of God. The third sense he suggests consists in "a move from a society where belief in God is unchallenged and indeed, unproblematic, to one in which it is understood to be one option among others, and frequently not the easiest to embrace."[2] He added to this that America as a whole is secularized, while the majority of Islamic countries provide a stark case of contrast. In all three senses of secular this is very much a Saudi issue, because God is understood to be everywhere, starting with the daily practice of believers and the constitution of the Kingdom.

We ought to take the shared interests and differences with Islam seriously if we are to get to the heart of the political and cultural challenge of the rise of Islam and the Saudi predicament. From the perspective of the Islamic world, many Muslims see the advance of secular Western values, particularly in respect to sexuality, along with a perceived spiritual vacuum in Western culture and capitalism, and believe there is an opportunity to fill this vacuum. Michel Houellebecq's novels *Platform* and *Submission* capture this point of a Western vacuum quite well. In the latter novel, in his search for meaning, the narrator explains:

> I was living in a country distinguished by a placid socialism, where ownership of material possessions was guaranteed by strict legislation, where the banking system was surrounded by powerful state guarantees. Unless I were to venture beyond what was lawful, I ran no risk of embezzlement or fraudulent bankruptcy. All in all, I needn't worry anymore. In fact, I never really had…why had I never shown any real passion in my life?[3]

This feeds into the Islamic narrative concerning the West, and the need for a more defining Islam than its secularized or Americanized versions on the one hand, and its radicalized and violent versions on the other. Young Muslim people, and others, are growing up in the West and they seek meaning in life, and they are finding it in the Islamic faith. This yearning has been the target of Saudi proselytization in recent times, supplying texts and materials to encourage people to follow the path of Islam.

This is a point we have to take on board if we are to understand the dynamics of the violence in recent years with attacks in France, Belgium, the United Kingdom, Spain, Germany and elsewhere. There are many theories and thoughts about how this radicalism has arisen, and it is a shared responsibility of Saudi and the West concerning the causes. Young people finding Islamic faith itself are not the problem. It is the content and the channeling of the expressions of Islamic faith that are troubling for Islam and the West alike. What Saudi has supplied in materials and ideas has been unprocessed for the most part, and thus it has influenced people's embrace of Islam but now how the new believer is guided to follow the path. The Islamic State forces have understood this and manipulated the guidance toward a radically fideist and troubling version of Islam. Saudi provided the opportunity, Islamic State took the advantage. The success of Islamic State has not been so much a direct military or operational threat in the West, it is essentially a very effective communications strategy. Like Al-Qaeda, the Western media did a top job of branding it, giving it a reality that belied its loose confederation. After some months of reporting about "Islamic State" and "ISIS" interchangeably, the news outlets started to refer to "so-called" Islamic State, but it was too late as the media had already done the branding job. This then relayed into an image projected into Europe to disaffected youth, who were inspired by this branded Islamic organization. They inspired such events that made headline news in Paris, Brussels and elsewhere. Islamic State was not running all these operations, they were inspiring young people, many of whom have never visited or lived in an Islamic society before, through a meaningful connection. They continue to manipulate such disaffected individuals by design, not by accident.

In turn, Europe is quite dizzy from the attacks on its culture and its secularity, which it had taken for granted for so long. We have witnessed the emergence of fear and ignorance, with mistakes being made. The controversy over women wearing the abaya or burkinis, which became a very public cultural dispute when bans were introduced on the Côte d'Azur in the Summer of 2016, highlights differences in values. It raised broader questions of who can tell a woman what to wear, but also gave rise to comment from Muslim women that they choose to wear the religious dress. While some women in Saudi may see the dress code as an imposition, many will say it expresses their Muslim identity, and it is Western women who are telling them what they should wear. This said, we need to look carefully at the history of the Saudi form of dress, since the current regulations are a mixture of Koranic injunction, a long tradition and ideas of more recent origin. The political challenges thus range from the highest level of learning in Europe right down to what women are wearing on the beach. This is where the war is being fought, but is it a clash of civilizations and religions? No. Much of it is a distraction.

We need to get back to a more authentic understanding and analysis of religion if we are to understand its role, positive and negative, in society. To reiterate, the problem is that religion is often excluded or ill-thought out in analysis, and before proceeding it is important to spend some time here in understanding why this is the case. The reason for the difficulty in discussing religion is largely down to the assumption of the secularization thesis, first fully articulated by Max Weber. It is important here to dissect the thesis as Weber developed it for two reasons at this stage, which will be helpful as we work our way through the problem of interpreting religion. First, his secularization thesis has been so influential in the social sciences, unfortunately putting a rather large plank in the social scientist's eye, to borrow from a well-known biblical text. Second, his analysis was deeply flawed in its grasp of theology and historical religion, and demonstrates the problems of getting it wrong.

To explore secularity, and the related issues in this chapter, I will look through the lens of three writers in particular, two Western and one Islamic:

- Max Weber
- Peter Berger
- Ibn Khaldūn

The intention here is not to undertake an exhaustive study of each of these thinkers, but to highlight their key ideas and how they can shed light on capitalism, religion and secularity generally, and Islam specifically. Weber first articulated the secularization thesis, and studied the connection between religion and capitalism. Peter Berger has made a series of useful investigations into secularism, explaining the decline of the thesis and connected these questions to the Christian tradition as well as other religious traditions, though to a lesser extent. Lastly, Ibn Khaldūn is an Islamic writer who can offer us a basis on which to analyze an Islamic route through the secularization challenge and the economic ones as well, thereby providing an Islamic underpinning to some of the thinking to the argument offered in this book.

Weber's Secularization Thesis: Anatomy of an Error

Weber's "secularization thesis" originated in article form in 1904–1905 and appeared in book form in 1920–1921 as *The Protestant Ethic and the Spirit of Capitalism*.[4] While not without controversy it became widely accepted in modern thinking in the West about secularism. He was trying to understand why capitalism had taken its strongest hold in northern Protestant countries rather than in those countries which held allegiance to the Roman Catholic tradition. He separated the pursuit of wealth under capitalism from pre-capitalistic society. In capitalism, Weber explained it is only under capitalism that we see the rational organization of formally free labor. He then famously connected Christian Reformation doctrine to the emergence of capitalism and its spirit. The doctrine of vocation, or *beruf* in the German of Luther, is the main link Weber made between Protestantism and capitalism. However, *beruf* means much more than one's job. In Luther's doctrine it is a radical, neighbor-centered ethic that displaces good works from the realm of the merely spiritual into the realm of the material, the social and the ordinary. God calls us to the ordinary task of life, and the Reformation extended the notion of priestly calling to activities of the laity. The ordinariness of this doctrine connected to the priesthood of all believers, which means serving God does not require us to be ordained or enter the monastery to pursue our calling with God. Vocation thus broadens God's reach in our lives. Luther's view was that God works through our vocation to care for the divine creation. It has the reformation doctrine of justification by faith alone at its heart, as in our vocation we do not work to show our status with God or prove our election, instead we are humbly responding as vessels to God's ordering of creation. What vocation does for the individual, it does for society, meaning the Reformation had broken down the division of society as church, nobility and commoners and promoted greater egalitarianism and fairer division of labor.

Weber traced what he saw as the influence of these religious ideas on the economic spirit or ethos of an economic system, specifically intending to link the spirit of modern economic life with what he called the rational ethics of ascetic Protestantism. He argued that capitalism entailed the accumulation of wealth for its own sake, and Calvinist Protestantism supplied the moral basis for the capitalist spirit, resulting in the work ethic and effort to show one's chosen nature by performing "good works" to demonstrate one was chosen or one of the elect of God. Weber discussed vocation or the Christian "calling" as this sign of being one of the elect. Weber had set his focus on Calvin and later puritans rather than Luther, and herein lay his fundamental theological error. Weber was analyzing forms of Protestantism of his own time rather than that of the reformation period. The Lutheranism that Weber grew up with in Germany was infused with pietism, which imported into Lutheranism some of the Calvinist thinking about calling and the elect. Theology aside, Weber argued that the new spirit driving capitalism led to the creation of self-reliance, as the individualization of the economy created a correlation with the rise of impersonal capital. Hence, the market does not simply set prices, it is for Weber "the market of life."[5] However, instead of seeing the problem in terms of social class, as Karl Marx did, Weber saw the problem as one of impersonal capital and a systemic web of interests; hence he discusses "capital" rather than "the capitalist." Weber was not arguing, as modern-day protesters do, that unlimited greed defines capitalism, if anything there is a need for restraint. The "greedy bankers" on Wall Street were wrong because they forsook this principle, but I venture Weber would say the same about the many indi-

viduals who "flipped" their homes and treated their houses like an investment rather than a home in the years leading up to the 2008 recession.
What defines capitalism, for Weber, is the pursuit of profit, forever
renewed, by means of the rational capitalistic enterprise. Other defining
characteristics were encapsulated by Benjamin Franklin's saying that time
is money and the other dictum, such as honesty is the best policy. One of
the core actors in this economy was the secular entrepreneur.

The individual in capitalism also opposes authority. Thus, in the capitalist economy there is a necessary nurturing of the individual and the
need of the individual to adapt. Weber drew a parallel between Calvin's
notion of *deus absconditus* or hidden God and the impersonal rule of
invisible capital. The individual is in an identical situation in respect to
the capitalist economy and predestination, which Weber identified as the
state of "unprecedented inner isolation of the single individual."[6] Like
Marx, Weber thought of capitalism in terms of the capitalist enterprise or
Betrieb, in other words the industrial organization of commerce. Thus, the
rentier economy was not for Weber, nor Marx, an authentic form of capitalism. Weber also believed freedom to be important, and the fact that
freedom was essential to capitalism made the problem difficult. Capitalism
had supplanted the patriarchal and hierarchical way of life before the capitalistic era, but he also saw capitalism as being in a transitional period.
This period was one, he believed, of technical change which would come
to an end. Subsequent history clearly demonstrates that capitalism continues to make technical innovation. The problem for understanding
Weber is that he could not see capitalism as a stable and lasting form of
social organization, which it has been for the past quarter millennia.

We can question Weber's enquiry in terms of how we can understand
the relationship between religion and capitalism. The Weberian summa-
tion of capitalism is at odds with the Islamic mindset regarding commerce generally. Weber explained:

Such natures as are filled with the "capitalist spirit" *today* tend to be, if not
directly hostile to the church, then indifferent. The thought of the "pious
boredom" of paradise has little attraction to a nature rejoicing in action; to
such people religion appears as a means of diverting people from their work
on this earth.[7]

This view of the capitalist is not one shared in Islam. The Koran includes many sayings and rules in regard to commerce, and it has generally a positive view of commercial activity, so long as it is practiced fairly. The anti-capitalist view is twofold, that it is practiced unfairly and it is intrinsically wrong in some way. Islam is at pains to deal positively with the former, and does not necessarily contest the latter in spirit as stated in Weber. Instead there is another reason it can be judged intrinsically wrong by Islam and that is the charging of interest. There are themes in capitalism that deeply trouble Islamic economists, and while the common perception relates to the ban on interest, it is the intention that is key. Interest is banned, along with speculation and derivatives, because the believer should not second-guess God. This makes capitalism not a problem of a diverting spirit, it is much more fundamental that that. Despite this, some Islamic economists have tied themselves to socialist ideas to offer an alternative, but that too is flawed because Socialism is a secular ideology and based on a confidence in humanity not shared by Islamic theology. There is certainly scope to explore Islamic economic thinking, but for the most part Islamic finance is a niche market that plays with language more than intent, charging fees instead of interest at a level where the two equate with similar levels of profit. This is not the place for such an exploration, but it should be noted.

The main part of the Weber thesis has proved to be in error, though in both academic and public discourses, there remains either implicitly or explicitly the notion that secularization and the advancement of human ideas and action should exclude religion. As Peter Berger portrayed the situation:

> It's a particular kind of elite. The top of that elite are people mostly in the social sciences and humanities. Natural scientists are not so much in that groove. The problem, I think, has to do with—again—pluralism. It has to do with the relativization of worldviews and values, which is most conscious to intellectuals who are in literature, or sociology, or anthropology, or history, rather than chemists, let's say, or physicists who are not as much affected by this relativization. I think an explanation can be made along those lines.[8]

If this is so, then while these elites embrace relativism almost religiously, we are still waiting for religion itself to become irrelevant or disappear. It has been so deeply ingrained in academic discourse that the outcome has been not the sidelining of religion, but the inadequacy of understanding of religion by social scientists and others. Social scientists and other thinkers ceased to learn about religion or engage with it in any truly meaningful sense, and are now still running to catch up with recent events. Despite the lengths to which Weber studied religion, the founding father of social sciences set the tone for the future by fostering a misunderstanding of religion and connecting two things that are loosely connected but ill-fitted to the conclusions he wished to draw. Weber understood religion to be holistic and that it makes claims on the self in contradistinction to politics, which only covers part of the whole self and ethics. This is certainly true of both Christianity and Islam, though in different ways.

Luther himself set up the theological problem very well for us when he wrote that the Christian cobbler makes good shoes, not bad shoes with little crosses on them. Social scientists have tended to understand the relationship between faith and action in reverse, and this approach can be traced back to Weber. Religion still had a place in their work, but it was clearly demarcated and increasingly was being pushed out by secularism. Thus religious ideas and input was increasingly ignored; and religious language became more archaic to the modern ear. This created a problem for religious people who sought a way to be relevant, leading to the mainstream forms of faith secularizing to keep up with culture, a reversal of the idea that people should keep up with God in traditional religion. The point of the Weberian trajectory, and that of social and political scientists, is that religion was always present, and those who assumed it had largely disappeared were themselves making narrow cultural assumptions, hence they could not see the plank firmly embedded in their own eye. Some have since decided religion was making a comeback; but even this is wrong. What they should have discovered is that religion had never gone away in the first place except within their narrow disciplines.

As Ghosh highlights,[9] Weber's treatment of Christianity is supranational, a place where the primacy of religious values is unquestioned. In Europe with its state religion it is easy to see how Christianity became housetrained, and its values subordinated to national interest and values, but this is not the Gospel brought by Jesus as understood by many Christians, nor is it the Koran of Mohammed followed by Muslims. The religion stands above all, and the world is judged by God not God by the world. This world for many Muslims is seen as troubled and threatened in broader terms than the economic ones, it is a question of culture and behaviors which are set in opposition to traditional Islam. The reason why the Iranians called Saudi's religious practice "American Islam" is not just a reference to American political influence, it is an attack on the secular and cultural influence which they believe has devalued the Islamic faith in the eyes of those who believed they were following the true path and who seek authentic Islam. Saudi has capitulated to this culture in Iranian eyes, though Iran is a capitalist country so clearly it has not seen the bigger picture either. Iran may miss the big picture, but since the Iranian revolution, and more so after 9/11, we have witnessed the Weberian assumption being turned on its head. The Iranian revolution and the subsequent rise of Islam and Islamic radicalism are a firm rebuttal of the Weberian thesis, but sadly in the process we have lost a dimension of understanding in the social sciences and in public discourse as a result. The Islamic religious revolt, whether we are talking about Iranian revolutionaries or Muslims in Saudi and America, is against secularism and America is seen as the progressive cultural warrior of secularism. To answer this mood, I will look first at Berger as a Christian thinker and then seek if there might be a resolution in Ibn Khaldūn.

Peter Berger: Dissecting the Decline of Secularism

Like Weber, Peter Berger explains religion in terms of the totality of human life, suggesting "religion is the audacious attempt to conceive of the entire universe as being humanly significant."[10] In his book *The Scared Canopy*, Berger highlights the problem of religion and world-maintenance, based on the argument that religion makes a whole claim and competes in a pluralistic world. Berger explains that in creating the sacred canopy, Protestantism has significantly contributed to the secularization of the West:

> At the risk of some simplification, it can be said that Protestantism divested itself as much as possible from the three most ancient and most powerful concomitants of the sacred—mystery, miracle, and magic. This process has been aptly caught in the phrase, 'disenchantment of the world...'[11]

Instead, mainline Protestantism has replaced the core of the Gospel:

> which has to do with the cosmic redefinition of reality, with either politics or psychology or a kind of vague morality, which is not what I think the Christian Gospel is basically about.[12]

Sacred Canopy is Berger's earliest work, and he later changes his mind. Berger labels himself "an unreconstructed Weberian" and argued it is clear that "some values foster modern economic development more than others."[13] However, the values that may have been evident in early capitalism are not necessarily essential in today's phase of capitalism, and so he suggests "The past is malleable and flexible, changing as our recollection interprets and re-explains what has happened."[14] He offers an explanation of how things changed and a shift from blind acceptance to questioning the secularization thesis:

> When I started out doing sociology of religion—like two hundred years ago—everyone else had the same idea. And I more or less assumed that it was correct. It wasn't a completely crazy assumption; there were many reasons why people said that. But it took me about twenty years to come to the conclusion that the data doesn't support this, and other people came to the same conclusion.... The world today is not heavily secularized, with two interesting exceptions that have to be explained. One is geographical, it's Western and Central Europe, and the other is an international intellectual class that is heavily secularized.... The rest of the world is massively religious. In some areas of the world, more religious than ever. The theory is wrong.[15]

To replace secularization theory and explain religion in the modern world, Berger suggests we need the theory of pluralism. He argues that secularity is not necessarily the product of modernity but pluralism is necessarily the product, by which he means the coexistence in the same society of different worldviews and value systems. Pluralism is what changes the status of religion and challenges every religious tradition. As Berger notes, "The problem with modernity is not that God is dead, as some people hoped and other people feared. There are too many gods, which is a challenge, but a different one."[16]

Thomas Kuhn, in his *The Structure of Scientific Revolutions*, goes further and argues that when one theoretical paradigm collapses under the weight of evidence, it opens up the possibility of new paradigms. In the Christian context Berger explains this means:

If a church is too closely linked to the state, every time people get annoyed at the state, they get annoyed with the church that is established by the state. It's very simple. And that's not good for religion, and it's not good for the state, for different but similar reasons. That's the most important reason, I think.[17]

In the Islamic context, Berger suggests:

The most massive change is in the Muslim world…you get now an intelligentsia in Muslim majority countries, which is heavily Islamic or even Islamist in the radical sense.[18]

This radicalization is thus rooted in theology and identity, not some madness or bloodlust. As Berger explains:

The Islamic revival is by no means restricted to the less modernized or "backward" sectors of society, as progressive intellectuals still like to think. On the contrary, it is very strong in cities with a high degree of modernization, and in a number of countries it is particularly visible among people with a western-style higher education.[19]

This said, Berger observes that "Islam has had a difficult time coming to terms with key modern institutions, such as pluralism, democracy, and the market economy."[20] In other words, there is a tension between the recovery of Islamic identity and the pluralist impacts of modernity. If we dig deeper we can perhaps see, to use Edward Said's term, the orientalism of Berger's assessment. Is it the case that Islam, whatever we mean by this, has a problem with these Western ideas and institutions, or is it that such ideas and institutions have not developed as they should have done? To follow this line thought we turn to the pioneering work undertaken by Islamic scholar Ibn Khaldūn, to see if we can arrive at a picture of modernity by way of an Islamic route.

Ibn Khaldūn: An Islamic Voice, Realist and Father of Social Sciences

Ibn Khaldūn, whose full name was Walī al-Dīn ʿAbd al-Raḥmān ibn Muḥammad ibn Muḥammad ibn Abī Bakr Muḥammad ibn al-Ḥasan Ibn Khaldūn, was born in Tunis in 1332 and died 1406 in Cairo. The Khaldūniyyah quarter in Tunis where he was born still stands largely unchanged, reputedly including the house where he was born. Ibn Khaldūn has the reputation of being the greatest of Arab historians and wrote one of the earliest nonreligious philosophies of history, his masterpiece, the *Muqaddimah* or "Introduction." The book was intended to form the introduction to a larger volume called the *Kitab al-Ibar*, or "Book of Lessons." Ibn Khaldūn analyzed systematically the functioning of an economy and offered a coherent general economic theory to explain and predict the rise and the fall of civilizations, nations and empires. The historian Arnold Toynbee described the *Muqaddimah* as "undoubtedly the greatest work of its kind that has ever yet been created by any mind in any time or place."[21] In 1964, Joseph Spengler praised Ibn Khaldūn as the greatest economist of medieval Islam,[22] eulogizing, "…one is compelled to infer from a comparison of Ibn Khaldūn's economic."[23] However, it was Schumpeter who "discovered" him a few months before his death.[24] Ibn Khaldūn also wrote a rich and extensive history of Muslim North Africa.

At a time when Saudi Arabia is going through its own problems, it is useful for us to look at this scholar who was born into an influential Saudi clan and had experience of turbulent times in Islamic Spain, as well the Black Death. His work exploring the scientific rules behind the rise and fall of social systems, and the patterns of historical change in terms of human society and social transformation, offers us insight into contemporary dynamics in Saudi and the region. Ibn Khaldūn understood changes in society occur cyclically during normal times and also through distinct events that rupture the system. At the heart of his system was 'asabiyya, which means the social cohesion and cooperation that drives human civilization. Luxury and other factors create a process of decline as social cohesion suffers, which in turn creates a new order of things. Khaldūn's theory explained the effects of government policies on the economy and predicted how a state could survive. He opposed state involvement in trade and production activities and thought that bureaucrats cannot understand commercial activities because they do not have the same motivations as businessmen. He predicted relative decline of economic surplus and the decline of countries in which state involvement in trade and production exists. He saw a large army as an impediment to the expansion of trade, production and economic surplus. In his analysis of economics, Ibn Khaldūn stated:

> it should be known that at the beginning of the dynasty, taxation yields a large revenue from small assessments. At the end of the dynasty, taxation yields a small revenue from large assessments.[25]

This insight was one that the 1970s economist Arthur Laffer later credited Ibn Khaldūn for inspiring the Laffer curve, which Laffer used to illustrate the tradeoff between tax rates and the total tax revenues actually collected by the government.

In explaining the dynamics of society and history, Ibn Khaldūn explained that empires rise when their peoples have a sense of social cohesion or asabiyyah, but once the society has been established on the basis of this cohesion then slowly it begins to lose this social cohesion and the society becomes increasingly sedentary and weakened, thus leading the society to be overthrown by new social groups. He thus held a cyclical view of history and society. Ibn Khaldūn explains the relationship between the state of society and social organization:

Human society is necessary since the individual acting alone could acquire neither the necessary food nor security. Only the division of labour, in and through society, makes this possible. The state arises through the need of a restraining force to curb the natural aggression of humanity. A state is inconceivable without a society, while a society is well-nigh impossible without a state. Social phenomena seem to obey laws which, while not as absolute as those governing natural phenomena, are sufficiently constant to cause social events to follow regular and well-defined patterns and sequences.[26]

Leadership exists through superiority, which comes from group feeling. This overall group feeling and superiority then trumps each individual group feeling. This group feeling can be transferred within the nation as luxury causes royal authority to weaken and gets overthrown, and this leads to a new rule. Ibn Khaldūn explains further:

Rulers and dynasties are strongly entrenched. Their foundations can be undermined and destroyed only through strong efforts backed by the group feeling of tribes and families… Similarly, prophets in their religious propaganda depended on groups and families, though they were the ones who could have been supported by God with anything in existence, if He had wished, but in His wisdom He permitted matters to take their customary course.[27]

If there is no support then the dynasties perish, while those who manipulate religious feeling deserve perdition. Religious reforms are a divine matter and occur through God's work in the world and the religious community.

Thus, Ibn Khaldūn outlines five stages of dynasty:

1. Success as the opposition is overthrown.
2. Complete control over the people.
3. Leisure and tranquility with the fruits of rule enjoyed.
4. Contentment and peacefulness as rulers tread the path of their predecessors.
5. Waste and squandering, with the ruin of the foundations built by the ancestors.

In this last stage, Ibn Khaldūn explains "the dynasty is seized by senility and the chronic disease from which it can hardly ever rid itself, for which it can find no cure, and, eventually, it is destroyed."[28] Any royal authority he explained must be founded firstly on might and feeling, and secondly on money. On the latter, he argued that from the beginning the dynasty has a desert attitude, aspects of which we still find in Saudi today:

> It has the qualities of kindness to subjects, planned moderation in expenditure, and respect for other people's property. It avoids onerous taxation and the display of cunning or shrewdness in the collection of money and the accounting (required) from officials. Nothing at this time calls for extravagant expenditure. Therefore, the dynasty does not need much money.[29]

Later, he explained, comes domination and expansion as royal authority flourishes and takes on more luxuries, and ultimately the ruler must impose taxes to maintain revenues. Saudi has started to take this route, but has a state apparatus and economic challenge to confront.

Using the framework of Ibn Khaldūn, we can ponder that Saudi today has started to impose new taxes and can be accused of not managing its economy properly by using funds to tackle short-term problems rather than trying to ensure the fruits of the dynasty remain plentiful. Using this framework we can go further here and consider the intent of Islam, and how the people may become part of a new social cohesion. Following the path is a case of having restraint and fortitude, according to Ibn Khaldūn:

> When the Muslims got their religion from Muhammad, the restraining influence came from themselves, as a result of encouragement and discouragement he gave them in the Qur'an…. (The influence of) religion, then, decreased among men, and they came to use restraining laws. The religious law became a branch of learning and a craft to be acquired through instruction and education. People turned to sedentary life and assumed the character of submissiveness to law. This led to a decrease in their fortitude.[30]

Government and education laws destroy this fortitude, unlike religious laws because of the qualities inherent in the religion. The Bedouins lived far from government and education and were thus joined in greater community. Like the Bedouins those who fight for Islamic State and other groups are gathered in community of religious and social cohesion that far outweighs the cohesion of those Muslims in sedentary societies elsewhere, who have less cohesion and behave in a more individualist way. This explains why simply saying "not my religion" or "not real Islam" are ineffective responses to these movements. Saudi has become in the framework of Ibn Khaldūn a sedentary society, far from the values and social cohesion of the Bedouins, and if his analysis is right then we are in the last stages of this implosion opening the way for a new dynasty to capture the spirit of the people gathered together with a new social cohesion. King Salman clearly hopes the young generation of royals will capture a new spirit balanced with continuity in the Islamic tradition, embodied in the authority of house of Saud.

An Economic Catalyst for Social Change

The twentieth century was a century which saw the emergence of what critics have broadly called fundamentalism, in both Islam and Christianity, as well as other faiths. It is perhaps trite to say that just as one man's terrorist is another man's freedom fighter, so one man's view of fundamentalism is another man's faith. I have already suggested a preference for fideism as a descriptive term. Whatever name it is called, there has been a complicated relationship between Saudi and the West, but also a complicated one with its Arab neighbors. The political context of Saudi in the twentieth century can be traced against the emergence of Islam on the world stage, culminating in the Iranian revolution and entering the twenty-first century with 9/11. In the Islamic world, Arab thinkers emerged in the wake of the First World War in Western Europe which suggested to them that Europeans were not the superior race at all and led to the emergence of colonial rebellion and resistance, resulting in a somewhat chaotic region. The early writings of this modern fundamentalism were Rashid Rida in *On the Caliphate* (1922–1923) and 'Abd Al-Raziq in *Islam and the Bases of Government* (1924–1925). Meanwhile the political origins of this modern Islamic movement can be traced back to the rise of the Muslim Brethren, Al-Mawdudi and Sayyid Qutb. Anthony Black argues that the Ottoman Empire had left behind a power vacuum and a "loose bundle of ethnic, religious and territorial political identities...The final blow was the recognition by the United Nations, after the civil war of 1948, of the state of Israel."[31] Arab leaders now had a host of agendas that were anti-colonialist, nationalist, socialist and a political Islam. In some quarters Islam became tied to socialism with the suggestion, also made one should add about Jesus, that Muhammad was the "first social-ist." The twentieth-century writers of Islamic economics also gravitated toward socialism, as discussed, and it was hard to distinguish quite where the socialism ends and the Islamism starts. The impact of the 1979 Iranian Revolution on the West was to clarify the demarcation, by reject-ing socialism and raising Islam and Islamic fundamentalism to promi-nence at the same time. Thus, Western generations whose only real contact with Islam was a distant textbook awareness of the crusades sud-denly found Islam was still a force in the world. However, it wasn't until 9/11 that it became the geopolitical question for the world it is today, as opposed to one usually left to regional and religious specialists.

The result is that the decline of the European grand narratives has led to the emergence of an idea that has retained some credibility with large swathes of people. The idea of Islam as a total system resonates with people who desire a grand narrative today, just as people in the West once hankered for socialism, communism and fascism, except this is a religious rather than a secular grand narrative. In an era which Western thinkers call post-Christian and postmodern, these grand secular ideologies and narratives have dissipated, disappeared or morphed into a variety of nar-ratives coalesced around different identity interests. Yet, in the Arab world it seems the grand narrative of Islam and fideism still holds some appeal. Equally paradoxical is the fact that in a global era of social media, this grand narrative of Islam and fideism has become very sophisticated in its use of messaging and channels to spread its ideology. It appears that this old narrative has appealed to an anchorless generation with its prom-ises of totality and certainty. Saudi Arabia is at the top of the user list of most social media, taking their messages and interests from this techno-logical public square as the officials continue censoring old media. At the same time, the general population of Saudi is not organizing action or challenging the state, for reasons rooted in the very meaning of the state in Saudi. Family and hereditary principles are the bases of authority in Saudi, and Black draws attention to membership of the ruling clan and an absence of an independent bourgeoisie, which creates a different conception of "civil society" and state relationship. Hence, we can see why there are cross-purposes in the many failing attempts in international civil group dialogues to problem-solve. Black explains, "The organism which, if any, holds a 'monopoly of the legitimate means of coercion' is not Weber's impersonal bureaucratic state but a network led by an individual—what Ibn Khaldūn called an 'asabiyya'."[32] This is what the modern Middle East state is in truth, and Black explains some observers "have gone so far to argue that one cannot create the state as an independent order in the Islamic world."[33]

So, if Saudi youth or others were to challenge the house of Saud, could they create a new state in Westphalian terms? What may create the change are not the actions of the state or political response, but how the impact of the economy is managed by the government and the response from the people based on asabiyya. The economic change in Saudi Arabia means the house of Saud needs to manage a balancing act between upholding a recovered Islam and its own political survival. In other words, it is a battle between culture and economics, and the outcome of the next few years will determine the basis of Saudi society in the future and whether it survives or implodes. To begin to see how this might play out means understanding the dynamics of the different ways of approaching Islam and getting to the meaning of the Saudi mind. Let us consider three recent ways of looking at Saudi Arabia.

First, writing back in 2000, published the same year as 9/11, Fred Halliday explained:

> In Saudi Arabia today there has been a subtle shift away from reliance on a legitimacy based on religion and the place of Wahhabism, towards a stress on the Al Saud family, the warrior component of the regime, as the sole legitimating instance.[34]

Halliday assesses the question through the lens of the house of Saud as the state actor of Saudi, and suggests how we are to understand the role of interaction of state and non-state actors, the diffusion of ideas, and how perceptions of the local and the foreign can play out politically in diverse locales and trans-national discourses. If Halliday is right then we would need to consider that the house of Saud has long since moved the ground from a religious nation to a political one, based on the politics of Kingdom rather than democracy.

Second, in his exploration of the spread of Islam, Bonnefoy described the history and geographic dynamics of the border between Yemen and Saudi Arabia, offering a picture of how the "spread" of Wahhabi Salafism from Saudi Arabia emerges not as a case of an exported ideology, but rather as a tapestry of local norms and practices shaping and being reshaped by engagement in transnational religious discourses. His observation is interesting, because it resonates with how Islam evolved, if one describes it as a non-miraculous or non-revelatory occurrence. Richard Bell, a Christian scholar at Edinburgh University who undertook historical and form critical work of the Koran in the early twentieth century, linked the Koran to Christianity in the Arab world and explained that Muhammad:

> ...claimed to be an Arab prophet and he was. We shall see him consciously borrowing – he is quite frank about it. But to begin with, the materials which he uses, though they may remind us ever and again of Jewish and Christian phrases and ideas, are in reality Arab material. They may have been originally derived from outside Arabia, but they had by Muhammad's time become part of the Arab mind.[35]

Of course, academic study sees from the outside, testing and doubting the claims to truth or unique nature of revelation, and treats the believer and the revelation sociologically. However, the believer is not behaving sociologically, they are behaving theologically, they believe the revelation and it shapes their worldview.

Lastly, there is a tendency in many studies of Saudi Arabia to assume, as Greg Gause and Toby C. Jones point out, that the Kingdom is a tradi-tional culture dominated by a "timeless Islam" and we need to dig deeper as such studies:

> tend to look uncritically at the importance of religion, and even take the official state narrative that the Al Saud are the guardians of the faith and that Saudi society is essentially "conservative" as an article of faith.[36]

The Saudi way of life and approach to governing and policy is to blend the old and the new, with the aim of retaining a distinctively Islamic approach to life while evolving albeit slowly as a Kingdom. The solution to the political and economic problems, from a Saudi perspective, is not to "westernize" Saudi to solve its economic problems. To suggest what it should do is a case of taking a culturally superior stance on the matter. The question we can ask is how Saudi is going to look through the Islamic lens at the global economic problem it faces and come up with a solution. Will it just muddle by? Traditionally there has been a large aspect of this attitude in their approach. It is recognized such an approach won't do anymore, but does this mean Vision 2030 will succeed as a programmatic and systematic approach to solving the economic challenges the Kingdom faces? Or, is it a strategy of wishful thinking that papers over the reality that Saudi is muddling through while talking big? However we answer these points and raise doubts about competence to deliver any real pro-gram of change, one thing that is distant in the horizon is the possibility of political unrest and rebellion.

One would have thought that oil price shocks in a nation like that experienced in Saudi in the past would have been enough to create unrest. The oil is so much at the heart of the economic structure of the country that it seems a natural rallying point for political unrest and challenge, yet as discussed this has never happened to date in Saudi. The few uprisings we have seen in recent decades have tended to be more narrowly political and religious than economically driven. The new factor here is a change in the economy that puts pressure on a power structure that cannot sim-ply throw money at the problem. There have been three such periods of upheaval, where uprisings and unrest have occurred:

- 1979–1980: Shia uprisings
- 1990–1991: First Gulf War and after
- 2001: The 9/11 attacks and thereafter

If we look back briefly at these uprisings, we can detect a final theme. The Shia uprisings were in the Eastern Province, along with the November 1979 takeover of the Grand Mosque in Mecca, and they related to the Iranian revolution and 1979 being the millennial hijri year of 1400. The first Gulf War and the period following reflected discontent with foreign, especially American, influence and intrusion in the Kingdom and the region. There were a number of petitions in part encouraged by King Fahd, but also protests such as women defying the driving "ban," and other protests related to social and political issues, and growing Islamist pressure promoting the need for Islamic ways, with the only real economic issues relating to the need for a more Islamic economy. There was also concern about the Saudi support for un-Islamic regimes in the region, notably Algeria, Egypt and Syria. The third period of unrest was post 9/11, which again saw petitions raised and concern about foreign influence. Saudi was able to fund its response to unrest because of the oil and financial reserves, allowing it to absorb the economic consequences of downturns, and was also in the position to influence the price mechanism of its primary resource. What is perhaps surprising is that Saudi passed through these periods of trial without any significant impact in the religiopolitical structure of the country, and it is perhaps because it is a religiopolitical structure that it was able to survive these economic shocks.

Thus, it may be easy to fall into thinking that this is another episode to be overcome. I have argued throughout this book that this time things are different. These were political upheavals that in reality had little to do with the economic situation, they occurred in periods when the oil prices were relatively buoyant. The current crisis is unlike these earlier difficulties, and this is what makes the crisis that started in 2014 so intriguing. The specifically economic aspects of past periods of concern were also solved by throwing expatriate workers at the problem, but this will not work this time in the long-term. Saudization doesn't just mean putting Saudis into positions, they've been doing that for years and used expats to do the real work. Saudization means actually getting things done, which in turn means the people of Saudi needing to change their mindset in a way that makes the Kingdom self-sufficient and able to improve economically. It is this narrower economic concern that raises significant problems, because Saudization is not changing the mindset rapidly enough and markets move faster than government solutions. The problem for Saudi is that having the oil wealth created a degree of dependence, and a lack of any real curiosity in diversifying their economy or advancing an entrepreneurial spirit to innovate their economy. The alternative which I have touched on in these last chapters is whether, with the help of Ibn Khaldūn, there is an Islamic option, and to answer this we now turn to draw these strands together in the concluding chapter.

Notes

1. A Conversation with Peter L. Berger "How My Views Have Changed" Gregor Thuswaldner http://thecresset.org/2014/Lent/Thuswaldner_L14.html
2. Taylor (2007, p. 3).
3. Houellebecq (2016, p. 25).
4. Weber (2010).
5. Ghosh (2017, p. 64).
6. Weber (2010, p. 28).
7. Weber(2010, p. 284).
8. Ibid., *The Cresset.*
9. Ghosh (2017, p. 79f.).
10. Berger (1967, p. 28).
11. Berger (1967, p. 111).
12. Ibid., *The Cresset.*
13. Berger (1999, p. 16).
14. Berger (1967, p. 111).
15. Ibid., *The Cresset.*
16. Ibid., *The Cresset.*
17. Ibid., *The Cresset.*
18. Ibid., *The Cresset.*
19. Berger (1999, p. 7f.).
20. Berger (1999, p. 8).
21. Toynbee, *A Study of History, Vol 3: The Growths of Civilizations* (Oxford: Oxford University Press, 1953) p. 322. See also https://mukaddimenot-lari.files.wordpress.com/2013/04/toynbee-and-ibn-khaldun.pdf
22. http://faculty.georgetown.edu/imo3/ibn.htm
23. Spengler, Joseph J. "Economic Thought in Islam: Ibn Khaldūn," *Comparative Studies in Society and History*, vol. 6, no. 3 (April 1964).
24. Schumpeter (1954, pp. 136, 788).
25. Ibn Khaldūn (1967, p. 230).

26. Ibn Khaldūn (1967, p. 101).
27. Ibn Khaldūn (1967, p. 127).
28. Ibn Khaldūn (1967, p. 142).
29. Ibn Khaldūn (1967, pp. 248–9).
30. Ibn Khaldūn (1967, p. 96).
31. Black (2001, pp. 308–9).
32. Ibn Khaldūn (1967, p. 310).
33. Black (2001, p. 310).
34. Halliday (2000, p. 41).
35. Bell (1968, p. 69).
36. Haykel et al. (2015, p. 34).

Bibliography

al-Rasheed, Madawi, ed. 2008. *Kingdom Without Borders: Saudi Arabia's Political, Religious and Media Frontiers*. London: Hurst.
al-Wadi'i, Muqbil. 2005. *Mushahadaiî iî al-Mamlaka al-'Arabiyya al-Sa'udiyya*. Sanaa: Dar al-athar.
An-Na'im, Abdullahi Ahmed. 2008. *Islam and the Secular State: Negotiating the Future of Shari'a*. Cambridge, MA: Harvard University Press.
Barber, Benjamin R. 2001. *Jihad vs McWorld: Terrorism's Challenge to Democracy*. New York: Ballantine Books.
Bell, Richard. 1968. *The Origin of Islam in Its Christian Environment: The Gunning Lectures, Edinburgh University 1925*. London: Macmillan, 1926; reprint: London: Cass, 1968.
Berger, Peter L. 1967. *The Sacred Canopy: Elements of a Sociological Theory of Religion*. New York: Anchor Books.
———. 1973. *The Social Reality of Religion*. London: Penguin.
———., ed. 1999. *The Desecularization of the World: Resurgent Religion and World Politics*. Grand Rapids: Eerdmans.
Black, Antony. 2001. *The History of Islamic Political Thought: From the Prophet to the Present*. Edinburgh: Edinburgh University Press.
Bowering, Gerhard, ed. 2015. *Islamic Political Thought: An Introduction*. Princeton: Princeton University Press.
Craze, Jonathan, and Mark Huband. 2009. *The Kingdom: Saudi Arabia and the Challenge of the 21st Century*. London: Hurst & Co.
Cunningham, Robert B., and Yasin K. Sarayrah. 1993. *Wasta: The Hidden Force in Middle Eastern Society*. Westport: Praeger.

Esposito, John L. 2002. *Unholy War: Terror in the Name of Islam*. New York: Oxford University Press.

Ghosh, Peter. 2017. *Max Weber and the Protestant Ethic: Twin Histories*. Oxford: Oxford University Press.

Halliday, Fred. 2000. *Nation and Religion in the Middle East*. Boulder: Lynne Rienner Publishers.

Hamid, Shadi. 2016. *Islamic Exceptionalism: How the Struggle Over Islam Is Reshaping the World*. New York: St. Martin's Press.

Haykel, Bernard, Thomas Hegghammer, and Stéphane Lacroix. 2015. *Saudi Arabia in Transition: Insights on Social, Political, Economic and Religious Change*. Cambridge: Cambridge University Press.

Heggenhammer, Thomas. 2010. *Jihad in Saudi Arabia: Violence and Pan-Islamism Since 1979*. New York: Cambridge University Press.

———. 2015. *Saudi Arabia in Transition: Insights on Social, Political, Economic and Religious Change*. New York: Cambridge University Press.

Houellebecq, Michel. 2016. *Submission*. New York: Picador.

Hourani, Albert. 2002. *A History of the Arab Peoples*. Cambridge, MA: Belknap Press.

Karsh, Effraim. 2006. *Islamic Imperialism: A History*. New Haven: Yale University Press.

Kepel, Gilles. 2004. *The War for Muslim Minds: Islam and the West*. Trans. Pascal Ghazaleh. Cambridge, MA: Belknap Press.

Khaldūn, Ibn. 1967. *The Muqaddimah: An Introduction to History*. Princeton: Princeton University Press.

Kuhn, Thomas. 1996. *The Structure of Scientific Revolutions*. Chicago: University of Chicago Press.

Lacey, Robert. 2009. *Inside the Kingdom: Kings, Clerics, Terrorists, Modernists, and the Struggle for Saudi Arabia*. New York: Viking.

Lackner, Helen. 1978. *A House Built on Sand. A Political Economy of Saudi Arabia*. London: Ithaca Press.

Lewis, Bernard. 2002. *The Arabs in History*. New York: Oxford University Press.

Luciani, Giacomo, ed. 1990. *The Arab State*. Berkeley: University of California Press.

Maher, Shiraz. 2016. *Salafi-Jihadism: The History of an Idea*. London: Hurst & Company.

Mansfield, Peter. 1985. *The Arabs*. London: Penguin Books.

Matthiesen, Toby. 2015. *The Other Saudis: Shiism, Dissent and Sectarianism*. New York: Cambridge University Press.

Naqvi, S.N.H. 1994. *Ethics and Economics: An Islamic Synthesis*. Leicester: The Islamic Foundation.

Nasr, Vali. 2009. *The Rise of Islamic Capitalism: Why the New Muslim Middle Class Is the Key to Defeating Extremism*. New York: Free Press.

Patai, Raphael. 1973. *The Arab Mind*. New York: Scribner.

Plantinga, Alvin, and Nicholas Wolterstorff, eds. 1983. *Faith and Rationality: Reason and Belief in God*. Notre Dame: University of Notre Dame Press.

Quaesem, Muhammad Abdul. 1983. *The Jewels of the Qur'an: Al-Ghazali's Theory*. London: Islamic Book Trust.

Said, Edward W. 1979. *Orientalism*. Princeton: Princeton University Press.

———. 1981. *Covering Islam: How the Media and the Experts Determine How We See the Rest of the World*. New York: Pantheon Books.

Salame, Ghassan, ed. 1994. *Democracy Without Democrats? The Renewal of Politics in the Muslim World*. London: I.B. Tauris.

Schumpeter, Joseph A. 1954. *History of Economic Analysis*. New York: Oxford University Press.

Shabbir, Akhtar. 1985. In *Philosophy Bridging the World Religions*, ed. P. Koslowski. Dordrecht: Kluwer.

Southern, R.W. 1978. *Western Views of Islam in the Middle Ages*. Cambridge, MA: Harvard University Press.

Taylor, Charles. 2007. *A Secular Age*. Cambridge, MA: Belknap Press.

Watt, W. Montgomery. 1953. *The Faith and Practice of Al-Ghazali*. London: George Allen and Unwin.

Weber, Max. 2010. *The Protestant Ethic and the Spirit of Capitalism*. Oxford: Oxford University Press.

Wilson, Bryan. 1966. *Religion in a Secular Society*. London: Watts.

12

An Islamic Behavioral Perspective

David Hume[1] stated that only religious fanatics believe they have the knowledge to make judgments as to how the world best works, and in this they provide a threat to political stability. This statement gets to the heart of the disconnect between the understanding and relationship of the Western secular liberal economic order and the Islamic religiously conservative rentier order in Saudi and elsewhere in what is commonly termed "the Islamic world." I have used the term fideist to capture the overarching Saudi Islamic worldview, rather than fanatic, fundamentalist and the host of other names used to frame the debate and various religious players involved. Part of this Saudi fideism is a desire to maintain an Islamic worldview, and to take from the West what is beneficial and reject what is not. The economic strain in Saudi will make this process much more difficult, and Saudi will become more vulnerable to secular forces, which makes maintaining the Islamic identity harder, and opening ways to those who would terrorize the Kingdom into rejecting all that is Western and secular. The house of Saud has managed the Kingdom through gradualism and occasional spurts of reform, and by repelling those forces that threaten it. It allowed radicals to exist in the Kingdom while the Saudis themselves proselytized, but once threatened the action taken by the authorities was swift and brutal. The house of Saud could do

© The Author(s) 2018   279
D. Cowan, *The Coming Economic Implosion of Saudi Arabia*,
https://doi.org/10.1007/978-3-319-74709-5_12

all these things because they have power in the sense of *'asabiyyah*, and because they have oil wealth. The former is under threat by sectarian political movements and the latter by global economic dynamics, with the thread of religion linking these threats together. The problem is whether these religious and political dynamics are in conflict with the economic policies and thinking needed to change the economic dynamics of Saudi. If the outcome of any conflict between culture and economics is the triumph of capitalism then in all likelihood Saudi will change as an Islamic state. If culture wins then the economy will implode. The contrast is stark.

Globalized Islam Under Stress

The future of Saudi Arabia is a religious, economic and geopolitical conundrum, and one that not only faces the Kingdom but faces the world. It concerns us all. What happens to Saudi Arabia to a great extent is a story of what will happen to Islam. There are over one-and-a-half billion Muslims in the world, about one-fifth of the human population, and to varying degrees they face Saudi Arabia, specifically Mecca, for their prayers on a daily basis. This global corporate act, if one thinks about it, is very impressive. It is a single focus, a single direction in the world, a corporate body bowing in the name of God and community. Saudi is a Kingdom and not a liberal democracy. It is an Islamic nation, not a secular one. Yet Saudi is not an insular state, it is a global player and has a global role as a leader of Islam; perhaps akin to the way the Soviet Union proselytized communism and the United States continues to do so for Western liberal democracy. Many actors and observers in this economic drama agree that in striving for future economic success Saudi faces some stark choices and challenges. The Vision 2030 view, not necessarily shared by all Saudis, is that Saudi can pursue a radically revolutionary agenda akin to the Thatcherite revolution in Britain, which changed the mindset of a nation; whether people thought it desirable or not this is what happened. There has been an increase in projects and investment that suggest a willingness to change, and there are public signs of changes in attitude, such as the recent changes to the ban on women driving and licensing of cinemas expected in 2018,[2] and these changes should not be underestimated in their significance. However, there are many signs of concern, as people face a rise in the cost of living and paying some taxes.

Saudi legitimates its claim to authority over global Islam by reason of having custodianship of the two holy sites, and being the global focus of this daily attention. In recent decades the Kingdom has seen itself as a global promoter of Islam, offering funds and materials to promote the faith, to persuade and proselytize. The horror of 9/11, undertaken mostly by Saudi nationals, the emergence of the terror networks called Al-Qaeda and Daesh or Islamic State and the increasing number of attacks in the West have all made this global ambition more controversial and more fragile. The problem for the global ambitions of the Kingdom today is that it is under stress as a result of a falling oil price and an economy in need of economic diversity. The Kingdom has a population used to believing it is blessed by God by means of oil but now worried about its economic future and the likely end of its welfare state. This in turn, along with the emerging interests of Iran, is impacting the Kingdom's geopolitical status. This is more than the usual tussles and demarcation disputes of reformers and traditionalists, it is between those who believe there is a bright future ahead only if change takes place and those who believe the Kingdom can gradually adapt and survive as it always has done. What is clear is that Saudi cannot stay as it is, even if there are many who would like it to remain as it is.

One of the popular narratives at the turn of the millennium, which barely merits repeating here, was that of a clash of civilizations between Islam and the old Christian and now secular West. However, there is not so much a clash of civilizations, as many fear or speculate upon, as much as there is a talking past or ignorance of each other's civilization and values. One reason our civilizations or nations talk past each other is that the differences between religions is a difference about revelation and the relationship with God. Secularists and many academics fail to grasp effectively the role of religion, and it seems hard for many critics to grasp the self-understanding, which in the Islamist sense is neatly captured by the term "Islamic Exceptionalism," suggested by Shadi Hamid.[3] The difference between religion and secularity is that the latter assumes there is little historical truth to the sacred texts and little validity to the doctrinal claims, in other words they assume the religion is essentially false or outmoded and only to be understood from a human point of view. This is a problem of conflicting worldviews. To understand Saudi Arabia and Islam it is necessary to get into the Saudi mindset and understand Saudis have a different worldview, they behave differently.

If we fail in this task of understanding this worldview and the current predicament, then I argue the Kingdom will implode, and the world will become an even more dangerous place. This is not to draw a judgment, it is to put the onus on us all, to play on words, to have a dialogue about the future of Saudi Arabia and Islamic communities which will make for a safer world. Creating Manichean views of good versus evil, Iran versus Saudi, Sunni versus Shia, terrorists versus law-abiding nations and other such divisions is not the most useful way to analyze the problems the world faces. In terms of the problems with and within Islam the problems are rooted in deeper sectarian differences, and the failure of Saudi as an economy or state would open up a sectarian divide like never before.

Finding the Path Forward

If Saudi is an "American Islam," does it need to become even more American or capitalist to get itself out of trouble and create the economic model it needs? If things are to move in such a direction then difficulties will surface in the relationship between religion and secularity. Another set of difficulties will arise from the relationship between religion and economics, specifically capitalism. America is rooted in a Christian, largely Calvinist, tradition in religious terms. America is also a political democracy, rooted in Lockean political philosophy, and this tempered the Calvinism of the nation and has been in constant dialogue over the centuries with its religious tradition. America is also a nation that emerged at the same time as capitalism. It is commonly understood, by supporters and critics alike, to be the archetypal capitalist nation. Saudi is an Islamic Kingdom, not a democracy. Where America has a church and state division, aimed at allowing plurality, Saudi is a theocracy banning other faiths from the public space and limiting them in the private space. Where America was built by an American mind that took faith and capitalism hand in hand, and had a can-do spirit to build its economy, Saudi had its modern wealth handed to it on a plate and created a rentier state, a state of reliance of its people on its leaders, governed by a spirit of *Inshallah*, if God wills it. This is not to say Americans are hard-working and clever while the Saudis are lazy or incompetent, the situation is a lot more complicated than such shallow supposition.

If Saudi is to build a new future, its *Vision 2030*, it essentially has three choices, which are:

1. The China option: State capitalism combined with Islamic ideology
2. The Soviet option: the economy implodes
3. The Islamic economic option: explore Islamic solutions

These approaches get to the heart of the spirit of the economy that will move the Kingdom forward or backward, the first two being secular options. The first option I call the China option which to a certain extent is behind the ideas and proposed solutions of the *Vision 2030*. It is also to a great extent behind the Western commentary on the policies Saudi needs to adopt, as the Thatcher comment suggests. The second option is not viable for the Kingdom, nor is it good for the rest of the world, and would most likely create even greater instability in the region and in the world. The last option will sound scary to a world currently paranoid about the term Islamic applied to anything, but we can explore whether this is the best option and that Saudi needs to be more, not less, Islamic. If the first option is already in play then one can expect that to be the way forward, and it certainly appears to be the government approach. The second option is unthinkable, which suggests to me the creative solution might lie with the third option. I will examine each in detail momentarily.

How this third option might work requires a more theological understanding of Islam, but we can also make use of the discourse of sociology discussed in the last chapter to connect the dots. The problem arises that just as there is much Western discourse that sees Islam as the problem, so too is there much sociological and ethical discourse that tends toward anti-capitalist thinking. This also resonates with much Christian theological academic work and ecclesiastical statements, which tend to be anti-capitalist. Indeed, if the economy is commented on at all in theological circles it is hard to find a prominent theologian in the capitalist era speaking well of capitalism prior to the fall of the Berlin Wall and the end of the Soviet Union. This has changed since, with a more nuanced approach, though still with an underlying animus toward capitalism. During the years of communism one could imagine another economic world, because there appeared to be an alternative, albeit one that was arguably deeply flawed. The victory of capitalism suggested there was only one economic system, and hence theologians and ethicists had to deal with a new paradigm. In most respects little really changed, instead critics had to adjust their language while remaining largely economically illiterate. We would be better served if such critics had had a more realistic grasp of economics over recent decades.

Islam does not have the same animus toward capitalism specifically or commerce more generally, which should make it an interesting dialogue partner for critics of capitalism. Islam is ethically anti-capitalist in the sense it bans usury, but this is tempered by having a generally favorable view of commerce from the start. It is also tempered by rules of commerce on which basis there should be constraints on commerce and commercial actors, but this is so in all areas of human life. The prophet himself, and his wife, were merchants and traders, and Mohammed helped arbitrate many business disputes, defining the ethical issues involved. All this could suggest there may once again be an alternative economic system based on an Islamic economic, except the current Islamic financial and economic system lacks the depth and robustness to be anything more than a pious niche. This explains why there was a tendency in the past to hitch its wagon to socialism in a coalition of discordant ideologies. There may be some attempts to have Islam fill the void left by the implosion of communism, and Saudi Arabia could be the crucible out of which an Islamic economy emerges. Such an argument will no doubt cause alarm in some circles, and raise questions whether this means a clash of economic ideas and systems. We need to be careful in quickly jumping to references about clashes between ideas, since as noted there has already been much discussion of the clash of civilization thesis, which brings to mind the crusades and Christianity versus Islam. Many Americans already see their Christian nation under threat from Islam, and they protest against the use of Sharia law in

America and other democracies. The suggestion of an Islamic economy in their view would take the crisis another step in the wrong direction, and underpin another ideological split in the world. There may be a middle way, in the way Saudi, Malaysia and Indonesia have tried to forge a mixed Islamic/capitalist economy, but there are not strong signs that Saudi wants to go much further in this direction. Any dissonance between capitalism and Saudi's Islam probably doesn't trouble the Saudi leadership too much. The possibility of an implosion will meet in most quarters with a desire that what the world needs is an economically viable Saudi Arabia.

The Two Secular Options

It is possible that Saudi will evolve a form of capitalism that is more attuned to its religion and ideology, and in turn tackle the perceived problems of consumerism and inequality in Western secular capitalism. If Saudi is to avoid secularization and advance the need for a theological dialogue, it is worth exploring two secular scenarios which can help us model a dialogue. These two scenarios are based on systems that kept their ideology, the two communist regimes that fought the ideological battle against capitalism with different outcomes. These countries are China and the Soviet Union. China has developed through state capitalism, while the Soviet Union imploded, though Russia is currently rising again from the ashes as a global powerhouse. The Cold War world of détente and global rivalry is still with us, but it is an open question of where these capitalisms will go. This is not a question for this book, except as guidance to explore which type of capitalism Saudi will embrace as it seeks to change its economy. The Western or American model of secular capitalism is deemed problematic because it is in conflict with the Saudi Islamic worldview, which either means rejecting it or adapting it through a process of dialogue between capitalist and Islamic ideas, and this has been explored above. The two scenarios offered here for discussion are also a result of secularization, but offer us pointers on possible trajectories for a Saudi Arabia that wants to keep its ideology and power in place.

The China Option: State Capitalism

In 1979, Deng Xiaoping and the Chinese Communist Party (CCP) undertook market reforms that have been transitioning the country from communism to a more capitalist society,[4] but with some key differences to Western capitalism. The approach has been to keep communism as its creed and capitalism as its practice. This new economy has been labeled state capitalism. However, the state apparatus has been growing and was essentially becoming bloated. Back in a 2005 OECD report, the authors noted more diplomatically that in this time of transition:

> China's public expenditure policies have been rapidly evolving but still bear important vestiges from the central planning era. There is much public spending carried outside of the formal budget...[5]

It seems that not much has changed in this respect, with both the OECD report and current World Bank assessments observing market reforms are incomplete. The World Bank notes the current and 13th Five-Year Plan (2016–2020) focuses on the need to develop services to address environmental problems and social imbalances. The areas where specific targets have been set are reduction of pollution, increasing energy efficiency, improving access to education and healthcare and expansion of social protection. Like Western economies China struggles with the balance or disconnect between economic success and social and welfare provision. China has high levels of inequality and low income levels, with per capita income a fraction of that in advanced countries and 55 million poor in rural areas in 2015. Rapid urbanization, an aging population and internal migration of labor are also creating pressure on the country and its economy. It is, however, in many aspects growing successfully and has become the poster child for state capitalism. The World Bank praises the economic progress of China:

> GDP growth has averaged nearly 10 percent a year—the fastest sustained expansion by a major economy in history—and has lifted more than 800 million people out of poverty. China reached all the Millennium Development Goals (MDGs) by 2015 and made a major contribution to the achievement of the MDGs globally.[6]

As the *Economist* has reported, the Chinese no longer saw state-directed firms as a route to liberal capitalism but as a sustainable model. They have concluded capitalism can be made to work better, and many other emerging governments are in agreement. The *Economist* outlines the approach the communist state has taken to the transition from communism to capitalism:

> China's infrastructure companies win contracts the world over. The best national champions are outward-looking, acquiring skills by listing on foreign exchanges and taking over foreign companies. And governments are selective in their corporate holdings. Overall, the Chinese state has loosened its grip on the economy: its bureaucrats concentrate on industries where they can make a difference.[7]

Meanwhile, the people of China have embraced capitalism. A Pew 2014 research study showed roughly three-quarters of the Chinese (76%) agree that most people are better off in a free market economy.[8] As many Western economies are perceived to be retreating into nationalism, the Chinese government is championing globalization. There are no signs of China giving up its ideology or its continued move toward state capitalism, and many nations including Saudi have been eager to forge closer ties with China. In March 2017, King Salman met with President Xi Jinping in Beijing, though little business has been done by the two nations, with no historical ties and a sense of mutual distrust. Given China's strength they will be the dominant partner in any deals, and so there is a risk for Saudi that there will be largely one-way traffic at a time when they are in great need of inward investment.

Such state capitalism is strong in the energy sector, where governments already own the world's largest oil companies and control three-quarters of the world's energy reserves. It is unsurprising then that Aramco would be subject to further use by the government to tackle the economy. Saudi Aramco will continue to be controlled and managed exclusively by the Saudi government, with the main aim to raise cash. The market-determined valuation will allow them to borrow more on the sovereign bond markets, despite their 95% holding in Aramco remaining barred from being used as collateral. The largest state capitalist exercise in Saudi is theautonomous Royal Commission, which has invested in two large new industrial cities, Jubail on the east coast and Yanbu on the west coast. The government has also invested in infrastructure, such as roads and the Riyadh metro, as well as increased eightfold the Kingdom's electricity generating capacity over the last five years. The government is handing contracts mostly to Saudi companies to boost the economy; thus 70% of the contracts in Jubail and Yanbu have gone to Saudi companies. However, for very large and complex projects, they are bringing in foreign companies as their primary partner.

Returning to the Thatcher theme, when the United Kingdom undertook a program of privatization, the former Prime Minister Harold Macmillan referred to it as "selling off the family silver." The Saudis are not planning to sell off the family silver, but they are certainly using one of its biggest pieces of silver in Saudi Aramco to tackle the economic woes ahead. The attempt in the Vision 2030 strategy by the Saudis of balancing the need to make their people modern capitalists while maintaining traditional religious and social values means looking for new models, since at this level of analysis there are many disconnects between Saudi worldview and capitalism. It is questionable whether this balancing act can be successful, but the Vision 2030 and sell-off of shares in Saudi Aramco could be signs of a growing state capitalism, though to date it seems rather than being a model or strategy it is simply a case of the government throwing excessive amounts of funds on top of a welfare and social structure that remains largely untouched. When the Saudi government launched its plan for a public offering of shares in Saudi Aramco they stated it would make it the largest company in the world,[9] the *Financial Times* reported:

Some Saudi officials believe Saudi Aramco's initial public offering could break records by valuing it at as much as $2tn, although the Financial Times has put the figure at between $880bn and $1.1tn. Against this backdrop, advisers to the government and the company are warning that unless Saudi Aramco broadly resembles an orthodox oil and gas producer at the IPO, by jettisoning its role as state enabler, it risks being unattractive for international investors.[10]

Part of the background is the need to raise funds and look for ways to diversify the economy, but it also suggests state capitalism is problematic as the *FT* report alludes. The question is further complicated by the on/off narrative surrounding the IPO itself.[11]

Other companies owned, part-owned by or aligned with the state enjoy growing market power in major economic sectors in the world's fastest-growing economies. There has also been substantial growth in the use of "sovereign wealth funds," a recent term for state-owned investment portfolios accounting for one-eighth of global investment, and that figure is increasing. The use of such financial instruments and use of assets is a trend impacting both international politics and the global economy. It allows governments to use these means to flex economic power and enhance state activity and authority. State capitalism is not to be confused with resources nationalism or nationalization, they are very different things. State capitalism is not necessarily a new thing either. The East India Company, democratic Japan in the 1950s and Imperial Germany in the 1870s are previous examples of state capitalism, though today's version is much bigger in scale and works with more sophisticated tools. While there any many areas both historically and in the present time where the state is involved in the economy, especially the much-vaunted public/private partnerships, state capitalism takes matters further from conventional free market capitalism. It involves public bodies that may look like private sector actors but still maintain a core public sector mindset. At the same time, it promotes a level of dependency for private firms on the government for their success, leaving them less attuned to competition and real markets, and beholden to high levels of influence by politicians.

However, as Ian Bremmer writing in *Foreign Affairs* explains, state capitalism can be seen as a threat to market capitalism and to the growth of democracy in the developing world, stating:

> The State is using markets to create wealth that can be directed as political officials see fit … the ultimate motive is not economic (maximising growth) but political (maximising the State's power and the leadership's chances of survival). This is a form of capitalism but one in which the State acts as the dominant economic player and uses markets primarily for political gain.[12]

Most governments attempt to strike a balance between the economic institutions that generate wealth and the political institutions that regulate economic actors and redistribute wealth. After all, it is not good economics to kill off the golden goose, though politics often results in just such an outcome. Yet in the West it has long been assumed by supporters of capitalism that market economics and liberal democracy go hand in hand. The success of China and the evolving state capitalism of Saudi suggest this is not necessarily the case. The working thesis of China is the "convergence theory," which plotted a course of abandoning a planned economy and created a market economy, which also assumes liberal democracy is integral to a successful economic model. This means incorporating the rule of law, many progressive and fundamental human rights and increased freedom. Western thinkers assume this all necessarily works together, but we find here a classic case of David Hume's suggestion that one cannot derive an ought from an is. As Paulo Urio plots the narrative of the convergence theory:

> ...for about 30 years market mechanisms have been implemented and expanded in China with great success in spite of the absence of liberal democracy, while the Chinese political system has retained many of the authoritarian characteristics it had already in 1949.[13]

While the Soviet Union case suggests the thesis is correct, China contradicts it and suggests the euphoria over a capitalist victory and liberal democracy combined was premature and we have problems to solve.

Likewise, we can look at commonalities between Saudi and China and ponder there is something else going on:

1. Concentration of power
2. Human rights abuse
3. Repressive use of power
4. Maintaining an ideological worldview

If such authoritarian structures of communist repression can go hand in hand with capitalism, then perhaps what we have is not so much a benign state capitalism but rather a hegemonic capitalist state. Saudi can maintain its authority and worldview and grow economically at the same time if they succeed where China has. If they fail then we could see the other route, the implosion of an authoritarian ideological regime.

The Soviet Option: A Systemic Implosion

If we entertain the notion Saudi may well implode, then we can examine this by drawing some useful parallels with the demise of the Soviet Union. While not exact likenesses, there are enough similarities for such a comparison to offer lessons for Saudi. Capitalism was in ideological competition with communism, and it triumphed over the ideology and the nation that embraced it, the Soviet Union. We can consider whether there will be a similar triumph of capitalism over an Islamic state as well. There are six parallels that can be drawn:

1. The Soviet identity was protected and reinforced because the West was just there. The Soviets saw capitalism the same as the Americans, namely, a Manichean dichotomy allowing the secular state to create social cohesion internally.

   Saudi has a more positive relationship historically with the West, especially America. However, there is still a sense in which a Manichean dichotomy is seen to operate.
2. It was only a matter of time before the freedoms, lifestyles and wealth of the West would entice the people of the Soviet Union.

   The Saudi young who have experienced the West come back with a broadly positive experience, and the prevalence of social media means there is more interaction with the West and Western ideas, with the youth either reacting against a corrupt Western way of life or looking to see Saudi change. Women are particularly influential here, though one should understand that there are many women who remain as committed to Saudi tradition.
3. The Soviet welfare state was under stress, along with the rest of the economy. The healthcare system was admired, but again there were cost and access issues.

This is the Achilles heel of Saudi. The welfare state has been generously maintained, and there has been a dependence on the state to make sure people don't suffer too much during economic problems.

4. The capitalist economy is driven by innovation and entrepreneurship, and a wise understanding of the role of risk in the economy. These elements were missing in an economy where the joke was "you pretend to work, we pretend to pay you."

   The mindset of Inshallah and the history of playing at being managers by depending on expats to do the work are the key to determining whether Saudi can innovate.

5. However, the West and Soviets lived in ideological coexistence. Although President Ronald Reagan is credited in certain quarters in America of beating the Soviets, he wasn't that interested in destroying it, instead he assumed like everybody else the Soviets would go along as usual and he wanted to maintain a peaceful coexistence.

   There are constant calls for Saudi to change its approach to women and human rights, which lay at the heart of the Obama administration's problems. The Trump administration is unlikely to take up these causes in the same way. There are many realists who would argue it is up to Saudi to decide these things as sovereign states, and thus the status quo of ideological coexistence will prevail.

6. Changes in leadership were pivotal. Gorbachev was the fourth leader of the Soviet Union for a period of two and half years. He represented a change of the old guard and the end of gerontocracy, but he also simply represented the end, the implosion of the Soviet Union. The reason why the Soviet Union imploded was that it had been crushed under the weight of its own ideology and a flawed economic system. It is not fanciful to see in this picture the problems of Saudi Arabia, which also has a strong ideology at its foundations and a flawed economy.

   The lineage of the al Sauds has long been a subject of discussion, but the transfer of power to King Salman and line of succession handed to Prince Nayef appeared to settle matters at the time for most people. However, Prince Nayef was never going to take the path to the throne, and Prince Mohammed is now in line, signifying the end of a gerontocracy in Saudi and the taking of power by a youthful leadership. This may lead to more energy and change, but equally it could weaken the sense of *'asabiyyah*, and as Archie Brown notes in *The Rise and Fall of Communism*, "The moment of greatest danger for an authoritarian regime is when it undertakes reform."[14]

The Soviet Union broke up into the constituent nations it had drawn into its union, leaving Russia as the largest and most powerful remnant. After communism Russia became what observers called a gangster economy, but it has since stabilized somewhat, particularly under Vladimir Putin. Saudi had built *'asabiyyah* through tribal connections forged through diplomacy and violence that go deep into the Saudi history and psyche, rather than the power broking and use of force which forged the Soviet Union. The centrality of the house of Saud and the relationship with the tribes suggest the popular revolt which tumbled the Berlin Wall and destroyed the political structure of communism will not happen in Saudi any time soon. However, the parallels drawn with the Soviet Union are uncomfortable enough to provide food for thought for anyone speculating about where Saudi goes from here as its economy faces stress and its people strive for change.

The Islamic Option

Saudi may follow China and expand state capitalism, or it may implode and fail as a state and society. The former would be an accommodation with an Islamic worldview, the latter the result of an intransigence of worldview. The question is, will fortitude and God steer Saudi in a new course? Or, is there a different spirit needed to stop Saudi from falling deeper into trouble and able to take the economic path to success in 2030? Weber suggested there is a particular spirit in capitalism that brought the West to economic superiority, but one that has also led into a secular and vacuous society if Berger and Islamic critics are to be believed. The contemporary revolution happening in Saudi is an economic one, and we can look at where this revolution will lead. If the Protestant work ethic, however ill-conceived, played a part in the development of capitalism, can we then look to Islam to find a spirit of Saudi as an Islamic economy that will change not just its economy but also its culture? The way ahead for Saudi is fraught with difficulties and challenges to the culture as it is today. On the one hand it is embracing a capitalism that could undermine the Saud dynasty and also the culture, while on the other hand there continues to be a move toward the cohesive spirit of Saudi and *asabiyyah*. In looking at this I am not thinking of Islamic economics or finance as system, rather I am thinking of whether it is possible for Saudi to change economically and keep its culture undamaged by a more robust market economy.

Earlier I noted the Williams and Zinkin paper, and I should explain they naturally added a caveat emptor of their own when they explained (as many do) there is a difference between the teachings of Islam and the practice. This is no surprise, religion and hypocrisy often travel far together. On the positive side, I suggest there is a shift toward the stake-holder/social contract view of business in the West, and as such Islamic tenets may also be argued as compatible with the tenets of those who, rightly or wrongly, are pushing us to the edges of the stakeholder view or into the social contract view. This may produce useful dialogue points for those seeking the Islamic path through the economic problems. Likewise, those who push the agenda for corporate social responsibility and corporate welfare objectives will find such Islamic discourse lends itself to pursuing those objectives. However, the role of business ethics in Saudi, and Islamic countries generally, is akin to Western nations, whether we are talking about Western or Islamic notions of ethical demands. This is because Saudi companies have embraced the broad demands of international ethical standards already, along with Islamic standards, which are in tension with the daily practicalities of doing business and the economic challenges they now face. An Islamic framework of ethics can be looked to as a dialogue partner for change, but as such it faces similar barriers to the discussions in the West between business and the more radical statements of stakeholder theory and those holding a social contract theory. I contend more so the social contract theory, except in the Islamic case it is a contract underwritten, so to speak, by Allah.

The more challenging aspects of Saudi today are the more basic cultural ones. Urio in his study of China ends on a very upbeat note:

...the Chinese leadership is constantly trying to find a balance between the necessity of retaining power for the purpose of leading the country's economic development and the goal of progressively introducing spaces of freedom within Chinese society necessary for sustaining the modernization process. Unless some extremely grave mistakes are made in the future, which is unlikely to happen given the findings presented in this book, it is most likely that the completion of the reconciliation with Chinese characteristics is on its way, even if it will necessitate more effort, imagination and patience for the decades to come. And the long history of China has shown that the Chinese people possess these qualities.[15]

For Saudi, which in many respects is a youthful Kingdom, the question is how cohesive its culture will remain, what will happen with family ties and *asabiyyah* and how its people respond to the economic work demands. It is this last that threatens the most, and whether the Saudis have the qualities attributed to the Chinese remains to be seen.

The desire for the necessary skills and attitudes that will bring Saudi business closer to a Western economic model leads us to ponder whether Islamic nations generally, and Saudi in particular, are simply absorbing Western-style capitalism and its ethics. Ali et al., quoted in the Kayed and Hassan paper, argue that in "Saudi Arabia…the private sector in the Kingdom is driven to profit maximisation rather than Islamic prescriptions."[16] I would suggest this is happening out of a sense of economic realism, which the nation certainly needs in facing the economic problems that lie ahead. This is the background to the discussion of the first option, the thinking behind the Vision 2030. Pressure may mount as the social issues become more problematic, especially as the welfare system comes under pressure on the one side with taxes and cost of living on the other side. This presents more of a challenge, because the challenges are personal and behavioral. Economic life and religious life are both behavioral, and we have to unpack what this means in the Saudi economy and consider whether the current landscape is one of Saudi going with the Capitalist flow and embracing objectives and the pace of change predicated on Capitalist assumptions. There is probably little scope or appetite to offer an alternative economic vision, and even if there is it is perhaps too late in the day to be asking this question.

One thing is perhaps certain, that is Islamic thinkers ought to avoid the error of Islamic Socialism and equally the disorder of Islamic finance dressed up in Capitalism if there is to be a distinctive voice. Rather, more work needs to be done in advancing dialogue connected to the challenge posed. There are many possible endings for the trajectories of Saudi, but one thing is certain and that is it is only through such improved dialogue and a better understanding of Islam ultimately that this will turn out well. It doesn't help to bash Islam, but neither should others capitulate to a foreign faith, foreign that is to Western liberal democracy. It is about dialogue and a robust understanding of cultural difference and dissonance. In this book I have taken all three aspects of the economy, politics and religion together in order to seek understanding of the current and future challenges of Saudi Arabia. The Kingdom is at a crossroads economically, and in terms of economic philosophy so too is the West. Questions about the benefits of globalization, about equality and what the economy does for everyone are all being reconsidered in the West. The old market economy faith has come under scrutiny. It is hardly surprising then that Saudi should be asking the same questions, but it has a particular Islamic philosophy to help find their answer, but only under one condition, which applies to the same question in the West. The condition I suggest is whether the economy only operates in a capitalist way, and thus we have to live with the negative consequences. Or, is the economy at the service of our political model, whereby we can use the economy and policy to create a better future. Saudi wants to create a better future, and that future is an Islamic one. If the former condition applies then Saudi will be under threat politically, culturally and religiously as it seeks to make its economy more robust. If the latter condition exists then Saudi can shape success in an Islamic way. If Saudi and other nations fail to have effective dialogue then there is little hope that Saudi will survive the coming implosion.

A Saudi Spirit of Islamic Economy

If there is any authenticity to Islamic economics and finance then that would suggest perhaps an Islamic political economy is possible, in contrast to Western political economy. If this were to be right then it would also suggest there is an alternative to the market economy. If such a separate economic system or approach comes to the fore, it would not be the first time. Communism came along as an alternative to capitalism for some decades, but since communism's implosion capitalism has stood as the only economic model. If it is not possible to have a separate distinctively Islamic economic, and I doubt there is such a possibility, then Saudi is left with a looming economic conflict between an Islamic system that is oppositional but irrelevant and the power of Western political economies. A good reason for casting doubt on the possibility is that although there is an Islamic financial market it is only a niche market which does little else than salve the consciences of pious wealthy Muslims, which adds to the problems Islam faces. Saudi, Malaysia, Iran and others are economies which foster Islamic finance but they are an imbalanced dualism between capitalism and Islamic economies, and it is hard to see them establishing a viable alternative to capitalism.

Imagine though I am wrong and that there is to be a successful Islamic economy, is this something to fear? Would it provide an economic base to suggest an alternative society, or would it simply be implosive like communism because it fails to meet the reality? The advantage of capitalism, often overlooked by its critics, is that it is reasonably neutral, in that those who transact or do business with each other can do so without worrying too much about their beliefs or lifestyles. Capitalism is the most effective economic means of dealing with scarcity in a world of conflicting wants, needs and desires. Communism required a common understanding, and likewise in religious economics such as we find in Judaism and Islam. A "pure" Islamic economy would mean doing commerce or interacting economically with agreement on the Islamic norms that regulate and drive such a market. This includes agreement on what is not acceptable or haram, such as speculative investment and the charging of interest. Islamic economics is far from neutral. Historically, Arab traders were quite pragmatic in their business, to the extent that they did not live up to all the Koranic demands of commerce, though in many respects some aspects of the Islamic ethic remained. Before the oil there was capitalism, and before that there was trade in the Arab world, and much economic thinking and writing. However, as was the case with many political ideas, Arab secularists and Islamists drew on socialistic and

Marxist thinking when looking to link Islamic economic ideas with the economic system in the world.

The most likely trajectory is an increased tension between Saudi religion aligned to a monoculture and capitalism offering pluralism. Islamist regimes and groups tend to feed off such tension and economic discontent. We can start by understanding this trajectory by recognizing essentially, and without making a value judgment here, that capitalism is a disruptive force in religion. For example, long gone in Western capitalist societies are the quiet Sundays, set aside mainly for worship; the peace replaced by busy roads and church bells replaced by ringing cash tills. This was driven by the desire of people to be able to shop on their Sundays, and do other leisure things on both Saturday and Sunday. Likewise, we can ponder whether the Saudi daily rhythm that allows for prayer times will give way to the ever-pressing needs for discipline and speed to deliver products. Capitalism is a challenge for, though not necessarily antithetical to, religious life. It is not simply the materialism but also the imaginative and aspirational qualities of capitalism that challenge religious values and way of life. We see this aspirational element reflected in the advertising approach, such as MasterCard's "There are some things that money can't buy. For everything else there's MasterCard" and competitor Visa's "It's everywhere you want to be." Capitalism doesn't just seek to feed the stomach, it seeks to feed the soul, and we can express ourselves through capitalism, whether it is wearing Nike's "Just Do It" or caring for our skins with Clairol's "Does she or doesn't she?"

In response to this disruption, Western ethics and much of Christian literature on capitalism have historically looked upon business and trade negatively; indeed, in the twentieth century you will be hard pressed to find a major Christian theologian who had a good word to say about capitalism until the fall of communism. This is not quite the same case for Islam. According to Islam, Allah blesses trade and investment and the world of business, which is for the benefit of society. Indeed, the prophet was himself a trader, as was his first wife. As Ibn Khaldun explained, if people stop doing business, then civilization itself will slump. The activity of business, however, is judged by intention and not the results. It is not only acceptable, but required, to have lower profits with the right intention rather than maximum profits by bad intention and breaking the commands of faith. One approach, argued by authors Ali, Aali and Owaihan, is an Islamic view of the market that sees the market as based on justice, transparency and fair dealing, with the absence of exploitation. They contend that profit maximization, which lies at the heart of market capitalism, is not sanctioned by Islam and thus not the goal of an ethically guided business. Their argument is that no action in business can be separated from the social context, stating:

> Islamic ethics refers to specified rules that govern individuals and organizational conduct and seek to insure generosity, openness, and accountability in behavior and actions, while safeguarding societal interests.[17]

Ali identifies four foundations of Islamic ethics that not only meet with international standards but, the authors argue, exceed them as well: *ihsan* (goodness and generosity), relationship with others, equity and accountability.[18] Fair dealing is an everyday command, even in an Arab culture renowned for its market haggling where there are rules set by Islamic teaching. The object is to reach an agreeable price, not for one party to get the upper hand on the other. The Koran states "He that doeth good shall have ten times as much to his credit. He that doeth evil shall only be compensated according to his vice."[19] Hence, the warning "buyer beware" and other seemingly aggressive aspects of trading and capitalism are also ruled out by the Islamic business ethic. There are also forbidden products, much like the ethical investment requirements familiar in the West, whereby the drive toward profit is overridden by ethical demands. Hence, alcohol, arms, gambling and tobacco products are forbidden or *haram*. The Koran states "They ask thee concerning wine and gambling. Say: in them is great sin, and some profit for men; but the sin is greater than the profit."[20] Gambling and speculation are jointly forbidden because they involve getting monetary gain without proper effort and also attempting to predict what the outcome is, when that is God's will.[21] A similar concern leads to the ban on usury, though Islamic countries do generally allow interest-based banking. However, there is a growing Islamic banking and insurance market, though it remains as noted a niche market, and is problematic when it comes to the intent in reality.

Nations around the world are in dialogue with ethics in understanding how their markets and economies should operate, and Saudi is no different. Nations, including Saudi, adopt global standards in business ethics, but they often run counter to their political record and cultural norms, just as they do to Islamic ideas. On one level, we can say that the UN Global Compact and Islamic principles are in harmony. Williams and Zinkin in their study find no substantive conflict between the tenets of Islam and the UN Global Compact.[22] In fact, they go further and argue that "not only is Islam fully in accordance with the Corporate Social Responsibility (CSR) agenda as codified in the UN Global Compact, but it goes further in ways that could potentially lead to understanding between Islam and the West."[23] They conclude that Islam exceeds the requirements for three principle reasons:

- Islamic direction is wider in scope in respect to transparency and ethics of business transactions
- There is a clear codification of what is haram and halal
- There is an explicit mechanism in the *Sharia*, community enforcement and accountability in face of the day of judgment

Much work has been done to articulate a broader socioeconomic system based on Islam, pointing to the specifics in the Koran and other teachings such as rules on contracts, pricing, fair trading, taxation, speculation and charging of interest. It is difficult to construe simply an individualistic version of Islam, it is driven by a social vision. From an Islamic perspective, business is rooted in society and as such it is subject to the ethics of Islam as much as any other person or persons. Actions and decisions have to be undertaken through what Muhammad Umer Chapra calls the "moral filter" of Islam.[24] In practice this means that business is part of the needs of society, not a temptation, which means rampant consumerism is forbidden. Islam places consumption before consumerism, which Chapra states prioritizes necessities (*daruriyyat*), conveniences (*hajiyyat*) and refinements (*tahsiniyyat*). A study by Bhuian et al.[25] examined Saudi Arabian consumers' attitudes toward ethical business practices, government regulations and consumers' rights. Their findings revealed that in practice Saudi consumers exhibit positive attitudes toward ethical business practices related to advertising, product quality, government regulations and perceived status of consumer rights. What the business and consumer share in Islam is the core notion of trusteeship (Khilafah), whereby all people are regarded as trustees or guardians of the earth, acting as vicegerent with God. We have responsibility together. The action of a person, whether in business or not, is to fulfill the dual command to be a true servant of Allah and to act responsibly as a vicegerent of God. There is a balance or equilibrium (*'adl*) between these two missions. What Islam sets down are duties rather than rights.

There are many ways we could study an Islamic economic system, and there are many studies that do just that, so I will leave the discussion at this point. There is just one last aspect to highlight, which matches concerns I have highlighted in the area of employee engagement, that is, bad and good behaviors in organizations originate from the top.[26] They are legitimated and copied within the organization. Al-Khatib et al. studied attitudes of employees in the Gulf region countries of Saudi Arabia, Oman and Kuwait. The authors argue that ethical attitudes affect business performance, and they concluded from their study that the issue is a critical one in the Gulf, as employees follow their leaders and because their superiors are unable to challenge some wrongs in the business, employees' ethical consciousness is relaxed.[27] If Muslims, and others in the world, are vicegerents then this equally applies to hierarchy, and of course the wearing of thobes and abayas is rooted in a desire in Islam to show equality of all before Allah. Ostensibly, an Islamic company should reflect this attitude and have a more inclusive and cooperative view of employee relations, far from the Western model of boss versus employees, and of course the role of trade unions, which are forbidden in Saudi, though arguably not in Islam. Zulfiqar, in the context of writing a new labor code for Iraq, explains "Ideas of profit sharing, collective bargaining and even trade unions find justification in Islamic Law and have been instituted into the codes of many other Muslim countries."[28]

On the basis of what I have outlined, admittedly in some broad brushstrokes, it may be possible to construct an Islamic spirit for the economy, financial system and business organization. However, it would come up against the same question that the more radical versions of the stakeholder theory and social contract theory come up against: would it work?

Islam is a friend to commerce, and its' very roots lie as much in commerce as it does in bloodshed. When we ask "which Islam?" it is wrong to frame it as a choice between violent fundamentalism and reformation; rather it is a choice between authoritarian regimes versus Islamic commercial success and the recovery of a more authentic Islam that utilizes what it has done well and sheds what is no longer appropriate. The challenges of materialism to religious life, as well as the ways we consume, plays a role in our identity and begs the question of whether Islam offers an alternative system, is a fellow traveler for Capitalism, or, will become more secular like Christianity has in the West. This discussion presents us with a clear and fascinating agenda. Islamic thought suggests a different approach to the economic task, which aligns with the civil society approaches in the West, and as such they can be dialogue partners together in their challenge to global business and the shareholder view; though it also brings Saudi on a collision course with civil society globally due to the failures to comply with the global standards discussed. Another route for Islamic countries like Saudi is to take on more, not less, Islamizing of their economies.

In short, and in humility and a quest for a healthier engagement rather than personal hubris, I have proposed a six-point agenda[29] to guide future discussion. The aim of such an agenda is to allow interested partners to explore a deeper, and perhaps a more truly and faithfully radical, approach to the economic problems. Simply taking the China option will gloss over this discussion and could in the long run lead to failure. The points considered here also touch on the dissonance currently experienced in the West, and if Saudi takes up this agenda there is a possibility that it will enter into a more secure future than its counterparts in the West, and contribute to solutions in the West as well. The agenda I propose is thus:

1. Create greater open dialogue between Islamic and Western business ethicists, business schools, civil society groups and other interested parties.
2. Have open dialogue among Islamic ethicists and business practitioners on the points of disconnect highlighted in this book, such as gender, corporate values and human rights, and identify points of difference or alternative approaches in relation to "global standards."

3. Find more imaginative ways to promote dialogue within companies to understand diversity of culture and how people work together while remaining different in the source of their values and ethics.
4. Explore a clearer articulation of Islamic economic ideas and specific policies, and how they are distinctive in the context of globalization, other economic policy options and cultural settings. This means dealing with those facets of Islamic teachings that are in conflict with capitalism and how, if achievable, these can be reconciled or at least harmonious in some way. Capitalism has a strong neutral element to it, despite what its critics conjure up, and this ought to be explored.
5. Create a forum for all interested parties, Islamic and non-Islamic, to share approaches and discern how there can be harmony in the global economy based on acceptance of cultural and faith differences rather than fear and ignorance, so that we have a mosaic of ethical viewpoints that sustain rather than fracture the economic life of the world. This includes facing some of the inconvenient truths within Islam and how they can be understood in a contemporary interpretive framework without losing the basis of the faith and worldview of Muslims.
6. In our modern times, surely there is scope now for Islam to promote greater understanding and healing crossing the great Sunni/Shia divide, a schism which appeared after the death of Mohammed and the deliverance of the message of the Koran. There is the common ground. Muslims have been in conflict with each other from the beginning, but there is an opportunity to explore a greater unity based on the intent of the message rather than the cultures that have encrusted the message. The outcome could be a better Islam, and in turn a better secularity in Islamic societies.

I leave this as an open agenda for all those interested in understanding Islamic thinking about economic ideas and their ethical implications and also to those interested in understanding ethical conflict in a world dominated, justifiably or not, by capitalism.

Andrew Hammond in his book *The Islamic Utopia* may well be right to sound the alarm in face of change, whether it be a so-called Arab Spring or *Vision 2030*, when he writes the Saud leaders:

are happy to entrap all those who will expend mental energy on their realm in the intricacies of internal debates, Islamists versus liberals, progressive princes versus retrograde clerics and hawks, the Kremlinology of who's in and who's out, who's up and who's down. But it's largely a ruse to distract attention from the more fundamental issue of the arbitrary and massive powers of a hyper-dynasty haunted by fear of losing it all.[30]

If the economic revolution is to succeed, the Crown Prince Mohammad bin Salman in his apparent zeal for economic and religious reforms needs to maintain social and religious cohesion, and he and the Kingdom cannot underestimate the threat of economic implosion. If MbS fails in his mission the experiment may be over and the older generation will take charge again. King Salman could again change the line of succession. In this scenario, MbS will become the scapegoat and negotiations will take place to maintain the house of Saud and keep conservative forces in check. As custodian of the two holy sites of Islam, Saudi is the beating heart of global Islam, and if the Kingdom implodes the failure could be more terminal than anyone can imagine.

This agenda is offered not to defend the house of Saud, assist opponents or promote utopia. It is offered to all participants interested in the economic and religious problems of our modern world, in the belief that this agenda is an Islamic version of the same battle raging in the West between economic realism and those who would have business serve society rather than simply fund it. Saudi Arabia has an opportunity ahead to become an exemplar of an economy that can balance economic realities with a social balance, by connecting the passion of the people to economic ideas in the way the first Scottish enlightenment economists offered, but not by going back to the eighteenth century, rather by exploring the moral ideas in front of Saudis today. We cannot look narrowly through the economic lens to understand what is happening in Saudi Arabia at present, we need to look at the behaviors and through the three lenses. I have explored economic implosion, which could happen because the economy does not diversify effectively and the entrepreneurial needs are overrun by statist thinking. I have explored political implosion, which could happen because of the loss of the relationship with America, a weakening power base in the region as a result and antagonisms with Iran and other regional actors. I have explored religious implosion, which could happen because of fracture between families and other social aspects, loss of welfare provisions and changes in religious practices regarded as either too conservative or too liberal depending on the theological point of view taken and the impact of secularization on the youth and women of Saudi. As Saudis seek their way through the economic, political and religious changes ahead, they need to keep the six-point agenda offered, and the ethical questions raised, in mind because they are in fact the same elements that Ibn Khaldun outlined as forming social cohesion, and without that the Saudi economy will implode, and with it the house of Saud will fall and the Kingdom.

Notes

1. Hume (2006).
2. http://variety.com/2017/film/news/saudi-arabia-lifts-cinema-ban-1202635634/
3. Hamid (2016).
4. Pipes (2001).
5. *Challenges for China's Public Spending: Toward Greater Effectiveness and Equity*, OECD, 2005. http://www.oecd.org/eco/public-finance/challengesforchinaspublicspendingtowardgreatereffectivenessandequity.htm#obtain_publication
6. http://www.worldbank.org/en/country/china/overview
7. http://www.economist.com/node/21543160
8. http://www.pewresearch.org/fact-tank/2014/10/10/chinas-government-may-be-communist-but-its-people-embrace-capitalism/
9. https://www.bloomberg.com/news/articles/2016-10-06/saudi-aramco-ipo-will-offer-stake-in-all-of-company-s-operations
10. https://www.ft.com/content/c21840d2-5042-11e7-bfb8-9970 09366969?mhq5j=e1
11. https://resourcegovernance.org/blog/float-or-not-float-aramco-ipo-bellwether-state-owned-enterprise-governance
12. https://www.foreignaffairs.com/articles/united-states/2009-05-01/state-capitalism-comes-age
13. Urio (2010, p. 196).
14. Brown (2009, p. 486).
15. Urio (2010, p. 204).
16. Ibid., p. 471.

17. Ali, Abbas J. Al-Aali, Abdulrahman. Al-Owaihan, Abdullah. Islamic Perspectives on Profit Maximization *Journal of Business Ethics* (October 2013, Volume 117, Issue 3), p. 469.
18. As with "Christian Ethics" one can contest the use of the term "Islamic Ethics," as they are an ethic and so adding the term "Ethic" becomes redundant. An example of this approach is Siddiqui, Ataullah, Ethics in Islam: Key Concepts and Contemporary Challenges, *Journal of Moral Education* 26:4 (1997), pp. 423–431.
19. Koran 6:160.
20. Koran 2:219.
21. Usury also has Jewish and Christian roots. The concern is the interest in profit without work and does not reflect the sharing of risk between the lender and borrower. In Leviticus, the ban on usury applied to lending at interest among Jews, but was permissible to non-Jews. Islam applies this universally, though limited in practice to a disapproval by Islamic teaching and the ban in some Islamic states.
22. Williams, Geoffrey and Zinkin, John, Islam and CSR: A Study of the Compatibility Between the Tenets of Islam and the UN Global Compact, *Journal of Business Ethics* (2010) 91:519–533.
23. Ibid., p. 520.
24. Chapra (1985).
25. Bhuian, S., A. M. Alhassan and D. Kim: 2002, "The Relationship Between Ethical Business Practices, Government Regulations, and Consumer Rights: An Examination in Saudi Arabia," *Business and Professional Ethics* 21(1), 47–63.
26. Cowan (2009, p. 25f).
27. Jamal A. Al-Khatib, Mohammed Y. A. Rawwas and Scott J. Vitell, Organizational Ethics in Developing Countries: A Comparative Analysis, *Journal of Business Ethics*, Page [309] of 309–322.
28. Adnan A. Zulfiqar, *Religious Sanctification of Labor Law: Islamic Labor Principles and Model Provisions*, 9 J. Bus. L. 421 (2007). See also Rehman, Khalil Ur. *The Concept of Labor in Islam*, Xlibris Corporation (2010); Hakim Mohammed Said ed., *The Employee and the Employer – Islamic Concept*, Dar al-Fikr al-Islami, Pakistan (1972); *Work and Production: Selections on the Labor Law in Islam (Islamic concepts)* Al-Balagh Foundation (1997). Also, Bayu Taufiq Possumah, Abdul Ghafar Ismail and Shahida Shahimi, Bringing Work Back in Islamic Ethics, *Journal of Business Ethics*, January 2013, Volume 112, Issue 2, pp. 257–270; Elsaman, Radwa S.,

Corporate Social Responsibility in Islamic Law: Labor and Employment, 18 *New Eng. J. Int'l & Comp. L.* 97 (2012).

29. David Cowan *Setting the Agenda for Global Dialogue*, paper presented at Gulf Research Meeting 2015 held at Cambridge University: published in Kropf and Ramady (2015, p. 279).

30. Hammond (2012).

Bibliography

al-Rasheed, Madawi, ed. 2008. *Kingdom Without Borders: Saudi Arabia's Political, Religious and Media Frontiers.* London: Hurst.

Allawi, Ali A. 2009. *The Crisis of Islamic Civilization.* New Haven: Yale University Press.

An-Na'im, Abdullahi Ahmed. 2008. *Islam and the Secular State: Negotiating the Future of Shari`a.* Cambridge, MA: Harvard University Press.

Barber, Benjamin R. 2001. *Jihad vs McWorld: Terrorism's Challenge to Democracy.* New York: Ballantine Books.

Beisner, Robert L. 2009. *Dean Acheson: A Life in the Cold War.* Oxford: Oxford University Press.

Berger, Peter L. 1967. *The Sacred Canopy: Elements of a Sociological Theory of Religion.* New York: Anchor Books.

———. 1973. *The Social Reality of Religion.* London: Penguin.

———., ed. 1999. *The Desecularization of the World: Resurgent Religion and World Politics.* Grand Rapids: Eerdmans.

Black, Antony. 2001. *The History of Islamic Political Thought: From the Prophet to the Present.* Edinburgh: Edinburgh University Press.

Bowering, Gerhard, ed. 2015. *Islamic Political Thought: An Introduction.* Princeton: Princeton University Press.

Bremmer, Ian. 2010. *The End of the Free Market.* New York: Portfolio Penguin.

Bronson, Rachel. 2006. *Thicker Than Oil: America's Uneasy Relationship with Saudi Arabia.* New York: Oxford University Press.

Brown, Archie. 2009. *The Rise and Fall of Communism.* New York: Doubleday.

Champion, Daryl. 2003. *The Paradoxical Kingdom: Saudi Arabia and the Momentum of Reform.* London: Hurst and Company.

Chapra, Mohammed Umer. 1985. *Towards a Just Monetary System.* Leicester: Islamic Foundation.

———. 1992. *Islam and the Economic Challenge.* Leicester: International Institute of Islamic Thought.

Cook, M.A., ed. 1970. *Studies in the Economic History of the Middle East*. Oxford: Oxford University Press.

Cowan, David. 2009. *Economic Parables: The Monetary Teachings of Jesus Christ*. 2nd ed. Downers Grove: IVP.

Craze, Jonathan, and Mark Huband. 2009. *The Kingdom: Saudi Arabia and the Challenge of the 21ˢᵗ Century*. London: Hurst & Co.

Cunningham, Robert B., and Yasin K. Sarayrah. 1993. *Wasta: The Hidden Force in Middle Eastern Society*. Westport: Praeger.

Esposito, John L. 2002. *Unholy War: Terror in the Name of Islam*. New York: Oxford University Press.

Halliday, Fred. 2000. *Nation and Religion in the Middle East*. Boulder CO: Lynne Rienner Publishers.

Hamid, Shadi. 2016. *Islamic Exceptionalism: How the Struggle over Islam is Reshaping the World*. New York: St. Martin's Press.

Hammond, Andrew. 2012. *The Islamic Utopia: The Illusion of Reform in Saudi Arabia*. London: Pluto Press.

Haykel, Bernard, Thomas Hegghammer, and Stéphane Lacroix. 2015. *Saudi Arabia in Transition: Insights on Social, Political, Economic and Religious Change*. Cambridge: Cambridge University Press.

Hertog, Steffen. 2010. *Princes, Brokers, and Bureaucrats Oil and the State in Saudi Arabia*. Ithaca: Cornell University Press.

House, Karen Elliott. 2012. *On Saudi Arabia: Its People, Past, Religion, Fault Lines – And Future*. New York: Vintage Books.

Hume, David. 2006. *An Enquiry Concerning the Principles of Morals*. Oxford: Oxford University Press.

Karsh, Effraim. 2006. *Islamic Imperialism: A History*. New Haven: Yale University Press.

Kepel, Gilles. 2004. *The War for Muslim Minds: Islam and the West*. Trans. Pascal Ghazaleh. Cambridge, MA: Belknap Press.

Khaldun, Ibn. 1967. *The Muqaddimah: An Introduction to History*. Princeton: Princeton University Press.

Kropf, Annika, and Mohamed A. Ramady, eds. 2015. *Employment and Career Motivation in the Arab Gulf States: The Rentier Mentality Revisited*. Berlin: Gerlach Press.

Lacey, Robert. 2009. *Inside the Kingdom: Kings, Clerics, Terrorists, Modernists, and the Struggle for Saudi Arabia*. New York: Viking.

Lackner, Helen. 1978. *A House Built on Sand. A Political Economy of Saudi Arabia*. London: Ithaca Press.

Lewis, Bernard. 2002. *The Arabs in History*. New York: Oxford University Press.

Lippman, Thomas W. 2012. *Saudi Arabia on the Edge: The Uncertain Future of an American Ally*. Dulles: Potomac Books.

Maher, Shiraz. 2016. *Salafi-Jihadism: The History of an Idea*. London: Hurst & Company.

Mansfield, Peter. 1985. *The Arabs*. London: Penguin Books.

Mazaheri, Nimah. 2016. *Oil Booms and Business Busts: Why Resource Wealth Hurts Entrepreneurs in the Developing World*. Oxford: Oxford University Press.

Mitchell, Timothy. 2013. *Carbon Democracy: Political Power in the Age of Oil*. London: Verso.

Naqvi, S.N.H. 1994. *Ethics and Economics: An Islamic Synthesis*. Leicester: The Islamic Foundation.

Nasr, Vali. 2009. *The Rise of Islamic Capitalism: Why the New Muslim Middle Class Is the Key to Defeating Extremism*. New York: Free Press.

Plantinga, Alvin, and Nicholas Wolterstorff, eds. 1983. *Faith and Rationality: Reason and Belief in God*. Notre Dame: University of Notre Dame Press.

Pipes, Richard. 2001. *Communism: A History*. New York: Random House.

Said, Edward W. 1979. *Orientalism*. Princeton: Princeton University Press.

Salame, Ghassan, ed. 1994. *Democracy Without Democrats? The Renewal of Politics in the Muslim World*. London: I.B. Tauris.

Urio, Paolo. 2010. *Reconciling State, Market and Society in China: The Long March Toward Prosperity*. London: Routledge.

Vitalis, Robert. 2009. *America's Kingdom: Mythmaking on the Saudi Oil Frontier*. London: Verso.

Wilson, Bryan. 1966. *Religion in a Secular Society*. London: Watts.

Yahya, Sadowski. 1993. *Scuds or Butter? The Political Economy of Arms Control in the Middle East*. Washington, DC: Brookings Institution.

Yergin, Daniel. 1993. *The Prize: The Epic Quest for Oil, Money & Power*. New York: Touchstone.

Index[1]

---

[1] Note: Page numbers followed by 'n' refer to notes.

© The Author(s) 2018

D. Cowan, *The Coming Economic Implosion of Saudi Arabia*, https://doi.org/10.1007/978-3-319-74709-5

Printed by Printforce, the Netherlands